Making Sense of

CHRIST

and the

SPIRIT

Works by Wayne Grudem

Bible Doctrine: Essential Teachings of the Christian Faith

Christian Beliefs: Twenty Basics Every Christian Should Know

Counterpoints: Are Miraculous Gifts for Today? (General Editor)

Politics According to the Bible

Systematic Theology

Systematic Theology Laminated Sheet

Making Sense of Series

Making Sense of the Bible

Making Sense of Who God Is

Making Sense of Man and Sin

Making Sense of Christ and the Spirit

Making Sense of Salvation

Making Sense of the Church

Making Sense of the Future

MAKING SENSE OF
CHRIST
AND THE
SPIRIT

ONE OF SEVEN PARTS FROM GRUDEM'S
SYSTEMATIC THEOLOGY

WAYNE GRUDEM

ZONDERVAN.com/
AUTHORTRACKER
follow your favorite authors

ZONDERVAN

Making Sense of Christ and the Spirit
Copyright © 1994, 2011 by Wayne Grudem

Previously published in *Systematic Theology*

This title is also available as a Zondervan ebook. Visit www.zondervan.com/ebooks.

Requests for information should be addressed to:

Zondervan, *Grand Rapids, Michigan 49530*

This edition: ISBN 978-0-310-49314-3 (softcover)

The Library of Congress has cataloged the complete volume as:

Grudem, Wayne Arden.
     Systematic theology: an introduction to biblical doctrine / Wayne Grudem.
       p.   cm.
     Includes index.
     ISBN 978-0-310-28670-7
     1. Theology, Doctrinal. I. Title.
  BT75.2.G78 — 1994
  230'.046—dc20   94-8300

Cover design: Rob Monacelli
Interior design: Mark Sheeres

Printed in the United States of America

11 12 13 14 15 16 /DCI/ 33 32 31 30 29 28 27 26 25 24 23 22 21 20 19 18 17 16 15 14 13 12 11 10 9 8 7 6 5 4 3 2 1

CONTENTS

PREFACE

I have not written this book for other teachers of theology (though I hope many of them will read it). I have written it for students—and not only for students, but also for every Christian who has a hunger to know the central doctrines of the Bible in greater depth.

I have tried to make it understandable even for Christians who have never studied theology before. I have avoided using technical terms without first explaining them. And most of the chapters can be read on their own, so that someone can begin at any chapter and grasp it without having read the earlier material.

Introductory studies do not have to be shallow or simplistic. I am convinced that most Christians are able to understand the doctrinal teachings of the Bible in considerable depth, provided that they are presented clearly and without the use of highly technical language. Therefore I have not hesitated to treat theological disputes in some detail where it seemed necessary.

Yet this book is still an *introduction* to systematic theology. Entire books have been written about the topics covered in each chapter of this book, and entire articles have been written about many of the verses quoted in this book. Therefore each chapter is capable of opening out into additional study in more breadth or more depth for those who are interested. The bibliographies at the end of each chapter give some help in that direction.

The following six distinctive features of this book grow out of my convictions about what systematic theology is and how it should be taught:

1. A Clear Biblical Basis for Doctrines. Because I believe that theology should be explicitly based on the teachings of Scripture, in each chapter I have attempted to show where the Bible gives support for the doctrines under consideration. In fact, because I believe that the words of Scripture themselves have power and authority greater than any human words, I have not just given Bible references; I have frequently quoted Bible passages at length so that readers can easily examine for themselves the scriptural evidence and in that way be like the noble Bereans, who were "examining the scriptures daily to see if these things were so" (Acts 17:11). This conviction about the unique nature of the Bible as God's words has also led to the inclusion of a Scripture memory passage at the end of each chapter.

2. Clarity in the Explanation of Doctrines. I do not believe that God intended the study of theology to result in confusion and frustration. A student who comes out of a course in theology filled only with doctrinal uncertainty and a thousand unanswered questions is hardly "able to give instruction in sound doctrine and also to confute those who contradict it" (Titus 1:9). Therefore I have tried to state the doctrinal positions of this book clearly and to show where in Scripture I find convincing evidence for those positions. I do not expect that everyone reading this book will agree with me at every point of doctrine; I do think that every reader will understand the positions I am arguing for and where Scripture can be found to support those positions.

This does not mean that I ignore other views. Where there are doctrinal differences within evangelical Christianity I have tried to represent other positions fairly, to explain why I disagree with them, and to give references to the best available defenses of the opposing positions. In fact, I have made it easy for students to find a conservative evangelical statement on each topic from within their own theological traditions, because each chapter contains an index to treatments of that chapter's subject in thirty-four other theology texts classified by denominational background.

3. Application to Life. I do not believe that God intended the study of theology to be dry and boring. Theology is the study of God and all his works! Theology is meant to be lived and prayed and sung! All of the great doctrinal writings of the Bible (such as Paul's epistle to the Romans) are full of praise to God and personal application to life. For this reason I have incorporated notes on application from time to time in the text, and have added "Questions for Personal Application" at the end of each chapter, as well as a hymn related to the topic of the chapter. True theology is "teaching which accords with godliness" (1 Tim. 6:3), and theology when studied rightly will lead to growth in our Christian lives, and to worship.

4. Focus on the Evangelical World. I do not think that a true system of theology can be constructed from within what we may call the "liberal" theological tradition—that is, by people who deny the absolute truthfulness of the Bible, or who do not think the words of the Bible to be God's very words. For this reason, the other writers I interact with in this book are mostly within what is today called the larger "conservative evangelical" tradition—from the great Reformers John Calvin and Martin Luther, down to the writings of evangelical scholars today. I write as an evangelical and for evangelicals. This does not mean that those in the liberal tradition have nothing valuable to say; it simply means that differences with them almost always boil down to differences over the nature of the Bible and its authority. The amount of doctrinal agreement that can be reached by people with widely divergent bases of authority is quite limited. I am thankful for my evangelical friends who write extensive critiques of liberal theology, but I do not think that everyone is called to do that, or that an extensive analysis of liberal views is the most helpful way to build a positive system of theology based on the total truthfulness of the whole Bible. In fact, somewhat like the boy in Hans Christian Andersen's tale who shouted, "The Emperor has no clothes!" I think someone needs to say that it is doubtful that liberal theologians have given us any significant insights into the doctrinal teachings of Scripture that are not already to be found in evangelical writers.

It is not always appreciated that the world of conservative evangelical scholarship is so rich and diverse that it affords ample opportunity for exploration of different viewpoints and insights into Scripture. I think that ultimately we will attain much more depth of understanding of Scripture when we are able to study it in the company of a great number of scholars who all begin with the conviction that the Bible is completely true and absolutely authoritative. The cross-references to thirty-four other evangelical systematic theologies that I have put at the end of each chapter reflect this conviction: though they are broken down into seven broad theological traditions (Anglican/Episcopalian, Arminian/Wesleyan/Methodist, Baptist, Dispensational, Lutheran, Reformed/Presbyterian, and Renewal/Charismatic/ Pentecostal), they all would hold to the inerrancy of the Bible and would belong to what would be called a conservative evangelical position today. (In addition to these thirty-four conservative evangelical works, I have also added to each chapter a section of cross-references to two representative Roman Catholic theologies, because Roman Catholicism continues to exercise such a significant influence worldwide.)

5. Hope for Progress in Doctrinal Unity in the Church. I believe that there is still much hope for the church to attain deeper and purer doctrinal understanding, and to overcome old barriers, even those that have persisted for centuries. Jesus is at work perfecting his church "that he might present the church to himself in splendor, without spot or wrinkle or any such thing, that she might be holy and without blemish" (Eph. 5:27), and he has given gifts to equip the church "until we all attain to the unity of the faith and of the knowledge of the Son of God" (Eph. 4:13). Though the past history of the church may discourage us, these Scriptures remain true, and we should not abandon hope of greater agreement. In fact, in this century we have already seen much greater understanding and some greater doctrinal agreement between Covenant and Dispensational theologians, and between charismatics and noncharismatics; moreover, I think the church's understanding of biblical inerrancy and of spiritual gifts has also increased significantly in the last few decades. I believe that the current debate over appropriate roles for men and women in marriage and the church will eventually result in much greater understanding of the teaching of Scripture as well, painful though the controversy may be at the present time. Therefore, in this book I have not hesitated to raise again some of the old differences (over baptism, the Lord's Supper, church government, the millennium and the tribulation, and predestination, for example) in the hope that, in some cases at least, a fresh look at Scripture may provoke a new examination of these doctrines and may perhaps prompt some movement not just toward greater understanding and tolerance of other viewpoints, but even toward greater doctrinal consensus in the church.

6. A Sense of the Urgent Need for Greater Doctrinal Understanding in the Whole Church. I am convinced that there is an urgent need in the church today for much greater understanding of Christian doctrine, or systematic theology. Not only pastors and teachers need to understand theology in greater depth—the whole church does as well. One day by God's grace we may have churches full of Christians who can discuss, apply, and live the doctrinal teachings of the Bible as readily as they can discuss the details of their own jobs or hobbies—or the fortunes of their favorite sports team or television program. It is not that Christians lack the ability to understand doctrine; it is just that they must have access to it in an understandable form. Once that happens, I think that many Christians will find that understanding (and living) the doctrines of Scripture is one of their greatest joys.

> *"O give thanks to the LORD, for he is good; for his steadfast love endures for ever!" (Ps. 118:29).*

> *"Not to us, O LORD, not to us, but to your name give glory" (Ps. 115:1).*

WAYNE GRUDEM
Phoenix Seminary
4222 E. Thomas Road/Suite 400
Phoenix, Arizona 85018
USA

ABBREVIATIONS

BAGD	*A Greek-English Lexicon of the New Testament and Other Early Christian Literature.* Ed. Walter Bauer. Rev. and trans. Wm. Arndt, F. W. Gingrich, and F. Danker. Chicago: University of Chicago Press, 1979.
BDB	*A Hebrew and English Lexicon of the Old Testament.* F. Brown, S. R. Driver, and C. Briggs. Oxford: Clarendon Press, 1907; reprinted, with corrections, 1968.
BETS	*Bulletin of the Evangelical Theological Society*
BibSac	*Bibliotheca Sacra*
cf.	compare
CRSQ	*Creation Research Society Quarterly*
CT	*Christianity Today*
CThRev	*Criswell Theological Review*
DPCM	*Dictionary of Pentecostal and Charismatic Movements.* Stanley M. Burgess and Gary B. McGee, eds. Grand Rapids: Zondervan, 1988.
EBC	*Expositor's Bible Commentary.* Frank E. Gaebelein, ed. Grand Rapids: Zondervan, 1976.
ed.	edited by, edition
EDT	*Evangelical Dictionary of Theology.* Walter Elwell, ed. Grand Rapids: Baker, 1984.
et al.	and others
IBD	*The Illustrated Bible Dictionary.* Ed. J. D. Douglas, et al. 3 vols. Leicester: Inter-Varsity Press, and Wheaton: Tyndale House, 1980.
ISBE	*International Standard Bible Encyclopedia.* Revised edition. G. W. Bromiley, ed. Grand Rapids: Eerdmans, 1982.
JAMA	*Journal of the American Medical Association*
JBL	*Journal of Biblical Literature*
JETS	*Journal of the Evangelical Theological Society*
JSOT	*Journal for the Study of the Old Testament*
KJV	King James Version (Authorized Version)
LSJ	*A Greek-English Lexicon,* ninth edition. Henry Liddell, Robert Scott, H. S. Jones, R. McKenzie. Oxford: Clarendon Press, 1940.
LXX	Septuagint
mg.	margin or marginal notes
n.	note
n.d.	no date of publication given
n.p.	no place of publication given

NASB	New American Standard Bible
NDT	*New Dictionary of Theology.* S. B. Ferguson, D. F. Wright, J. I. Packer, eds. Leicester and Downers Grove, Ill.: InterVarsity Press, 1988.
NIDCC	*New International Dictionary of the Christian Church.* Ed. J. D. Douglas et al. Grand Rapids: Zondervan, 1974.
NIDNTT	*The New International Dictionary of New Testament Theology.* 3 vols. Colin Brown, gen. ed. Grand Rapids: Zondervan, 1975–78.
NIGTC	New International Greek Testament Commentaries
NIV	New International Version
NKJV	New King James Version
NTS	*New Testament Studies*
ODCC	*Oxford Dictionary of the Christian Church.* Ed. F. L. Cross. London and New York: Oxford University Press, 1977.
rev.	revised
RSV	Revised Standard Version
TB	*Tyndale Bulletin*
TDNT	*Theological Dictionary of the New Testament.* 10 vols. G. Kittel and G. Friedrich, eds.; trans. G. W. Bromiley. Grand Rapids: Eerdmans, 1964–76.
TNTC	Tyndale New Testament Commentaries
TOTC	Tyndale Old Testament Commentaries
trans.	translated by
TrinJ	*Trinity Journal*
vol.	volume
WBC	Word Biblical Commentary
WTJ	*Westminster Theological Journal*

Chapter 1

INTRODUCTION TO SYSTEMATIC THEOLOGY

What is systematic theology?
Why should Christians study it?
How should we study it?

EXPLANATION AND SCRIPTURAL BASIS

A. Definition of Systematic Theology

What is systematic theology? Many different definitions have been given, but for the purposes of this book the following definition will be used: *Systematic theology is any study that answers the question, "What does the whole Bible teach us today?" about any given topic.*[1]

This definition indicates that systematic theology involves collecting and understanding all the relevant passages in the Bible on various topics and then summarizing their teachings clearly so that we know what to believe about each topic.

1. Relationship to Other Disciplines. The emphasis of this book will not therefore be on *historical theology* (a historical study of how Christians in different periods have understood various theological topics) or *philosophical theology* (studying theological topics largely without use of the Bible, but using the tools and methods of philosophical reasoning and what can be known about God from observing the universe) or *apologetics*

---

[1]This definition of systematic theology is taken from Professor John Frame, now of Westminster Seminary in Escondido, California, under whom I was privileged to study in 1971–73 (at Westminster Seminary, Philadelphia). Though it is impossible to acknowledge my indebtedness to him at every point, it is appropriate to express gratitude to him at this point, and to say that he has probably influenced my theological thinking more than anyone else, especially in the crucial areas of the nature of systematic theology and the doctrine of the Word of God. Many of his former students will recognize echoes of his teaching in the following pages, especially in those two areas.

(providing a defense of the truthfulness of the Christian faith for the purpose of convincing unbelievers). These three subjects, which are worthwhile subjects for Christians to pursue, are sometimes also included in a broader definition of the term *systematic theology*. In fact, some consideration of historical, philosophical, and apologetic matters will be found at points throughout this book. This is because historical study informs us of the insights gained and the mistakes made by others previously in understanding Scripture; philosophical study helps us understand right and wrong thought forms common in our culture and others; and apologetic study helps us bring the teachings of Scripture to bear on the objections raised by unbelievers. But these areas of study are not the focus of this volume, which rather interacts directly with the biblical text in order to understand what the Bible itself says to us about various theological subjects.

If someone prefers to use the term *systematic theology* in the broader sense just mentioned instead of the narrow sense which has been defined above, it will not make much difference.[2] Those who use the narrower definition will agree that these other areas of study definitely contribute in a positive way to our understanding of systematic theology, and those who use the broader definition will certainly agree that historical theology, philosophical theology, and apologetics can be distinguished from the process of collecting and synthesizing all the relevant Scripture passages for various topics. Moreover, even though historical and philosophical studies do contribute to our understanding of theological questions, only Scripture has the final authority to define what we are to believe,[3] and it is therefore appropriate to spend some time focusing on the process of analyzing the teaching of Scripture itself.

Systematic theology, as we have defined it, also differs from *Old Testament theology, New Testament theology,* and *biblical theology*. These three disciplines organize their topics historically and in the order the topics are presented in the Bible. Therefore, in Old Testament theology, one might ask, "What does Deuteronomy teach about prayer?" or "What do the Psalms teach about prayer?" or "What does Isaiah teach about prayer?" or even, "What does the whole Old Testament teach about prayer and how is that teaching developed over the history of the Old Testament?" In New Testament theology one might ask, "What does John's gospel teach about prayer?" or "What does Paul teach about prayer?" or even "What does the New Testament teach about prayer and what is the historical development of that teaching as it progresses through the New Testament?"

"Biblical theology" has a technical meaning in theological studies. It is the larger category that contains both Old Testament theology and New Testament theology as we have defined them above. Biblical theology gives special attention to the teachings of *individual authors and sections* of Scripture, and to the place of each teaching in the *historical development* of Scripture.[4] So one might ask, "What is the historical development

---

[2]Gordon Lewis and Bruce Demarest have coined a new phrase, "integrative theology," to refer to systematic theology in this broader sense: see their excellent work, *Integrative Theology* (Grand Rapids: Zondervan, 1996). For each doctrine, they analyze historical alternatives and relevant biblical passages, give a coherent summary of the doctrine, answer philosophical objections, and give practical application.

[3]Charles Hodge says, "The Scriptures contain all the Facts of Theology" (section heading in *Systematic Theology,* 1:15). He argues that ideas gained from intuition or observation or experience are valid in theology only if they are supported by the teaching of Scripture.

[4]The term "biblical theology" might seem to be a natural and appropriate one for the process I have called

of the teaching about prayer as it is seen throughout the history of the Old Testament and then of the New Testament?" Of course, this question comes very close to the question, "What does the whole Bible teach us today about prayer?" (which would be *systematic theology* by our definition). It then becomes evident that the boundary lines between these various disciplines often overlap at the edges, and parts of one study blend into the next. Yet there is still a difference, for biblical theology traces the historical development of a doctrine and the way in which one's place at some point in that historical development affects one's understanding and application of that particular doctrine. Biblical theology also focuses on the understanding of each doctrine that the biblical authors and their original hearers or readers possessed.

Systematic theology, on the other hand, makes use of the material of biblical theology and often builds on the results of biblical theology. At some points, especially where great detail and care is needed in the development of a doctrine, systematic theology will even use a biblical-theological method, analyzing the development of each doctrine through the historical development of Scripture. But the focus of systematic theology remains different: its focus is on the collection and then the summary of the teaching of all the biblical passages on a particular subject. Thus systematic theology asks, for example, "What does the whole Bible teach us today about prayer?" It attempts to summarize the teaching of Scripture in a brief, understandable, and very carefully formulated statement.

2. Application to Life. Furthermore, systematic theology focuses on summarizing each doctrine as it should be understood by present-day Christians. This will sometimes involve the use of terms and even concepts that were not themselves used by any individual biblical author, but that are the proper result of combining the teachings of two or more biblical authors on a particular subject. The terms *Trinity, incarnation,* and *deity of Christ,* for example, are not found in the Bible, but they usefully summarize biblical concepts.

Defining systematic theology to include "what the whole Bible *teaches us* today" implies that application to life is a necessary part of the proper pursuit of systematic theology. Thus a doctrine under consideration is seen in terms of its practical value for living the Christian life. Nowhere in Scripture do we find doctrine studied for its own sake or in isolation from life. The biblical writers consistently apply their teaching to life. Therefore, any Christian reading this book should find his or her Christian life enriched and deepened during this study; indeed, if personal spiritual growth does not occur, then the book has not been written properly by the author or the material has not been rightly studied by the reader.

3. Systematic Theology and Disorganized Theology. If we use this definition of systematic theology, it will be seen that most Christians actually do systematic theology (or at least make systematic-theological statements) many times a week. For example: "The Bible says that everyone who believes in Jesus Christ will be saved." "The Bible says

---

"systematic theology." However, its usage in theological studies to refer to tracing the historical development of doctrines throughout the Bible is too well established, so that starting now to use the term biblical theology to refer to what I have called systematic theology would only result in confusion.

that Jesus Christ is the only way to God." "The Bible says that Jesus is coming again." These are all summaries of what Scripture says and, as such, they are systematic-theological statements. In fact, every time a Christian says something about what the whole Bible says, he or she is in a sense doing "systematic theology"—according to our definition—by thinking about various topics and answering the question, "What does the whole Bible teach us today?"[5]

How then does this book differ from the "systematic theology" that most Christians do? First, it treats biblical topics in a *carefully organized way* to guarantee that all important topics will receive thorough consideration. This organization also provides one sort of check against inaccurate analysis of individual topics, for it means that all other doctrines that are treated can be compared with each topic for consistency in methodology and absence of contradictions in the relationships between the doctrines. This also helps to ensure balanced consideration of complementary doctrines: Christ's deity and humanity are studied together, for example, as are God's sovereignty and man's responsibility, so that wrong conclusions will not be drawn from an imbalanced emphasis on only one aspect of the full biblical presentation.

In fact, the adjective *systematic* in systematic theology should be understood to mean something like "carefully organized by topics," with the understanding that the topics studied will be seen to fit together in a consistent way, and will include all the major doctrinal topics of the Bible. Thus "systematic" should be thought of as the opposite of "randomly arranged" or "disorganized." In systematic theology topics are treated in an orderly or "systematic" way.

A second difference between this book and the way most Christians do systematic theology is that it treats topics in *much more detail* than most Christians do. For example, an ordinary Christian as a result of regular reading of the Bible may make the theological statement, "The Bible says that everyone who believes in Jesus Christ will be saved." That is a perfectly true summary of a major biblical teaching. However, it can take several pages to elaborate more precisely what it means to "believe in Jesus Christ," and it could take several chapters to explain what it means to "be saved" in all of the many implications of that term.

Third, a formal study of systematic theology will make it possible to formulate summaries of biblical teachings with *much more accuracy* than Christians would normally arrive at without such a study. In systematic theology, summaries of biblical teachings must be worded precisely to guard against misunderstandings and to exclude false teachings.

Fourth, a good theological analysis must find and treat fairly *all the relevant Bible passages* for each particular topic, not just some or a few of the relevant passages. This

---

[5]Robert L. Reymond, "The Justification of Theology with a Special Application to Contemporary Christology," in Nigel M. Cameron, ed., *The Challenge of Evangelical Theology: Essays in Approach and Method* (Edinburgh: Rutherford House, 1987), pp. 82–104, cites several examples from the New Testament of this kind of searching through all of Scripture to demonstrate doctrinal conclusions: Jesus in Luke 24:25–27 (and elsewhere); Apollos in Acts 18:28; the Jerusalem Council in Acts 15; and Paul in Acts 17:2–3; 20:27; and all of Romans. To this list could be added Heb. 1 (on Christ's divine Sonship), Heb. 11 (on the nature of true faith), and many other passages from the Epistles.

often means that it must depend on the results of careful exegesis (or interpretation) of Scripture generally agreed upon by evangelical interpreters or, where there are significant differences of interpretation, systematic theology will include detailed exegesis at certain points.

Because of the large number of topics covered in a study of systematic theology and because of the great detail with which these topics are analyzed, it is inevitable that someone studying a systematic theology text or taking a course in systematic theology for the first time will have many of his or her own personal beliefs challenged or modified, refined or enriched. It is of utmost importance therefore that each person beginning such a course firmly resolve in his or her own mind to abandon as false any idea which is found to be clearly contradicted by the teaching of Scripture. But it is also very important for each person to resolve not to believe any individual doctrine simply because this textbook or some other textbook or teacher says that it is true, unless this book or the instructor in a course can convince the student from the text of Scripture itself. It is Scripture alone, not "conservative evangelical tradition" or any other human authority, that must function as the normative authority for the definition of what we should believe.

4. What Are Doctrines? In this book, the word *doctrine* will be understood in the following way: *A doctrine is what the whole Bible teaches us today about some particular topic.* This definition is directly related to our earlier definition of systematic theology, since it shows that a "doctrine" is simply the result of the process of doing systematic theology with regard to one particular topic. Understood in this way, doctrines can be very broad or very narrow. We can speak of "the doctrine of God" as a major doctrinal category, including a summary of all that the Bible teaches us today about God. Such a doctrine would be exceptionally large. On the other hand, we may also speak more narrowly of the doctrine of God's eternity, or the doctrine of the Trinity, or the doctrine of God's justice.[6]

Within the major doctrinal category of this book, many more specific teachings have been selected as appropriate for inclusion. Generally these meet at least one of the following three criteria: (1) they are doctrines that are most emphasized in Scripture; (2) they are doctrines that have been most significant throughout the history of the church and have been important for all Christians at all times; (3) they are doctrines that have become important for Christians in the present situation in the history of the church (even though some of these doctrines may not have been of such great interest earlier in church history). Some examples of doctrines in the third category would be the doctrine of the inerrancy of Scripture, the doctrine of baptism in the Holy Spirit, the doctrine of Satan and demons with particular reference to spiritual warfare, the doctrine of spiritual gifts in the New Testament age, and the doctrine of the creation of man as male and female in relation to the understanding of roles appropriate to men and women today.

---

[6]The word *dogma* is an approximate synonym for *doctrine*, but I have not used it in this book. *Dogma* is a term more often used by Roman Catholic and Lutheran theologians, and the term frequently refers to doctrines that have official church endorsement. *Dogmatic theology* is another term for *systematic theology*.

Finally, what is the difference between systematic theology and *Christian ethics?* Although there is inevitably some overlap between the study of theology and the study of ethics, I have tried to maintain a distinction in emphasis. The emphasis of systematic theology is on what God wants us to *believe* and to *know,* while the emphasis in Christian ethics is on what God wants us to *do* and what *attitudes* he wants us to have. Such a distinction is reflected in the following definition: *Christian ethics is any study that answers the question, "What does God require us to do and what attitudes does he require us to have today?" with regard to any given situation.* Thus theology focuses on ideas while ethics focuses on situations in life. Theology tells us how we should think while ethics tells us how we should live. A textbook on ethics, for example, would discuss topics such as marriage and divorce, lying and telling the truth, stealing and ownership of property, abortion, birth control, homosexuality, the role of civil government, discipline of children, capital punishment, war, care for the poor, racial discrimination, and so forth. Of course there is some overlap: theology must be applied to life (therefore it is often ethical to some degree). And ethics must be based on proper ideas of God and his world (therefore it is theological to some degree).

This book will emphasize systematic theology, though it will not hesitate to apply theology to life where such application comes readily. Still, for a thorough treatment of Christian ethics, another textbook similar to this in scope would be necessary.

B. Initial Assumptions of This Book

We begin with two assumptions or presuppositions: (1) that the Bible is true and that it is, in fact, our only absolute standard of truth; (2) that the God who is spoken of in the Bible exists, and that he is who the Bible says he is: the Creator of heaven and earth and all things in them. These two presuppositions, of course, are always open to later adjustment or modification or deeper confirmation, but at this point, these two assumptions form the point at which we begin.

C. Why Should Christians Study Theology?

Why should Christians study systematic theology? That is, why should we engage in the process of collecting and summarizing the teachings of many individual Bible passages on particular topics? Why is it not sufficient simply to continue reading the Bible regularly every day of our lives?

1. The Basic Reason. Many answers have been given to this question, but too often they leave the impression that systematic theology somehow can "improve" on the Bible by doing a better job of organizing its teachings or explaining them more clearly than the Bible itself has done. Thus we may begin implicitly to deny the clarity of Scripture or the sufficiency of Scripture.

However, Jesus commanded his disciples and now commands us also to *teach* believers to observe all that he commanded:

> Go therefore and make disciples of all nations, baptizing them in the name of
> the Father and of the Son and of the Holy Spirit, *teaching them* to observe all

that I have commanded you; and lo, I am with you always, to the close of the age. (Matt. 28:19–20)

Now to teach all that Jesus commanded, in a narrow sense, is simply to teach the content of the oral teaching of Jesus as it is recorded in the gospel narratives. However, in a broader sense, "all that Jesus commanded" includes the interpretation and application of his life and teachings, because in the book of Acts it is implied that it contains a narrative of what Jesus *continued* to do and teach through the apostles after his resurrection (note that 1:1 speaks of "all that Jesus *began* to do and teach"). "All that Jesus commanded" can also include the Epistles, since they were written under the supervision of the Holy Spirit and were also considered to be a "command of the Lord" (1 Cor. 14:37; see also John 14:26; 16:13; 1 Thess. 4:15; 2 Peter 3:2; and Rev. 1:1–3). Thus in a larger sense, "all that Jesus commanded" includes all of the New Testament.

Furthermore, when we consider that the New Testament writings endorse the absolute confidence Jesus had in the authority and reliability of the Old Testament Scriptures as God's words, and when we realize that the New Testament epistles also endorse this view of the Old Testament as absolutely authoritative words of God, then it becomes evident that we cannot teach "all that Jesus commanded" without including all of the Old Testament (rightly understood in the various ways in which it applies to the new covenant age in the history of redemption) as well.

The task of fulfilling the Great Commission includes therefore not only evangelism but also *teaching.* And the task of teaching all that Jesus commanded us is, in a broad sense, the task of teaching what the whole Bible says to us today. To effectively teach ourselves and to teach others what the whole Bible says, it is necessary to *collect* and *summarize* all the Scripture passages on a particular subject.

For example, if someone asks me, "What does the Bible teach about Christ's return?" I could say, "Just keep reading your Bible and you'll find out." But if the questioner begins reading at Genesis 1:1 it will be a long time before he or she finds the answer to his question. By that time many other questions will have needed answers, and his list of unanswered questions will begin to grow very long indeed. What does the Bible teach about the work of the Holy Spirit? What does the Bible teach about prayer? What does the Bible teach about sin? There simply is not time in our lifetimes to read through the entire Bible looking for an answer for ourselves every time a doctrinal question arises. Therefore, for us to learn what the Bible says, it is very helpful to have the benefit of the work of others who have searched through Scripture and found answers to these various topics.

We can teach others most effectively if we can direct them to the most relevant passages and suggest an appropriate summary of the teachings of those passages. Then the person who questions us can inspect those passages quickly for himself or herself and learn much more rapidly what the teaching of the Bible is on a particular subject. Thus the necessity of systematic theology for teaching what the Bible says comes about primarily because we are finite in our memory and in the amount of time at our disposal.

The basic reason for studying systematic theology, then, is that it enables us to teach ourselves and others what the whole Bible says, thus fulfilling the second part of the Great Commission.

2. The Benefits to Our Lives. Although the basic reason for studying systematic theology is that it is a means of obedience to our Lord's command, there are some additional specific benefits that come from such study.

First, studying theology helps us *overcome our wrong ideas.* If there were no sin in our hearts, we could read the Bible from cover to cover and, although we would not immediately learn everything in the Bible, we would most likely learn only true things about God and his creation. Every time we read it we would learn more true things and we would not rebel or refuse to accept anything we found written there. But with sin in our hearts we retain some rebelliousness against God. At various points there are—for all of us—biblical teachings which for one reason or another we do not want to accept. The study of systematic theology is of help in overcoming those rebellious ideas.

For example, suppose there is someone who does not want to believe that Jesus is personally coming back to earth again. We could show this person one verse or perhaps two that speak of Jesus' return to earth, but the person might still find a way to evade the force of those verses or read a different meaning into them. But if we collect twenty-five or thirty verses that say that Jesus is coming back to earth personally and write them all out on paper, our friend who hesitated to believe in Christ's return is much more likely to be persuaded by the breadth and diversity of biblical evidence for this doctrine. Of course, we all have areas like that, areas where our understanding of the Bible's teaching is inadequate. In these areas, it is helpful for us to be confronted with the *total weight of the teaching of Scripture* on that subject, so that we will more readily be persuaded even against our initial wrongful inclinations.

Second, studying systematic theology helps us to be *able to make better decisions later* on new questions of doctrine that may arise. We cannot know what new doctrinal controversies will arise in the churches in which we will live and minister ten, twenty, or thirty years from now, if the Lord does not return before then. These new doctrinal controversies will sometimes include questions that no one has faced very carefully before. Christians will be asking, "What does the whole Bible say about this subject?" (The precise nature of biblical inerrancy and the appropriate understanding of biblical teaching on gifts of the Holy Spirit are two examples of questions that have arisen in our century with much more forcefulness than ever before in the history of the church.)

Whatever the new doctrinal controversies are in future years, those who have learned systematic theology well will be much better able to answer the new questions that arise. The reason for this is that everything that the Bible says is somehow related to everything else the Bible says (for it all fits together in a consistent way, at least within God's own understanding of reality, and in the nature of God and creation as they really are). Thus the new question will be related to much that has already been learned from Scripture. The more thoroughly that earlier material has been learned, the better able we will be to deal with those new questions.

This benefit extends even more broadly. We face problems of applying Scripture to life in many more contexts than formal doctrinal discussions. What does the Bible teach about husband-wife relationships? About raising children? About witnessing to a friend at work? What principles does Scripture give us for studying psychology, or economics, or the natural sciences? How does it guide us in spending money, or in saving, or in tithing? In every area of inquiry certain theological principles will come to bear, and those who have learned well the theological teachings of the Bible will be much better able to make decisions that are pleasing to God.

A helpful analogy at this point is that of a jigsaw puzzle. If the puzzle represents "what the whole Bible teaches us today about everything" then a course in systematic theology would be like filling in the border and some of the major items pictured in the puzzle. But we will never know everything that the Bible teaches about everything, so our jigsaw puzzle will have many gaps, many pieces that remain to be put in. Solving a new real-life problem is analogous to filling in another section of the jigsaw puzzle: the more pieces one has in place correctly to begin with, the easier it is to fit new pieces in, and the less apt one is to make mistakes. In this book the goal is to enable Christians to put into their "theological jigsaw puzzle" as many pieces with as much accuracy as possible, and to encourage Christians to go on putting in more and more correct pieces for the rest of their lives. The Christian doctrines studied here will act as guidelines to help in the filling in of all other areas, areas that pertain to all aspects of truth in all aspects of life.

Third, studying systematic theology will *help us grow as Christians.* The more we know about God, about his Word, about his relationships to the world and mankind, the better we will trust him, the more fully we will praise him, and the more readily we will obey him. Studying systematic theology rightly will make us more mature Christians. If it does not do this, we are not studying it in the way God intends.

In fact, the Bible often connects sound doctrine with maturity in Christian living: Paul speaks of "*the teaching which accords with godliness*" (1 Tim. 6:3) and says that his work as an apostle is "to further the faith of God's elect and their knowledge of *the truth which accords with godliness*" (Titus 1:1). By contrast, he indicates that all kinds of disobedience and immorality are "contrary to sound doctrine" (1 Tim. 1:10).

In connection with this idea it is appropriate to ask what the difference is between a "major doctrine" and a "minor doctrine." Christians often say they want to seek agreement in the church on major doctrines but also to allow for differences on minor doctrines. I have found the following guideline useful:

> A major doctrine is one that has a significant impact on our thinking about other doctrines, or that has a significant impact on how we live the Christian life. A minor doctrine is one that has very little impact on how we think about other doctrines, and very little impact on how we live the Christian life.

By this standard doctrines such as the authority of the Bible, the Trinity, the deity of Christ, justification by faith, and many others would rightly be considered major doctrines. People who disagree with the historic evangelical understanding of any of these doctrines will have wide areas of difference with evangelical Christians who affirm these doctrines. By contrast, it seems to me that differences over forms of church government or some details about the Lord's Supper or the timing of the great tribulation concern minor doctrines. Christians who differ over these things can agree on perhaps every other area of doctrine, can live Christian lives that differ in no important way, and can have genuine fellowship with one another.

Of course, we may find doctrines that fall somewhere between "major" and "minor" according to this standard. For example, Christians may differ over the degree of significance that should attach to the doctrine of baptism or the millennium or the extent of the atonement. That is only natural, because many doctrines have *some* influence on other doctrines or on life, but we may differ over whether we think it to be a "significant" influence. We could even recognize that there will be a range of significance here and just say that the more influence a doctrine has on other doctrines and on life, the more "major" it becomes. This amount of influence may even vary according to the historical circumstances and needs of the church at any given time. In such cases, Christians will need to ask God to give them mature wisdom and sound judgment as they try to determine to what extent a doctrine should be considered "major" in their particular circumstances.

D. A Note on Two Objections to the Study of Systematic Theology

1. "The Conclusions Are 'Too Neat' to Be True." Some scholars look with suspicion at systematic theology when—or even because—its teachings fit together in a noncontradictory way. They object that the results are "too neat" and that systematic theologians must therefore be squeezing the Bible's teachings into an artificial mold, distorting the true meaning of Scripture to get an orderly set of beliefs.

To this objection two responses can be made: (1) We must first ask the people making the objection to tell us at what specific points Scripture has been misinterpreted, and then we must deal with the understanding of those passages. Perhaps mistakes have been made, and in that case there should be corrections.

Yet it is also possible that the objector will have no specific passages in mind, or no clearly erroneous interpretations to point to in the works of the most responsible evangelical theologians. Of course, incompetent exegesis can be found in the writings of the less competent scholars in *any* field of biblical studies, not just in systematic theology, but those "bad examples" constitute an objection not against the scholar's field but against the incompetent scholar himself.

It is very important that the objector be specific at this point because this objection is sometimes made by those who—perhaps unconsciously—have adopted from our culture a skeptical view of the possibility of finding universally true conclusions about anything, even about God from his Word. This kind of skepticism regarding theological truth is especially common in the modern university world where "systematic theology"—if it is studied at all—is studied only from the perspectives of philosophical theology and historical theology (including perhaps a historical study of the various ideas that were believed by the early Christians who wrote the New Testament, and by other Christians at that time and throughout church history). In this kind of intellectual climate the study of "systematic theology" as defined in this chapter would be considered impossible, because the Bible would be assumed to be merely the work of many human authors who wrote out of diverse cultures and experiences over the course of more than one thousand years: trying to find "what the whole Bible teaches" about any subject would be thought nearly as hopeless as trying to find "what all philosophers teach" about some question, for the answer in both cases would be thought to be not one view but many diverse and often conflicting views. This skeptical viewpoint must be rejected by evangelicals who see Scripture as the product of human *and* divine authorship, and therefore as a collection of writings that teach noncontradictory truths about God and about the universe he created.

(2) Second, it must be answered that in God's own mind, and in the nature of reality itself, *true* facts and ideas are all consistent with one another. Therefore if we have accurately understood the teachings of God in Scripture we should expect our conclusions to "fit together" and be mutually consistent. Internal consistency, then, is an argument for, not against, any individual results of systematic theology.

2. "The Choice of Topics Dictates the Conclusions." Another general objection to systematic theology concerns the choice and arrangement of topics, and even the fact that such topically arranged study of Scripture, using categories sometimes different from those found in Scripture itself, is done at all. Why are *these* theological topics treated rather than just the topics emphasized by the biblical authors, and why are the topics *arranged in this way* rather than in some other way? Perhaps—this objection would say—our traditions and our cultures have determined the topics we treat and the arrangement of topics, so that the results of this systematic-theological study of Scripture, though acceptable in our own theological tradition, will in fact be untrue to Scripture itself.

A variant of this objection is the statement that our starting point often determines our conclusions on controversial topics: if we decide to start with an emphasis on the divine authorship of Scripture, for example, we will end up believing in biblical inerrancy, but if we start with an emphasis on the human authorship of Scripture, we will end up believing there are some errors in the Bible. Similarly, if we start with an emphasis on God's sovereignty, we will end up as Calvinists, but if we start with an emphasis on man's ability to make free choices, we will end up as Arminians, and so forth. This objection makes it sound as if the most important theological questions could probably be decided by flipping a coin to decide where to start, since *different* and *equally valid* conclusions will inevitably be reached from the different starting points.

Those who make such an objection often suggest that the best way to avoid this problem is not to study or teach systematic theology at all, but to limit our topical studies to the field of biblical theology, treating only the topics and themes the biblical authors themselves emphasize and describing the historical development of these biblical themes through the Bible.

In response to this objection, much of the discussion in this chapter about the necessity to teach Scripture will be relevant. Our choice of topics need not be restricted to the main concerns of the biblical authors, for our goal is to find out what God requires of us in all areas of concern to us today.

For example, it was not the *main* concern of any New Testament author to explain such topics as "baptism in the Holy Spirit," or women's roles in the church, or the doctrine of the Trinity, but these are valid areas of concern for us today, and we must look at all the places in Scripture that have relevance for those topics (whether those specific terms are mentioned or not, and whether those themes are of primary concern to each passage we examine or not) if we are going to be able to understand and explain to others "what the whole Bible teaches" about them.

The only alternative—for we *will* think *something* about those subjects—is to form our opinions haphazardly from a general impression of what we feel to be a "biblical" position on each subject, or perhaps to buttress our positions with careful analysis of one or two relevant texts, yet with no guarantee that those texts present a balanced view of "the whole counsel of God" (Acts 20:27) on the subject being considered. In fact this approach—one all too common in evangelical circles today—could, I suppose, be called "unsystematic theology" or even "disorderly and random theology"! Such an alternative is too subjective and too subject to cultural pressures. It tends toward doctrinal fragmentation and widespread doctrinal uncertainty, leaving the church theologically immature, like "children, tossed to and fro and carried about with every wind of doctrine" (Eph. 4:14).

Concerning the objection about the choice and sequence of topics, there is nothing to prevent us from going to Scripture to look for answers to *any* doctrinal questions, considered in *any sequence.* The sequence of topics in this book is a very common one and has been adopted because it is orderly and lends itself well to learning and teaching. But the chapters could be read in any sequence one wanted and the conclusions should not be different, nor should the persuasiveness of the arguments—if they are rightly derived from Scripture—be significantly diminished. I have tried to write the chapters so that they can be read as independent units.

E. How Should Christians Study Systematic Theology?

How then should we study systematic theology? The Bible provides some guidelines for answering this question.

1. We Should Study Systematic Theology with Prayer. If studying systematic theology is simply a certain way of studying the Bible, then the passages in Scripture that talk about the way in which we should study God's Word give guidance to us in this task. Just as the psalmist prays in Psalm 119:18, "Open my eyes, that I may behold wondrous things out of your law," so we should pray and seek God's help in understanding his Word. Paul tells us in 1 Corinthians 2:14 that "the unspiritual man does not receive the gifts of the Spirit of God, for they are folly to him, and he is not able to understand them because they are spiritually discerned." Studying theology is therefore a spiritual activity in which we need the help of the Holy Spirit.

No matter how intelligent, if the student does not continue to pray for God to give him or her an understanding mind and a believing and humble heart, and the student does not maintain a personal walk with the Lord, then the teachings of Scripture will be misunderstood and disbelieved, doctrinal error will result, and the mind and heart of the student will not be changed for the better but for the worse. Students of systematic theology should resolve at the beginning to keep their lives free from any disobedience to God or any known sin that would disrupt their relationship with him. They should resolve to maintain with great regularity their own personal devotional lives. They should continually pray for wisdom and understanding of Scripture.

Since it is the Holy Spirit who gives us the ability rightly to understand Scripture, we need to realize that the proper thing to do, particularly when we are unable to understand some passage or some doctrine of Scripture, is to pray for God's help. Often what we need is not more data but more insight into the data we already have available. This insight is given only by the Holy Spirit (cf. 1 Cor. 2:14; Eph. 1:17–19).

2. We Should Study Systematic Theology with Humility. Peter tells us, "Clothe your-selves, all of you, with humility toward one another, for 'God opposes the proud, but gives grace to the humble'" (1 Peter 5:5). Those who study systematic theology will learn many things about the teachings of Scripture that are perhaps not known or not known well by other Christians in their churches or by relatives who are older in the Lord than they are. They may also find that they understand things about Scripture that some of their church officers do not understand, and that even their pastor has perhaps forgotten or never learned well.

In all of these situations it would be very easy to adopt an attitude of pride or superi-ority toward others who have not made such a study. But how ugly it would be if anyone were to use this knowledge of God's Word simply to win arguments or to put down a fel-low Christian in conversation, or to make another believer feel insignificant in the Lord's work. James' counsel is good for us at this point: "Let every man be quick to hear, slow to speak, slow to anger, for the anger of man does not work the righteousness of God" (James 1:19–20). He tells us that one's understanding of Scripture is to be imparted in humility and love:

> Who is wise and understanding among you? By his good life let him show his works in the meekness of wisdom. . . . But the wisdom from above is first pure, then peaceable, gentle, open to reason, full of mercy and good fruits, without uncertainty or insincerity. And the harvest of righteousness is sown in peace by those who make peace. (James 3:13, 17–18)

Systematic theology rightly studied will not lead to the knowledge that "puffs up" (1 Cor. 8:1) but to humility and love for others.

3. We Should Study Systematic Theology with Reason. We find in the New Testament that Jesus and the New Testament authors will often quote a verse of Scripture and then draw logical conclusions from it. They *reason* from Scripture. It is therefore not wrong to use human understanding, human logic, and human reason to draw conclusions from the statements of Scripture. Nevertheless, when we reason and draw what we think to be correct logical deductions from Scripture, we sometimes make mistakes. The deduc-tions we draw from the statements of Scripture are not equal to the statements of Scrip-ture themselves in certainty or authority, for our ability to reason and draw conclusions is not the ultimate standard of truth — only Scripture is.

What then are the limits on our use of our reasoning abilities to draw deductions from the statements of Scripture? The fact that reasoning to conclusions that go beyond the mere statements of Scripture is appropriate and even necessary for studying Scripture, and the fact that Scripture itself is the ultimate standard of truth, combine to indicate to us that *we are free to use our reasoning abilities to draw deductions from any passage of Scripture so long as these deductions do not contradict the clear teaching of some other passage of Scripture.*[7]

This principle puts a safeguard on our use of what we think to be logical deductions from Scripture. Our supposedly logical deductions may be erroneous, but Scripture itself cannot be erroneous. Thus, for example, we may read Scripture and find that God the Father is called God (1 Cor. 1:3), that God the Son is called God (John 20:28; Titus 2:13), and that God the Holy Spirit is called God (Acts 5:3–4). We might deduce from this that there are three Gods. But then we find the Bible explicitly teaching us that God is one (Deut. 6:4; James 2:19). Thus we conclude that what we *thought* to be a valid logical deduction about three Gods was wrong and that Scripture teaches both (a) that there are three separate persons (the Father, the Son, and the Holy Spirit), each of whom is fully God, and (b) that there is one God.

We cannot understand exactly how these two statements can both be true, so together they constitute a *paradox* ("a seemingly contradictory statement that may nonetheless be true").[8] We can tolerate a paradox (such as "God is three persons and one God") because we have confidence that ultimately God knows fully the truth about himself and about the nature of reality, and that in his understanding the different elements of a paradox are fully reconciled, even though at this point God's thoughts are higher than our thoughts (Isa. 55:8–9). But a true contradiction (such as, "God is three persons and God is not three persons") would imply ultimate contradiction in God's own understanding of himself or of reality, and this cannot be.

---

[7]This guideline is also adopted from Professor John Frame at Westminster Seminary.

[8]The *American Heritage Dictionary of the English Language,* ed. William Morris (Boston: Houghton-Mifflin, 1980), p. 950 (first definition). Essentially the same meaning is adopted by the *Oxford English Dictionary* (1913 ed., 7:450), the *Concise Oxford Dictionary* (1981 ed., p. 742), the *Random House College Dictionary* (1979 ed., p. 964), and the *Chambers Twentieth Century Dictionary* (p. 780), though all note that *paradox* can also mean "contradiction" (though less commonly); compare the *Encyclopedia of Philosophy,* ed. Paul Edwards (New York: Macmillan and The Free Press, 1967), 5:45, and the entire article "Logical Paradoxes" by John van Heijenoort on pp. 45–51 of the same volume, which proposes solutions to many of the classical paradoxes in the history of philosophy. (If *paradox* meant "contradiction," such solutions would be impossible.)

When I use the word *paradox* in the primary sense defined by these dictionaries today I realize that I am differing somewhat with the article "Paradox" by K. S. Kantzer in the *EDT,* ed. Walter Elwell, pp. 826–27 (which takes *paradox* to mean essentially "contradiction"). However, I am using *paradox* in an ordinary English sense and one also familiar in philosophy. There seems to me to be available no better word than *paradox* to refer to an apparent but not real contradiction.

There is, however, some lack of uniformity in the use of the term *paradox* and a related term, *antinomy,* in con-

temporary evangelical discussion. The word *antinomy* has sometimes been used to apply to what I here call *paradox,* that is, "seemingly contradictory statements that may nonetheless both be true" (see, for example, John Jefferson Davis, *Theology Primer* [Grand Rapids: Baker, 1981], p. 18). Such a sense for *antinomy* gained support in a widely read book, *Evangelism and the Sovereignty of God,* by J. I. Packer (London: Inter-Varsity Press, 1961). On pp. 18–22 Packer defines *antinomy* as "an appearance of contradiction" (but admits on p. 18 that his definition differs with the *Shorter Oxford Dictionary*). My problem with using *antinomy* in this sense is that the word is so unfamiliar in ordinary English that it just increases the stock of technical terms Christians have to learn in order to understand theologians, and moreover such a sense is unsupported by any of the dictionaries cited above, all of which define *antinomy* to mean "contradiction" (e.g., *Oxford English Dictionary,* 1:371). The problem is not serious, but it would help communication if evangelicals could agree on uniform senses for these terms.

A paradox is certainly acceptable in systematic theology, and paradoxes are in fact inevitable so long as we have finite understanding of any theological topic. However, it is important to recognize that Christian theology should never affirm a *contradiction* (a set of two statements, one of which denies the other). A contradiction would be, "God is three persons and God is not three persons" (where the term *persons* has the same sense in both halves of the sentence).

When the psalmist says, "The sum of your word is truth; and every one of your righteous ordinances endures for ever" (Ps. 119:160), he implies that God's words are not only true individually but also viewed together as a whole. Viewed collectively, their "sum" is also "truth." Ultimately, there is no internal contradiction either in Scripture or in God's own thoughts.

4. We Should Study Systematic Theology with Help from Others. We need to be thankful that God has put teachers in the church ("And God has appointed in the church first apostles, second prophets, third *teachers . . .*" [1 Cor. 12:28]. We should allow those with gifts of teaching to help us understand Scripture. This means that we should make use of systematic theologies and other books that have been written by some of the teachers that God has given to the church over the course of its history. It also means that our study of theology should include *talking with other Christians* about the things we study. Among those with whom we talk will often be some with gifts of teaching who can explain biblical teachings clearly and help us to understand more easily. In fact, some of the most effective learning in systematic theology courses in colleges and seminaries often occurs outside the classroom in informal conversations among students who are attempting to understand Bible doctrines for themselves.

5. We Should Study Systematic Theology by Collecting and Understanding All the Relevant Passages of Scripture on Any Topic. This point was mentioned in our definition of systematic theology at the beginning of the chapter, but the actual process needs to be described here. How does one go about making a doctrinal summary of what all the passages of Scripture teach on a certain topic? For topics covered in this book, many people will think that studying the chapters in this book and reading the Bible verses noted in the chapters is enough. But some people will want to do further study of Scripture on a particular topic or study some new topic not covered here. How could a student go about using the Bible to research its teachings on some new subject, perhaps one not discussed explicitly in any of his or her systematic theology textbooks?

The process would look like this: (1) Find all the relevant verses. The best help in this step is a good concordance, which enables one to look up key words and find the verses in which the subject is treated. For example, in studying what it means that man is created in the image and likeness of God, one needs to find all the verses in which "image" and "likeness" and "create" occur. (The words "man" and "God" occur too often to be useful for a concordance search.) In studying the doctrine of prayer, many words could be looked up (*pray, prayer, intercede, petition, supplication, confess, confession, praise, thanks, thanksgiving,* et al.) — and perhaps the list of verses would grow too long to be manageable, so that the student would have to skim the concordance entries without looking up the verses, or the search would probably have to be divided into sections or limited in some other way. Verses can also be found by thinking through the overall history of the Bible and then turning to sections where there would be information on the topic at hand — for example, a student studying prayer would want to read passages like the one about Hannah's prayer for a son (in 1 Sam. 1), Solomon's prayer at the dedication of the temple (in 1 Kings 8), Jesus' prayer in the Garden of Gethsemane (in Matt. 26 and parallels), and so forth. Then in addition to concordance work and reading other passages that one can find on the subject, checking the relevant sections in some systematic theology books will often bring to light other verses that had been missed, sometimes because none of the key words used for the concordance were in those verses.[9]

(2) The second step is to read, make notes on, and try to summarize the points made in the relevant verses. Sometimes a theme will be repeated often and the summary of the various verses will be relatively easy. At other times, there will be verses difficult to understand, and the student will need to take some time to study a verse in depth (just by reading the verse in context over and over, or by using specialized tools such as commentaries and dictionaries) until a satisfactory understanding is reached.

(3) Finally, the teachings of the various verses should be summarized into one or more points that the Bible affirms about that subject. The summary does not have to take the exact form of anyone else's conclusions on the subject, because we each may see things in Scripture that others have missed, or we may organize the subject differently or emphasize different things.

On the other hand, at this point it is also helpful to read related sections, if any can be found, in several systematic theology books. This provides a useful check against error and oversight, and often makes one aware of alternative perspectives and arguments that may cause us to modify or strengthen our position. If a student finds that others have argued for strongly differing conclusions, then these other views need to be stated fairly and then answered. Sometimes other theology books will alert us to historical or philosophical considerations that have been raised before in the history of the church, and these will provide additional insight or warnings against error.

The process outlined above is possible for any Christian who can read his or her Bible and can look up words in a concordance. Of course people will become faster and more accurate in this process with time and experience and Christian maturity, but it would be a tremendous help to the church if Christians generally would give much more time to searching out topics in Scripture for themselves and drawing conclusions in the way outlined above. The joy of discovery of biblical themes would be richly rewarding. Especially pastors and those who lead Bible studies would find added freshness in their understanding of Scripture and in their teaching.

6. We Should Study Systematic Theology with Rejoicing and Praise. The study of theology is not merely a theoretical exercise of the intellect. It is a study of the living God, and of the wonders of all his works in creation and redemption. We cannot study this subject dispassionately! We must love all that God is, all that he says and all that he does. "You shall love the LORD your God with all your heart" (Deut. 6:5). Our response to the study of the theology of Scripture should be that of the psalmist who said, "How precious to me are your thoughts, O God!" (Ps. 139:17). In the study of the teachings of

---

[9]I have read a number of student papers telling me that John's gospel says nothing about how Christians should pray, for example, because they looked at a concordance and found that the word *prayer* was not in John, and the word *pray* only occurs four times in reference to Jesus praying in John 14, 16, and 17. They overlooked the fact that John contains several important verses where the word *ask* rather than the word *pray* is used (John 14:13 – 14; 15:7, 16, et al.).

God's Word, it should not surprise us if we often find our hearts spontaneously breaking forth in expressions of praise and delight like those of the psalmist:

> The precepts of the LORD are right,
> rejoicing the heart. (Ps. 19:8)

> In the way of your testimonies I delight
> as much as in all riches. (Ps. 119:14)

> How sweet are your words to my taste,
> sweeter than honey to my mouth! (Ps. 119:103)

> Your testimonies are my heritage for ever;
> yea, they are the joy of my heart. (Ps. 119:111)

> I rejoice at your word
> like one who finds great spoil. (Ps. 119:162)

Often in the study of theology the response of the Christian should be similar to that of Paul in reflecting on the long theological argument that he has just completed at the end of Romans 11:32. He breaks forth into joyful praise at the richness of the doctrine which God has enabled him to express:

> O the depth of the riches and wisdom and knowledge of God! How unsearchable are his judgments and how inscrutable his ways!

> "For who has known the mind of the Lord,
> or who has been his counselor?"
> "Or who has given a gift to him
> that he might be repaid?"

> For from him and through him and to him are all things. To him be glory for ever. Amen. (Rom. 11:33–36)

QUESTIONS FOR PERSONAL APPLICATION

These questions at the end of each chapter focus on application to life. Because I think doctrine is to be felt at the emotional level as well as understood at the intellectual level, in many chapters I have included some questions about how a reader *feels* regarding a point of doctrine. I think these questions will prove quite valuable for those who take the time to reflect on them.

1. In what ways (if any) has this chapter changed your understanding of what systematic theology is? What was your attitude toward the study of systematic theology before reading this chapter? What is your attitude now?

2. What is likely to happen to a church or denomination that gives up learning systematic theology for a generation or longer? Has that been true of your church?

3. Are there any doctrines listed in the Contents for which a fuller understanding would help to solve a personal difficulty in your life at the present time? What

are the spiritual and emotional dangers that you personally need to be aware of in studying systematic theology?

4. Pray for God to make this study of basic Christian doctrines a time of spiritual growth and deeper fellowship with him, and a time in which you understand and apply the teachings of Scripture rightly.

SPECIAL TERMS

apologetics

biblical theology

Christian ethics

contradiction

doctrine

dogmatic theology

historical theology

major doctrine

minor doctrine

New Testament theology

Old Testament theology

paradox

philosophical theology

presupposition

systematic theology

BIBLIOGRAPHY

Baker, D. L. "Biblical Theology." In *NDT*, p. 671.

Berkhof, Louis. *Introduction to Systematic Theology.* Grand Rapids: Eerdmans, 1982, pp. 15–75 (first published 1932).

Bray, Gerald L., ed. *Contours of Christian Theology.* Downers Grove, Ill.: InterVarsity Press, 1993.

_____. "Systematic Theology, History of." In *NDT*, pp. 671–72.

Cameron, Nigel M., ed. *The Challenge of Evangelical Theology: Essays in Approach and Method.* Edinburgh: Rutherford House, 1987.

Carson, D. A. "Unity and Diversity in the New Testament: The Possibility of Systematic Theology." In *Scripture and Truth.* Ed. by D. A. Carson and John Woodbridge. Grand Rapids: Zondervan, 1983, pp. 65–95.

Davis, John Jefferson. *Foundations of Evangelical Theology.* Grand Rapids: Baker, 1984.

_____. *The Necessity of Systematic Theology.* Grand Rapids: Baker, 1980.

_____. *Theology Primer: Resources for the Theological Student.* Grand Rapids: Baker, 1981.

Demarest, Bruce. "Systematic Theology." In *EDT*, pp. 1064–66.

Erickson, Millard. *Concise Dictionary of Christian Theology.* Grand Rapids: Baker, 1986.

Frame, John. *Van Til the Theologian.* Phillipsburg, N.J.: Pilgrim, 1976.

Geehan, E. R., ed. *Jerusalem and Athens.* Nutley, N.J.: Craig Press, 1971.

Grenz, Stanley J. *Revisioning Evangelical Theology: A Fresh Agenda for the 21st Century.* Downers Grove, Ill.: InterVarsity Press, 1993.

House, H. Wayne. *Charts of Christian Theology and Doctrine.* Grand Rapids: Zondervan, 1992.

Kuyper, Abraham. *Principles of Sacred Theology.* Trans. by J. H. DeVries. Grand Rapids: Eerdmans, 1968 (reprint; first published as *Encyclopedia of Sacred Theology* in 1898).

Machen, J. Gresham. *Christianity and Liberalism.* Grand Rapids: Eerdmans, 1923. (This 180-page book is, in my opinion, one of the most significant theological studies ever written. It gives a clear overview of major biblical doctrines and shows the vital differences with Protestant liberal theology at every point, differences that still confront us today. It is required reading in all my introductory theology classes.)

Morrow, T. W. "Systematic Theology." In *NDT,* p. 671.

Poythress, Vern. *Symphonic Theology: The Validity of Multiple Perspectives in Theology.* Grand Rapids: Zondervan, 1987.

Preus, Robert D. *The Theology of Post-Reformation Lutheranism: A Study of Theological Prolegomena.* 2 vols. St. Louis: Concordia, 1970.

Van Til, Cornelius. *In Defense of the Faith,* vol. 5: *An Introduction to Systematic Theology.* N.p.: Presbyterian and Reformed, 1976, pp. 1–61, 253–62.

_____. *The Defense of the Faith.* Philadelphia: Presbyterian and Reformed, 1955.

Vos, Geerhardus. "The Idea of Biblical Theology as a Science and as a Theological Discipline." In *Redemptive History and Biblical Interpretation,* pp. 3–24. Ed. by Richard Gaffin. Phillipsburg, N.J.: Presbyterian and Reformed, 1980 (article first published 1894).

Warfield, B. B. "The Indispensableness of Systematic Theology to the Preacher." In *Selected Shorter Writings of Benjamin B. Warfield,* 2:280–88. Ed. by John E. Meeter. Nutley, N.J.: Presbyterian and Reformed, 1973 (article first published 1897).

_____. "The Right of Systematic Theology." In *Selected Shorter Writings of Benjamin B. Warfield,* 2:21–279. Ed. by John E. Meeter. Nutley, N.J.: Presbyterian and Reformed, 1973 (article first published 1896).

Wells, David. *No Place for Truth, or, Whatever Happened to Evangelical Theology?* Grand Rapids: Eerdmans, 1993.

Woodbridge, John D., and Thomas E. McComiskey, eds. *Doing Theology in Today's World: Essays in Honor of Kenneth S. Kantzer.* Grand Rapids: Zondervan, 1991.

SCRIPTURE MEMORY PASSAGE

Students have repeatedly mentioned that one of the most valuable parts of any of their courses in college or seminary has been the Scripture passages they were required to memorize. "I have hidden your word in my heart that I might not sin against you" (Ps. 119:11 NIV). In each chapter, therefore, I have included an appropriate memory passage so that instructors may incorporate Scripture memory into the course requirements wherever possible. (Scripture memory passages at the end of each chapter are taken from the RSV. These same passages in the NIV and NASB may be found in appendix 2.)

Matthew 28:18–20: *And Jesus came and said to them, "All authority in heaven and on earth has been given to me. Go therefore and make disciples of all nations, baptizing them in the name of the Father and of the Son and of the Holy Spirit, teaching them to observe all that I have commanded you; and lo, I am with you always, to the close of the age."*

HYMN

Systematic theology at its best will result in praise. It is appropriate therefore at the end of each chapter to include a hymn related to the subject of that chapter. In a classroom setting, the hymn can be sung together at the beginning or end of class. Alternatively, an individual reader can sing it privately or simply meditate quietly on the words.

For almost every chapter the words of the hymns were found in *Trinity Hymnal* (Philadelphia: Great Commission Publications, 1990),[10] the hymnal of the Presbyterian Church in America and the Orthodox Presbyterian Church, but most of them are found in many other common hymnals. Unless otherwise noted, the words of these hymns are now in public domain and no longer subject to copyright restrictions: therefore they may be freely copied for overhead projector use or photocopied.

Why have I used so many old hymns? Although I personally like many of the more recent worship songs that have come into wide use, when I began to select hymns that would correspond to the great doctrines of the Christian faith, I realized that the great hymns of the church throughout history have a doctrinal richness and breadth that is still unequaled. For several of the chapters in this book, I know of no modern worship song that covers the same subject in an extended way—perhaps this can be a challenge to modern songwriters to study these chapters and then write songs reflecting the teaching of Scripture on the respective subjects.

For this chapter, however, I found no hymn ancient or modern that thanked God for the privilege of studying systematic theology from the pages of Scripture. Therefore I have selected a hymn of general praise, which is always appropriate.

"O for a Thousand Tongues to Sing"

This hymn by Charles Wesley (1707–88) begins by wishing for "a thousand tongues" to sing God's praise. Verse 2 is a prayer that God would "assist me" in singing his praise throughout the earth. The remaining verses give praise to Jesus (vv. 3–6) and to God the Father (v. 7).

> O for a thousand tongues to sing
> My great Redeemer's praise,
> The glories of my God and King,
> The triumphs of His grace.
>
> My gracious Master and my God,
> Assist me to proclaim,
> To spread through all the earth abroad,
> The honors of Thy name.
>
> Jesus! the name that charms our fears,
> That bids our sorrows cease;

---

[10]This hymn book is completely revised from a similar hymnal of the same title published by the Orthodox Presbyterian Church in WW 1961.

'Tis music in the sinner's ears,
'Tis life and health and peace.

He breaks the pow'r of reigning sin,
He sets the prisoner free;
His blood can make the foulest clean;
His blood availed for me.

He speaks and, list'ning to His voice,
New life the dead receive;
The mournful, broken hearts rejoice;
The humble poor believe.

Hear him, ye deaf; his praise, ye dumb,
Your loosened tongues employ,
Ye blind, behold your Savior come;
And leap, ye lame, for joy.

Glory to God and praise and love
Be ever, ever giv'n
By saints below and saints above—
The church in earth and heav'n.

AUTHOR: CHARLES WESLEY, 1739, ALT.

Chapter 2

THE PERSON OF CHRIST

How is Jesus fully God and fully man, yet one person?

EXPLANATION AND SCRIPTURAL BASIS

We may summarize the biblical teaching about the person of Christ as follows: *Jesus Christ was fully God and fully man in one person, and will be so forever.*

The scriptural material supporting this definition is extensive. We will discuss first the humanity of Christ, then his deity, and then attempt to show how Jesus' deity and humanity are united in the one person of Christ.

A. The Humanity of Christ

1. Virgin Birth. When we speak of the humanity of Christ it is appropriate to begin with a consideration of the virgin birth of Christ. Scripture clearly asserts that Jesus was conceived in the womb of his mother Mary by a miraculous work of the Holy Spirit and without a human father.

"Now the birth of Jesus Christ took place in this way. When his mother Mary had been betrothed to Joseph, *before they came together* she was found to be with child *of the Holy Spirit*" (Matt. 1:18). Shortly after that an angel of the Lord said to Joseph, who was engaged to Mary, "Joseph, son of David, do not fear to take Mary your wife, for *that which is conceived in her is of the Holy Spirit*" (Matt. 1:20). Then we read that Joseph "did as the angel of the Lord commanded him; he took his wife, but knew her not until she had borne a son; and he called his name Jesus" (Matt. 1:24–25).

The same fact is affirmed in Luke's gospel, where we read about the appearance of the angel Gabriel to Mary. After the angel had told her that she would bear a son, Mary said, "How shall this be, since I have no husband?" The angel answered,

> "The Holy Spirit will come upon you,
>   and the power of the Most High will overshadow you;

therefore the child to be born will be called holy,
    the Son of God." (Luke 1:35; cf. 3:23)

The doctrinal importance of the virgin birth is seen in at least three areas.

1. It shows that salvation ultimately must come from the Lord. Just as God had promised that the "seed" of the woman (Gen. 3:15) would ultimately destroy the serpent, so God brought it about by his own power, not through mere human effort. The virgin birth of Christ is an unmistakable reminder that salvation can never come through human effort, but must be the work of God himself. Our salvation only comes about through the supernatural work of God, and that was evident at the very beginning of Jesus' life when "God sent forth his Son, born of woman, born under the law, to redeem those who were under the law, so that we might receive adoption as sons" (Gal. 4:4–5).

2. The virgin birth made possible the uniting of full deity and full humanity in one person. This was the means God used to send his Son (John 3:16; Gal. 4:4) into the world as a man. If we think for a moment of other possible ways in which Christ might have come to the earth, none of them would so clearly unite humanity and deity in one person. It probably would have been possible for God to create Jesus as a complete human being in heaven and send him to descend from heaven to earth without the benefit of any human parent. But then it would have been very hard for us to see how Jesus could be fully human as we are, nor would he be a part of the human race that physically descended from Adam. On the other hand, it probably would have been possible for God to have Jesus come into the world with two human parents, both a father and a mother, and with his full divine nature miraculously united to his human nature at some point early in his life. But then it would have been hard for us to understand how Jesus was fully God, since his origin was like ours in every way. When we think of these two other possibilities, it helps us to understand how God, in his wisdom, ordained a combination of human and divine influence in the birth of Christ, so that his full humanity would be evident to us from the fact of his ordinary human birth from a human mother, and his full deity would be evident from the fact of his conception in Mary's womb by the powerful work of the Holy Spirit.[1]

3. The virgin birth also makes possible Christ's true humanity without inherited sin. All human beings have inherited legal guilt and a corrupt moral nature from their first father, Adam (this is sometimes called "inherited sin" or "original sin"). But the fact that Jesus did not have a human father means that the line of descent from Adam is partially interrupted. Jesus did not descend from Adam in exactly the same way in which every other human being has descended from Adam. And this helps us to understand why the legal guilt and moral corruption that belongs to all other human beings did not belong to Christ.

This idea seems to be indicated in the statement of the angel Gabriel to Mary, where he says to her,

---

[1] This is not to say that it would have been *impossible* for God to bring Christ into the world in any other way, but only to say that God, in his wisdom, decided that this would be the best way to bring it about, and part of that is evident in the fact that the virgin birth does help us understand how Jesus can be fully God and fully man. Whether any other means of bringing Christ into the world would have been "possible" in some absolute sense of "possible," Scripture does not tell us.

> "The Holy Spirit will come upon you,
>   and the power of the Most High will overshadow you;
> *therefore the child to be born will be called holy,*
>   the Son of God." (Luke 1:35)

Because the Spirit brought about the conception of Jesus in the womb of Mary, the child was to be called "*holy.*"[2] Such a conclusion should not be taken to mean that the transmission of sin comes only through the father, for Scripture nowhere makes such an assertion. It is enough for us merely to say that *in this case* the unbroken line of descent from Adam was interrupted, and Jesus was conceived by the power of the Holy Spirit. Luke 1:35 connects this conception by the Holy Spirit with the holiness or moral purity of Christ, and reflection on that fact allows us to understand that through the absence of a human father, Jesus was not fully descended from Adam, and that this break in the line of descent was the method God used to bring it about that Jesus was fully human yet did not share inherited sin from Adam.

But why did Jesus not inherit a sinful nature from Mary? The Roman Catholic Church answers this question by saying that Mary herself was free from sin, but Scripture nowhere teaches this, and it would not really solve the problem anyway (for why then did Mary not inherit sin from her mother?).[3] A better solution is to say that the work of the Holy Spirit in Mary must have prevented not only the transmission of sin from Joseph

---

[2]I have quoted here the translation of the RSV, which I think to be correct (so NIV margin). But it is also grammatically possible to translate the words as "so the holy one to be born will be called the Son of God" (NIV; similarly, NASB). The Greek phrase is *dio kai to gennōmenon hagion klēthēsetai, huios theou.* The decision on which translation is correct depends on whether we take *to gennōmenon* as the subject, meaning "the child to be born," or whether we think that the subject is *to hagion,* "the holy one," with the participle *gennōmenon* then functioning as an adjective, giving the sense "the being-born holy one" (this is the way the NIV and NASB understand it).

Recently, more extensive lexical research seems to indicate that the expression *to gennōmenon* was a fairly common expression that was readily understood to mean "the child to be born." Examples of this use can be seen in Plotinus, *Nead,* 3.6.20–24; Plato, *Menexenus,* 237E; *Laws,* 6,775C; Philo, *On the Creation,* 100; *On the Change of Names,* 267; Plutarch, *Moralia,* "Advice to Bride and Groom," 140F; "On Affection for Offspring," 495E. More examples could probably be found with a more extensive computer search, but these should be sufficient to demonstrate that the mere grammatical possibility of translating Luke 1:35 the way the NIV and NASB do is not a strong argument in favor of their translations, because Greek-speaking readers in the first century would ordinarily have understood the words *to gennōmenon* as a unit meaning "the child to be born." Because of this fact, the RSV represents the sense that first-century readers would have understood from the sentence: "therefore *the child to be born* will be called holy." (I discovered these examples of

to gennōmenon by searching the Thesaurus Linguae Graecae data base on the Ibycus computer at Trinity Evangelical Divinity School.)

[3]The Roman Catholic Church teaches the doctrine of the *immaculate conception.* This doctrine does not refer to the conception of Jesus in Mary's womb, but to the conception of *Mary* in her mother's womb, and teaches that Mary was free from inherited sin. On December 8, 1854, Pope Pius IX proclaimed, "The Most Holy Virgin Mary was, in the first moment of her conception . . . in view of the merits of Jesus Christ . . . preserved free from all stain of original sin" (Ludwig Ott, *Fundamentals of Catholic Dogma,* trans. Patrick Lynch [Rockford: Tan, 1960FNT#], p. 190). (The Catholic Church also teaches that "in consequence of a Special Privilege of Grace from God, Mary was free from every personal sin during her whole life," p. 203.)

In response, we must say that the New Testament does highly honor Mary as one who has "found favor with God" (Luke 1:30) and one who is "Blessed . . . among women" (Luke 1:42), but nowhere does the Bible indicate that Mary was free from inherited sin. The expression, "Hail, O *favored one,* the Lord is with you!" (Luke 1:28) simply means that Mary has found much blessing from God; the same word translated "*favored*" in Luke 1:28 (Gk. *charitoō*) is used to refer to all Christians in Eph. 1:6: "his glorious grace which he *freely bestowed* on us in the Beloved." In fact, Ott says, "The doctrine of the Immaculate Conception of Mary is not explicitly revealed in Scripture" (p. 200), though he thinks it is implicit in Gen. 3:15 and Luke 1:28, 41.

(for Jesus had no human father) but also, in a miraculous way, the transmission of sin from Mary: "The Holy Spirit will come upon you . . . *therefore* the child to be born will be called *holy*" (Luke 1:35).

It has been common, at least in previous generations, for those who do not accept the complete truthfulness of Scripture to deny the doctrine of the virgin birth of Christ. But if our beliefs are to be governed by the statements of Scripture, then we will certainly not deny this teaching. Whether or not we could discern any aspects of doctrinal importance for this teaching, we should believe it first of all simply because Scripture affirms it. Certainly such a miracle is not too hard for the God who created the universe and everything in it—anyone who affirms that a virgin birth is "impossible" is just confessing his or her own unbelief in the God of the Bible. Yet in addition to the fact that Scripture teaches the virgin birth, we can see that it is doctrinally important, and if we are to understand the biblical teaching on the person of Christ correctly, it is important that we begin with an affirmation of this doctrine.

2. Human Weaknesses and Limitations.

a. Jesus Had a Human Body: The fact that Jesus had a human body just like our human bodies is seen in many passages of Scripture. He was born just as all human babies are born (Luke 2:7). He grew through childhood to adulthood just as other children grow: "And the child grew and became strong, filled with wisdom; and the favor of God was upon him" (Luke 2:40). Moreover, Luke tells us that "Jesus increased in wisdom *and in stature,* and in favor with God and man" (Luke 2:52).

Jesus became tired just as we do, for we read that "Jesus, *wearied* as he was with his journey, sat down beside the well" in Samaria (John 4:6). He became thirsty, for when he was on the cross he said, *"I thirst"* (John 19:28). After he had fasted for forty days in the wilderness, we read that "he was *hungry*" (Matt. 4:2). He was at times physically weak, for during his temptation in the wilderness he fasted for forty days (the point at which a human being's physical strength is almost entirely gone and beyond which irreparable physical harm will occur if the fast continues). At that time "angels came and ministered to him" (Matt. 4:11), apparently to care for him and provide nourishment until he regained enough strength to come out of the wilderness. When Jesus was on his way to be crucified, the soldiers forced Simon of Cyrene to carry his cross (Luke 23:26), most likely because Jesus was so weak following the beating he had received that he did not have strength enough to carry it himself. The culmination of Jesus' limitations in terms of his human body is seen when he died on the cross (Luke 23:46). His human body ceased to have life in it and ceased to function, just as ours does when we die.

Jesus also rose from the dead in a physical, human body, though one that was made perfect and was no longer subject to weakness, disease, or death. He demonstrates repeatedly to his disciples that he does have a real physical body: he says, "See my hands and my feet, that it is I myself; handle me, and see; for *a spirit has not flesh and bones as you see that I have*" (Luke 24:39). He is showing them and teaching them that he has "flesh and bones" and is not merely a "spirit" without a body. Another evidence of this fact is that "they gave him a piece of broiled fish, and he took it and ate before them" (Luke 24:42; cf. v. 30; John 20:17, 20, 27; 21:9, 13).

In this same human body (though a resurrection body that was made perfect), Jesus also ascended into heaven. He said before he left, "I am leaving the world and going to the Father" (John 16:28; cf. 17:11). The way in which Jesus ascended up to heaven was calculated to demonstrate the continuity between his existence in a physical body here on earth and his continuing existence in that body in heaven. Just a few verses after Jesus had told them, "A spirit has not flesh and bones as you see that I have" (Luke 24:39), we read in Luke's gospel that Jesus "led them out as far as Bethany, and lifting up his hands he blessed them. While he blessed them, he parted from them, and was carried up into heaven" (Luke 24:50–51). Similarly, we read in Acts, "As they were looking on, he was lifted up, and a cloud took him out of their sight" (Acts 1:9).

All of these verses taken together show that, as far as Jesus' human body is concerned, it was like ours in every respect before his resurrection, and after his resurrection it was still a human body with "flesh and bones," but made perfect, the kind of body that we will have when Christ returns and we are raised from the dead as well.[4] Jesus continues to exist in that human body in heaven, as the ascension is designed to teach.

b. Jesus Had a Human Mind: The fact that Jesus *"increased in wisdom"* (Luke 2:52) says that he went through a learning process just as all other children do—he learned how to eat, how to talk, how to read and write, and how to be obedient to his parents (see Heb. 5:8). This ordinary learning process was part of the genuine humanity of Christ.

We also see that Jesus had a human mind like ours when he speaks of the day on which he will return to earth: "But of that day or that hour no one knows, not even the angels in heaven, nor the Son, but only the Father" (Mark 13:32).[5]

c. Jesus Had a Human Soul and Human Emotions: We see several indications that Jesus had a human soul (or spirit). Just before his crucifixion, Jesus said, "Now is my soul *troubled"* (John 12:27). John writes just a little later, "When Jesus had thus spoken, he was *troubled* in spirit" (John 13:21). In both verses the word *troubled* represents the Greek term *tarassō*, a word that is often used of people when they are anxious or suddenly very surprised by danger.[6]

Moreover, before Jesus' crucifixion, as he realized the suffering he would face, he said, "My soul is very sorrowful, even to death" (Matt. 26:38). So great was the sorrow he felt that it seemed as though, if it were to become any stronger, it would take his very life.

Jesus had a full range of human emotions. He "marveled" at the faith of the centurion (Matt. 8:10). He wept with sorrow at the death of Lazarus (John 11:35). And he prayed with a heart full of emotion, for "in the days of his flesh, Jesus offered up prayers and

---

[4]See chapter 4, pp. 109–14, on the nature of the resurrection body.

[5]See further discussion of this verse below, pp. 65–66.

[6]The word *tarassō*, "troubled," is used, for example, to speak of the fact that Herod was "troubled" when he heard that the wise men had come looking for the new king of the Jews (Matt. 2:3); the disciples "were troubled" when they suddenly saw Jesus walking on the sea and thought he was a ghost (Matt. 14:26); Zechariah was "troubled" when he suddenly saw an angel appear in the temple in Jerusalem (Luke 1:12); and the disciples were "troubled" when Jesus suddenly appeared among them after his resurrection (Luke 24:38). But the word is also used in John 14:1, 27, when Jesus says, "Let not your hearts be *troubled*." When Jesus was troubled in his spirit, therefore, we must not think that there was any lack of faith or any sin involved, but it was definitely a strong human emotion that accompanied a time of extreme danger.

supplications, *with loud cries and tears,* to him who was able to save him from death, and he was heard for his godly fear" (Heb. 5:7).

Moreover, the author tells us, "Although he was a Son, *he learned obedience* through what he suffered; and being made perfect he became the source of eternal salvation to all who obey him" (Heb. 5:8–9). Yet if Jesus never sinned, how could he "learn obedience"? Apparently as Jesus grew toward maturity he, like all other human children, was able to take on more and more responsibility. The older he became the more demands his father and mother could place on him in terms of obedience, and the more difficult the tasks that his heavenly Father could assign to him to carry out in the strength of his human nature. With each increasingly difficult task, even when it involved some suffering (as Heb. 5:8 specifies), Jesus' human moral ability, his ability to obey under more and more difficult circumstances, increased. We might say that his "moral backbone" was strengthened by more and more difficult exercise. Yet in all this he never once sinned.

The complete absence of sin in the life of Jesus is all the more remarkable because of the severe temptations he faced, not only in the wilderness, but throughout his life. The author of Hebrews affirms that Jesus "*in every respect* has been tempted as we are, yet without sin" (Heb. 4:15). The fact that he faced temptation means that he had a genuine human nature that could be tempted, for Scripture clearly tells us that "God cannot be tempted with evil" (James 1:13).

d. People Near Jesus Saw Him As Only a Man: Matthew reports an amazing incident in the middle of Jesus' ministry. Even though Jesus had taught throughout all Galilee, "healing every disease and every infirmity among the people," so that "great crowds followed him" (Matt. 4:23–25), when he came to his own village of Nazareth, the people who had known him for many years did not receive him:

> And when Jesus had finished these parables, he went away from there, and coming to his own country he taught them in their synagogue, so that they were astonished, and said, "*Where did this man get this wisdom and these mighty works?* Is not this the carpenter's son? Is not his mother called Mary? And are not his brothers James and Joseph and Simon and Judas? And are not all his sisters with us? Where then did this man get all this?" And *they took offense at him.* . . . And he did not do many mighty works there, *because of their unbelief.* (Matt. 13:53–58)

This passage indicates that those people who knew Jesus best, the neighbors with whom he had lived and worked for thirty years, saw him as no more than an ordinary man — a good man, no doubt, fair and kind and truthful, but certainly not a prophet of God who could work miracles and certainly not God himself in the flesh. Although in the following sections we will see how Jesus was fully divine in every way — was truly God and man in one person — we must still recognize the full force of a passage like this. For the first thirty years of his life Jesus lived a human life that was so ordinary that the people of Nazareth who knew him best were amazed that he could teach with authority and work miracles. They knew him. He was one of them. He was "the carpenter's son" (Matt. 13:55), and he was himself "the carpenter" (Mark 6:3), so ordinary that they could ask, "Where then did this man get all this?" (Matt. 13:56). And John tells us, "*Even his brothers* did not believe in him" (John 7:5).

Was Jesus fully human? He was so fully human that even those who lived and worked with him for thirty years, even those brothers who grew up in his own household, did not realize that he was anything more than another very good human being. They apparently had no idea that he was God come in the flesh.

3. Sinlessness. Though the New Testament clearly affirms that Jesus was fully human just as we are, it also affirms that Jesus was different in one important respect: he was without sin, and he never committed sin during his lifetime. Some have objected that if Jesus did not sin, then he was not *truly* human, for all humans sin. But those making that objection simply fail to realize that human beings are now in an *abnormal* situation. God did not create us sinful, but holy and righteous. Adam and Eve in the Garden of Eden before they sinned were *truly* human, and we now, though human, do not match the pattern that God intends for us when our full, sinless humanity is restored.

The sinlessness of Jesus is taught frequently in the New Testament. We see suggestions of this early in his life when he was "filled with wisdom" and "the favor of God was upon him" (Luke 2:40). Then we see that Satan was unable to tempt Jesus successfully, but failed, after forty days, to persuade him to sin: "And when the devil had ended every temptation, he departed from him until an opportune time" (Luke 4:13). We also see in the synoptic gospels (Matthew, Mark, and Luke) no evidence of wrongdoing on Jesus' part. To the Jews who opposed him, Jesus asked, "Which of you convicts me of sin?" (John 8:46), and received no answer.

The statements about Jesus' sinlessness are more explicit in John's gospel. Jesus made the amazing proclamation, "I am the light of the world" (John 8:12). If we understand light to represent both truthfulness and moral purity, then Jesus is here claiming to be the source of truth and the source of moral purity and holiness in the world—an astounding claim, and one that could only be made by someone who was free from sin. Moreover, with regard to obedience to his Father in heaven, he said, "I always do what is pleasing to him" (John 8:29; the present tense gives the sense of continual activity, "I *am always doing* what is pleasing to him"). At the end of his life, Jesus could say, "I have kept my Father's commandments and abide in his love" (John 15:10). It is significant that when Jesus was put on trial before Pilate, in spite of the accusations of the Jews, Pilate could only conclude, "I find no crime in him" (John 18:38).

In the book of Acts Jesus is several times called the "Holy One" or the "Righteous One," or is referred to with some similar expression (see Acts 2:27; 3:14; 4:30; 7:52; 13:35). When Paul speaks of Jesus coming to live as a man he is careful not to say that he took on "sinful flesh," but rather says that God sent his own Son "*in the likeness of sinful flesh and for sin*" (Rom. 8:3). And he refers to Jesus as "him . . . who knew no sin" (2 Cor. 5:21).

The author of Hebrews affirms that Jesus was tempted but simultaneously insists that he did not sin: Jesus is "one who in every respect has been tempted as we are, *yet without sin*" (Heb. 4:15). He is a high priest who is "holy, blameless, unstained, separated from sinners, exalted above the heavens" (Heb. 7:26). Peter speaks of Jesus as "a lamb without blemish or spot" (1 Peter 1:19), using Old Testament imagery to affirm his freedom from any moral defilement. Peter directly states, *"He committed no sin; no guile was found on his lips"* (1 Peter 2:22). When Jesus died, it was "the righteous for the unrighteous, that he might bring us to God" (1 Peter 3:18). And John, in his first epistle, calls him "Jesus Christ the righteous" (1 John 2:1) and says, "In him there is no sin" (1 John 3:5). It is hard to deny, then, that the sinlessness of Christ is taught clearly in all the major sections of the New Testament. He was truly man yet without sin.

In connection with Jesus' sinlessness, we should notice in more detail the nature of his temptations in the wilderness (Matt. 4:1–11; Mark 1:12–13; Luke 4:1–13). The essence of these temptations was an attempt to persuade Jesus to escape from the hard path of obedience and suffering that was appointed for him as the Messiah. Jesus was "led by the Spirit for forty days in the wilderness, tempted by the devil" (Luke 4:1–2). In many respects this temptation was parallel to the testing that Adam and Eve faced in the Garden of Eden, but it was much more difficult. Adam and Eve had fellowship with God and with each other and had an abundance of all kinds of food, for they were only told not to eat from one tree. By contrast, Jesus had no human fellowship and no food to eat, and after he had fasted for forty days he was near the point of physical death. In both cases the kind of obedience required was not obedience to an eternal moral principle rooted in the character of God, but was a test of pure obedience to God's specific directive. With Adam and Eve, God told them not to eat of the tree of the knowledge of good and evil, and the question was whether they would obey simply because God told them. In the case of Jesus, "led by the Spirit" for forty days in the wilderness, he apparently realized that it was the Father's will that he eat nothing during those days but simply remain there until the Father, through the leading of the Holy Spirit, told him that the temptations were over and he could leave.

We can understand, then, the force of the temptation, "If you are the Son of God, command this stone to become bread" (Luke 4:3). Of course Jesus was the Son of God, and of course he had the power to make any stone into bread instantly. He was the one who would soon change water into wine and multiply the loaves and the fishes. The temptation was intensified by the fact that it seemed as though, if he did not eat soon, his very life would be taken from him. Yet he had come to obey God perfectly in our place, and to do so *as a man*. This meant that he had to obey in his human strength alone. If he had called upon his divine powers to make the temptation easier for himself, then he would not have obeyed God fully *as a man*. The temptation was to use his divine power to "cheat" a bit on the requirements and make obedience somewhat easier. But Jesus, unlike Adam and Eve, refused to eat what appeared to be good and necessary for him, choosing rather to obey the command of his heavenly Father.

The temptation to bow down and worship Satan for a moment and then receive authority over "all the kingdoms of the world" (Luke 4:5) was a temptation to receive power not through the path of lifelong obedience to his heavenly Father, but through wrongful submission to the Prince of Darkness. Again, Jesus rejected the apparently easy path and chose the path of obedience that led to the cross.

Similarly, the temptation to throw himself down from the pinnacle of the temple (Luke 4:9–11) was a temptation to "force" God to perform a miracle and rescue him in a spectacular way, thus attracting a large following from the people without pursuing the hard path ahead, the path that included three years of ministering to people's needs, teaching with authority, and exemplifying absolute holiness of life in the midst of harsh opposition. But Jesus again resisted this "easy route" to the fulfillment of his goals as the Messiah (again, a route that would not actually have fulfilled those goals in any case).

These temptations were really the culmination of a lifelong process of moral strengthening and maturing that occurred throughout Jesus' childhood and early adulthood, as he "increased in wisdom . . . and in favor with God" (Luke 2:52) and as he "*learned obedience* through what he suffered" (Heb. 5:8). In these temptations in the wilderness and in the various temptations that faced him through the thirty-three years of his life, Christ obeyed God in our place and as our representative, thus succeeding where Adam had failed, where the people of Israel in the wilderness had failed, and where we had failed (see Rom. 5:18–19).

As difficult as it may be for us to comprehend, Scripture affirms that in these temptations Jesus gained an ability to understand and help us in our temptations. "*Because he himself has suffered and been tempted,* he is able to help those who are tempted" (Heb. 2:18). The author goes on to connect Jesus' ability to sympathize with our weaknesses to the fact the he was tempted as we are:

> For we have not a high priest who is unable to sympathize with our weaknesses, but one who in every respect has been tempted as we are, yet without sin. Let us then [lit., 'therefore'] with confidence draw near to the throne of grace, that we may receive mercy and find grace to help in time of need. (Heb. 4:15–16)

This has practical application for us: in every situation in which we are struggling with temptation, we should reflect on the life of Christ and ask if there were not similar situations that he faced. Usually, after reflecting for a moment or two, we will be able to think of some instances in the life of Christ where he faced temptations that, though they were not the same in every detail, were very similar to the situations that we face every day.[7]

4. Could Jesus Have Sinned? The question is sometimes raised, "Was it possible for Christ to have sinned?" Some people argue for the *impeccability* of Christ, in which the word *impeccable* means "not able to sin."[8] Others object that if Jesus were not able to sin, his temptations could not have been real, for how can a temptation be real if the person being tempted is not able to sin anyway?

---

[7]Particularly with respect to family life, it is helpful to remember that Joseph is nowhere mentioned in the Gospels after the incident in the temple when Jesus was twelve years old. It is especially interesting that Joseph is omitted from the verses that list Jesus' mother and other family members, even naming his brothers and sisters (see Matt. 13:55–56; Mark 6:3; cf. Matt. 12:48). It would seem very strange, for example, that "the mother of Jesus" was at the wedding at Cana in Galilee (John 2:1) but not his father, if his father were still living (cf. John 2:12). This suggests that sometime after Jesus was twelve Joseph had died, and that for a period in his life Jesus grew up in a "single-parent home." This would mean that, as he became older, he assumed more and more of the responsibility of male leadership in that family, earning a living as a "carpenter" (Mark 6:3) and no doubt helping care for his younger brothers and sisters as well. Therefore, although Jesus was never married, he no doubt experienced a wide range of family situations and conflicts similar to those experienced by families today.

[8]The Latin word *peccare* means "to sin."

In order to answer this question we must distinguish what Scripture clearly affirms, on the one hand, and, on the other hand, what is more in the nature of possible inference on our part. (1) Scripture clearly affirms that Christ never actually sinned (see above). There should be no question in our minds at all on this fact. (2) It also clearly affirms that Jesus was tempted, and that these were real temptations (Luke 4:2). If we believe Scripture, then we must insist that Christ "*in every respect has been tempted as we are,* yet without sin" (Heb. 4:15). If our speculation on the question of whether Christ could have sinned ever leads us to say that he was not truly tempted, then we have reached a wrong conclusion, one that contradicts the clear statements of Scripture.

(3) We also must affirm with Scripture that "God cannot be tempted with evil" (James 1:13). But here the question becomes difficult: if Jesus was fully God as well as fully man (and we shall argue below that Scripture clearly and repeatedly teaches this), then must we not also affirm that (in some sense) Jesus also "could not be tempted with evil"?

This is as far as we can go in terms of clear and explicit affirmations of Scripture. At this point we are faced with a dilemma similar to a number of other doctrinal dilemmas where Scripture seems to be teaching things that are, if not directly contradictory, at least very difficult to combine together in our understanding. For example, with respect to the doctrine of the Trinity, we affirmed that God exists in three persons, and each is fully God, and there is one God. Although those statements are not contradictory, they are, nonetheless, difficult to understand in connection with each other, and although we can make some progress in understanding how they fit together, in this life, at least, we have to admit that there can be no final understanding on our part. Here the situation is somewhat similar. We do not have an actual contradiction. Scripture does not tell us that "Jesus was tempted" and that "Jesus was not tempted" (a contradiction if "Jesus" and "tempted" are used exactly in the same sense in both sentences). The Bible tells us that "Jesus was tempted" and "Jesus was fully man" and "Jesus was fully God" and "God cannot be tempted." This combination of teachings from Scripture leaves open the possibility that as we understand the way in which Jesus' human nature and divine nature work together, we might understand more of the way in which he could be tempted in one sense and yet, in another sense, not be tempted. (This possibility will be discussed further below.)

At this point, then, we pass beyond the clear affirmations of Scripture and attempt to suggest a solution to the problem of whether Christ could have sinned. But it is important to recognize that the following solution is more in the nature of a suggested means of combining various biblical teachings and is not directly supported by explicit statements of Scripture. With this in mind, it is appropriate for us to say:[9] (1) If Jesus' human nature had existed by itself, independent of his divine nature, then it would have been a human nature just like that which God gave Adam and Eve. It would have been free from sin but nonetheless *able to sin.* Therefore, if Jesus' human nature had existed by itself, there was the abstract or theoretical possibility that Jesus could have sinned, just as Adam and Eve's human natures were able to sin. (2) But Jesus' human nature never existed apart from union with his divine nature. From the moment of his conception, he existed as truly

---

[9]In this discussion I am largely following the conclusions of Geerhardus Vos, *Biblical Theology* (Grand Rapids: Eerdmans, 1948), pp. 339–42.

God and truly man as well. Both his human nature and his divine nature existed united in one person. (3) Although there were some things (such as being hungry or thirsty or weak) that Jesus experienced in his human nature alone and were not experienced in his divine nature (see below), nonetheless, an act of sin would have been a moral act that would apparently have involved the whole person of Christ. Therefore, if he had sinned, it would have involved both his human and divine natures. (4) But if Jesus as a person had sinned, involving both his human and divine natures in sin, then God himself would have sinned, and he would have ceased to be God. Yet that is clearly impossible because of the infinite holiness of God's nature. (5) Therefore, if we are asking if it was *actually* possible for Jesus to have sinned, it seems that we must conclude that it was not possible. The union of his human and divine natures in one person prevented it.

But the question remains, "How then could Jesus' temptations be real?" The example of the temptation to change the stones into bread is helpful in this regard. Jesus had the ability, by virtue of his divine nature, to perform this miracle, but if he had done it, he would no longer have been obeying in the strength of his human nature alone, he would have failed the test that Adam also failed, and he would not have earned our salvation for us. Therefore, Jesus refused to rely on his divine nature to make obedience easier for him. In like manner, it seems appropriate to conclude that Jesus met every temptation to sin, not by his divine power, but on the strength of his human nature alone (though, of course, it was not "alone" because Jesus, in exercising the kind of faith that humans should exercise, was perfectly depending on God the Father and the Holy Spirit at every moment). The moral strength of his divine nature was there as a sort of "backstop" that would have prevented him from sinning in any case (and therefore we can say that it was not possible for him to sin), but he did not rely on the strength of his divine nature to make it easier for him to face temptations, and his refusal to turn the stones into bread at the beginning of his ministry is a clear indication of this.

Were the temptations real then? Many theologians have pointed out that only he who successfully resists a temptation to the end most fully feels the force of that temptation. Just as a champion weightlifter who successfully lifts and holds over head the heaviest weight in the contest feels the force of it more fully than one who attempts to lift it and drops it, so any Christian who has successfully faced a temptation to the end knows that that is far more difficult than giving in to it at once. So it was with Jesus: every temptation he faced, he faced to the end, and triumphed over it. The temptations were real, even though he did not give in to them. In fact, they were most real *because* he did not give in to them.

What then do we say about the fact that "God cannot be tempted with evil" (James 1:13)? It seems that this is one of a number of things that we must affirm to be true of Jesus' divine nature but not of his human nature. His divine nature could not be tempted with evil, but his human nature could be tempted and was clearly tempted. How these two natures united in one person in facing temptations, Scripture does not clearly explain to us. But this distinction between what is true of one nature and what is true of another nature is an example of a number of similar statements that Scripture requires us to make (see more on this distinction, below, when we discuss how Jesus could be God and man in one person).

5. Why Was Jesus' Full Humanity Necessary? When John wrote his first epistle, a heretical teaching was circulating in the church to the effect that Jesus was not a man. This heresy became known as *docetism*.[10] So serious was this denial of truth about Christ, that John could say it was a doctrine of the antichrist: "By this you know the Spirit of God: every spirit which confesses *that Jesus Christ has come in the flesh* is of God, and every spirit which does not confess Jesus is not of God. This is the spirit of antichrist" (1 John 4:2–3). The apostle John understood that to deny Jesus' true humanity was to deny something at the very heart of Christianity, so that no one who denied that Jesus had come in the flesh was sent from God.

As we look through the New Testament, we see several reasons why Jesus had to be fully man if he was going to be the Messiah and earn our salvation. We can list seven of those reasons here.

a. For Representative Obedience: Jesus was our representative and obeyed for us where Adam had failed and disobeyed.[11] We see this in the parallels between Jesus' temptation (Luke 4:1–13) and the time of testing for Adam and Eve in the garden (Gen. 2:15–3:7). It is also clearly reflected in Paul's discussion of the parallels between Adam and Christ, in Adam's disobedience and Christ's obedience:

> Then as one man's trespass led to condemnation for all men, so *one man's act of righteousness* leads to acquittal and life for all men. For as by one man's disobedience many were made sinners, so *by one man's obedience* many will be made righteous. (Rom. 5:18–19)

This is why Paul can call Christ "the last Adam" (1 Cor. 15:45) and can call Adam the "first man" and Christ the "second man" (1 Cor. 15:47). Jesus had to be a man in order to be our representative and obey in our place.

b. To Be a Substitute Sacrifice: If Jesus had not been a man, he could not have died in our place and paid the penalty that was due to us. The author of Hebrews tells us that "For surely it is not with angels that he is concerned but with the descendants of Abraham. Therefore he *had to* be made like his brethren in every respect, so that he might become a merciful and faithful high priest in the service of God, to make expiation [more accurately, 'propitiation'] for the sins of the people" (Heb. 2:16–17; cf. v. 14). Jesus had to become a man, not an angel, because God was concerned with saving men, not with saving angels. But to do this he *"had to"* be made like us in every way, so that he might become "the propitiation" for us, the sacrifice that is an acceptable substitute for us. Though this idea will be discussed more fully in chapter 3, on the atonement, it is important here to realize that unless Christ was fully man, he could

---

[10]The word *docetism* comes from the Greek verb *dokeō*, "to seem, to appear to be." Any theological position that says that Jesus was not really a man, but only appeared to be a man, is called a "docetic" position. Behind docetism is an assumption that the material creation is inherently evil, and therefore the Son of God could not have been united to a true human nature.

No prominent church leader ever advocated docetism, but it was a troublesome heresy that had various supporters in the first four centuries of the church. Modern evangelicals who neglect to teach on the full humanity of Christ can unwittingly support docetic tendencies in their hearers.

[11]See chapter 3, pp. 73–74.

not have died to pay the penalty for man's sins. He could not have been a substitute sacrifice for us.

c. To Be the One Mediator Between God and Men: Because we were alienated from God by sin, we needed someone to come between God and ourselves and bring us back to him. We needed a mediator who could represent us to God and who could represent God to us. There is only one person who has ever fulfilled that requirement: "There is one God, and *there is one mediator* between God and men, the man Christ Jesus" (1 Tim. 2:5). In order to fulfill this role of mediator, Jesus had to be fully man as well as fully God.

d. To Fulfill God's Original Purpose for Man to Rule Over Creation: God put mankind on the earth to subdue it and rule over it as God's representatives. But man did not fulfill that purpose, for he instead fell into sin. The author of Hebrews realizes that God intended everything to be in subjection to man, but he admits, "As it is, we do not yet see everything in subjection to him" (Heb. 2:8). Then when Jesus came as a man, he was able to obey God and thereby have the right to rule over creation *as a man,* thus fulfilling God's original purpose in putting man on the earth. Hebrews recognizes this when it says that now "we see Jesus" in the place of authority over the universe, "crowned with glory and honor" (Heb. 2:9; cf. the same phrase in v. 7). Jesus in fact has been given "all authority in heaven and on earth" (Matt. 28:18), and God has "put all things under his feet and has made him the head over all things for the church" (Eph. 1:22). Indeed, we shall someday reign with him on his throne (Rev. 3:21) and experience, in subjection to Christ our Lord, the fulfillment of God's purpose that we reign over the earth (cf. Luke 19:17, 19; 1 Cor. 6:3). Jesus had to be a man in order to fulfill God's original purpose that man rule over his creation.

e. To Be Our Example and Pattern in Life: John tells us, "He who says he abides in him ought to walk *in the same way in which he walked*" (1 John 2:6), and reminds us that "when he appears we shall be like him," and that this hope of future conformity to Christ's character even now gives increasing moral purity to our lives (1 John 3:2–3). Paul tells us that we are continually being "changed into his likeness" (2 Cor. 3:18), thus moving toward the goal for which God saved us, that we might "be conformed to the image of his Son" (Rom. 8:29). Peter tells us that especially in suffering we have to consider Christ's example: "Christ also suffered for you, *leaving you an example,* that you should follow in his steps" (1 Peter 2:21). Throughout our Christian life, we are to run the race set before us "looking to Jesus the pioneer and perfecter of our faith" (Heb. 12:2). If we become discouraged by the hostility and opposition of sinners, we are to "consider him who endured from sinners such hostility against himself" (Heb. 12:3). Jesus is also our example in death. Paul's goal is to become "*like him* in his death" (Phil. 3:10; cf. Acts 7:60; 1 Peter 3:17–18 with 4:1). Our goal should be to be like Christ all our days, up to the point of death, and to die with unfailing obedience to God, with strong trust in him, and with love and forgiveness to others. Jesus had to become a man like us in order to live as our example and pattern in life.

f. To Be the Pattern for Our Redeemed Bodies: Paul tells us that when Jesus rose from the dead he rose in a new body that was "imperishable . . . raised in glory . . . raised in power . . . raised a spiritual body" (1 Cor. 15:42–44). This new resurrection body that Jesus had when he rose from the dead is the pattern for what our bodies will be like when we are raised from the dead, because Christ is "the first fruits" (1 Cor. 15:23)—an agricultural metaphor that likens Christ to the first sample of the harvest, showing what the other fruit from that harvest would be like. We now have a physical body like Adam's, but we will have one like Christ's: "Just as we have borne the image of the man of dust, we shall also bear the image of the man of heaven" (1 Cor. 15:49). Jesus had to be raised as a man in order to be the "first-born from the dead" (Col. 1:18), the pattern for the bodies that we would later have.

g. To Sympathize As High Priest: The author of Hebrews reminds us that "because he himself has suffered and been tempted, he is able to help those who are tempted" (Heb. 2:18; cf. 4:15–16). If Jesus had not been a man, he would not have been able to know *by experience* what we go through in our temptations and struggles in this life. But because he has lived as a man, he is able to sympathize more fully with us in our experiences.[12]

6. Jesus Will Be a Man Forever. Jesus did not give up his human nature after his death and resurrection, for he appeared to his disciples as a man after the resurrection, even with the scars of the nail prints in his hands (John 20:25–27). He had "flesh and bones" (Luke 24:39) and ate food (Luke 24:41–42). Later, when he was talking with his disciples, he was taken up into heaven, still in his resurrected human body, and two angels promised that he would return in the same way: "This Jesus, who was taken up from you into heaven, *will come in the same way* as you saw him go into heaven" (Acts 1:11). Still later, Stephen gazed into heaven and saw Jesus as "the Son of man standing at the right hand of God" (Acts 7:56). Jesus also appeared to Saul on the Damascus Road and said, "I am Jesus, whom you are persecuting" (Acts 9:5)—an appearance that Saul (Paul) later coupled with the resurrection appearances of Jesus to others (1 Cor. 9:1; 15:8). In John's vision in Revelation, Jesus still appears as "one like a son of man" (Rev. 1:13), though he is filled with great glory and power, and his appearance causes John to fall at his feet in awe (Rev. 1:13–17). He promises one day to drink wine again with his disciples in his Father's kingdom (Matt. 26:29) and invites us to a great marriage supper in heaven (Rev. 19:9). Moreover, Jesus will continue forever in his offices as prophet, priest, and king, all of them carried out by virtue of the fact that he is both God and man forever.[13]

---

[12]This is a difficult concept for us to understand, because we do not want to say that Jesus acquired additional knowledge or information by becoming man: certainly as omniscient God he knew every fact there was to know about the experience of human suffering. But the book of Hebrews does say, "*Because* he himself has suffered and been tempted, he is able to help those who are tempted" (Heb. 2:18), and we must insist that that statement is true—there is a relationship between Jesus' suffering and his ability to sympathize with us and help us in temptation. Apparently the author is speaking not of any additional factual or intellectual knowledge, but of an ability to recall a personal experience that he had himself gone through, an ability he would not have if he had not had that personal experience. Some faint parallel to this might be seen in the fact that a man who is a medical doctor, and has perhaps even written a textbook on obstetrics, might know far more *information* about childbirth than any of his patients. Yet, because he is a man, he will never share in that actual experience. A woman who has herself had a baby (or, to give a closer parallel, a woman physician who first writes a textbook and then has a baby herself) can sympathize much more fully with other women who are having babies.

[13]See chapter 5, pp. 124–32, on the offices of Christ.

All of these texts indicate that Jesus did not *temporarily* become man, but that his divine nature was *permanently* united to his human nature, and he lives forever not just as the eternal Son of God, the second person of the Trinity, but also as Jesus, the man who was born of Mary, and as Christ, the Messiah and Savior of his people. Jesus will remain fully God and fully man, yet one person, forever.

B. The Deity of Christ

To complete the biblical teaching about Jesus Christ, we must affirm not only that he was fully human, but also that he was fully divine. Although the word does not explicitly occur in Scripture, the church has used the term *incarnation* to refer to the fact that Jesus was God in human flesh. The *incarnation* was the act of God the Son whereby he took to himself a human nature.[14] The scriptural proof for the deity of Christ is very extensive in the New Testament. We shall examine it under several categories.[15]

1. Direct Scriptural Claims. In this section we examine direct statements of Scripture that Jesus is God or that he is divine.[16]

a. The Word *God (Theos)* Used of Christ: Although the word *theos*, "God," is usually reserved in the New Testament for God the Father, nonetheless, there are several passages where it is also used to refer to Jesus Christ. In all of these passages the word "God" is used in the strong sense to refer to the one who is the Creator of heaven and earth, the ruler over all. These passages include John 1:1; 1:18 (in older and better manuscripts); 20:28; Romans 9:5; Titus 2:13; Hebrews 1:8 (quoting Ps. 45:6); and 2 Peter 1:1.[17] There are at least these seven clear passages in the New Testament that explicitly refer to Jesus as God. [18]

One Old Testament example of the name *God* applied to Christ is seen in a familiar messianic passage: "For to us a child is born, to us a son is given; and the government will be upon his shoulder, and his name will be called 'Wonderful Counselor, *Mighty God . . .*'" (Isa. 9:6).

b. The Word *Lord (Kyrios)* Used of Christ: Sometimes the word *Lord* (Gk. *kyrios*) is used simply as a polite address to a superior, roughly equivalent to our word *sir* (see Matt.

---

[14]The Latin word *incarnāre* means "to make flesh," and is derived from the prefix *in-* (which has a causative sense, "to cause something to be something") and the stem *caro, carnis-,* "flesh."

[15]In the following section I have not distinguished between claims to deity made by Jesus himself and claims made about him by others: while such a distinction is helpful for tracing development in people's understanding of Christ, for our present purposes both kinds of statements are found in our canonical New Testament Scriptures and are valid sources for building Christian doctrine.

[16]An excellent discussion of New Testament evidence for the deity of Christ, drawn especially from the titles of Christ

in the New Testament, is found in Donald Guthrie, *New Testament Theology* (Leicester and Downers Grove, Ill.: InterVarsity Press, 1981), pp. 235–365.

[17]Titus 1:3, in connection with the fact that v. 4 calls Christ Jesus "our Savior" and the fact that it was Jesus Christ who commissioned Paul to preach the gospel, might also be considered another example of the use of the word *God* to refer to Christ.

[18]For discussion of passages that refer to Jesus as "God," see Murray J. Harris, *Jesus as God* (Grand Rapids: Baker, 1992), for the most extensive exegetical treatment ever published dealing with New Testament passages that refer to Jesus as "God."

13:27; 21:30; 27:63; John 4:11). Sometimes it can simply mean "master" of a servant or slave (Matt. 6:24; 21:40). Yet the same word is also used in the Septuagint (the Greek translation of the Old Testament, which was commonly used at the time of Christ) as a translation for the Hebrew *yhwh,* "Yahweh," or (as it is frequently translated) "the Lord," or "Jehovah." The word *kyrios* is used to translate the name of the Lord 6,814 times in the Greek Old Testament. Therefore, any Greek-speaking reader at the time of the New Testament who had any knowledge at all of the Greek Old Testament would have recognized that, in contexts where it was appropriate, the word "Lord" was the name of the one who was the Creator and Sustainer of heaven and earth, the omnipotent God.

Now there are many instances in the New Testament where "Lord" is used of Christ in what can only be understood as this strong Old Testament sense, "the Lord" who is Yahweh or God himself. This use of the word "Lord" is quite striking in the word of the angel to the shepherds of Bethlehem: "For to you is born this day in the city of David a Savior, who is Christ *the Lord*" (Luke 2:11). Though these words are familiar to us from frequent reading of the Christmas story, we should realize how surprising it would be to any first-century Jew to hear that someone born as a baby was the "Christ" (or "Messiah"),[19] and, moreover, that this one who was the Messiah was also "the Lord"—that is, the Lord God himself! The amazing force of the angel's statement, which the shepherds could hardly believe, was to say, essentially, "Today in Bethlehem a baby has been born who is your Savior and your Messiah, and who is also God himself." It is not surprising that "all who heard it wondered at what the shepherds told them" (Luke 2:18).

When Mary comes to visit Elizabeth several months before Jesus is to be born, Elizabeth says, "Why is this granted me, that the mother of *my Lord* should come to me?" (Luke 1:43). Because Jesus was not even born, Elizabeth could not be using the word "Lord" to mean something like human "master." She must rather be using it in the strong Old Testament sense, giving an amazing sense to the sentence: "Why is this granted me, that the mother of the Lord God himself should come to me?" Though this is a very strong statement, it is difficult to understand the word "Lord" in this context in any weaker sense.

We see another example when Matthew says that John the Baptist is the one who cries out in the wilderness, "Prepare the way of *the Lord,* make his paths straight" (Matt. 3:3). In doing this John is quoting Isaiah 40:3, which speaks about the Lord God himself coming among his people. But the context applies this passage to John's role of preparing the way for Jesus to come. The implication is that when Jesus comes, *the Lord himself* will come.

Jesus also identifies himself as the sovereign Lord of the Old Testament when he asks the Pharisees about Psalm 110:1, "The Lord said to *my Lord,* Sit at my right hand, till I put your enemies under your feet" (Matt. 22:44). The force of this statement is that "God the Father said to God the Son [David's Lord], 'Sit at my right hand. . . .'" The Pharisees know he is talking about himself and identifying himself as one worthy of the Old Testament title *kyrios,* "Lord."

Such usage is seen frequently in the Epistles, where "the Lord" is a common name to refer to Christ. Paul says "there is one God, the Father, from whom are all things and for

---

[19]The word *Christ* is the Greek translation of the Hebrew word *Messiah.*

whom we exist, and *one Lord*, Jesus Christ, through whom are all things and through whom we exist" (1 Cor. 8:6; cf. 12:3, and many other passages in the Pauline epistles).

A particularly clear passage is found in Hebrews 1, where the author quotes Psalm 102, which speaks about the work of the Lord in creation and applies it to Christ:

> You, Lord, founded the earth in the beginning,
> and the heavens are the work of your hands;
> they will perish, but you remain;
> they will all grow old like a garment,
> like a mantle you will roll them up,
> and they will be changed.
> But you are the same,
> and your years will never end. (Heb. 1:10–12)

Here Christ is explicitly spoken of as the eternal Lord of heaven and earth who created all things and will remain the same forever. Such strong usage of the term "Lord" to refer to Christ culminates in Revelation 19:16, where we see Christ returning as conquering King, and "On his robe and on his thigh he has a name inscribed, King of kings and *Lord of lords.*"

c. Other Strong Claims to Deity: In addition to the uses of the word *God* and *Lord* to refer to Christ, we have other passages that strongly claim deity for Christ. When Jesus told his Jewish opponents that Abraham had seen his (Christ's) day, they challenged him, "You are not yet fifty years old, and have you seen Abraham?" (John 8:57). Here a sufficient response to prove Jesus' eternity would have been, "Before Abraham was, I was." But Jesus did not say this. Instead, he made a much more startling assertion: "Truly, truly, I say to you, before Abraham was, *I am*" (John 8:58). Jesus combined two assertions whose sequence seemed to make no sense: "Before something in the past happened [Abraham was], something in the present happened [I am]." The Jewish leaders recognized at once that he was not speaking in riddles or uttering nonsense: when he said, "I am," he was repeating the very words God used when he identified himself to Moses as "*I AM who I AM*" (Ex. 3:14). Jesus was claiming for himself the title "I AM," by which God designates himself as the eternal existing One, the God who is the source of his own existence and who always has been and always will be. When the Jews heard this unusual, emphatic, solemn statement, they knew that he was claiming to be God. "So they took up stones to throw at him; but Jesus hid himself, and went out of the temple" (John 8:59).[20]

Another strong claim to deity is Jesus' statement at the end of Revelation, "I am the Alpha and the Omega, the first and the last, the beginning and the end" (Rev. 22:13). When this is combined with the statement of God the Father in Revelation 1:8, "I am the Alpha and the Omega," it also constitutes a strong claim to equal deity with

---

[20]The other "I am" sayings in John's gospel, where Jesus claims to be the bread of life (6:35), the light of the world (8:12), the door of the sheep (10:7), the good shepherd (10:11), the resurrection and the life (11:25), the way, the truth, and the life (14:6), and the true vine (15:1), also contribute to the overall picture of deity that John paints of Christ: see Guthrie, *New Testament Theology,* pp. 330–32.

God the Father. Sovereign over all of history and all of creation, Jesus is the beginning and the end.

In John 1:1, John not only calls Jesus "God" but also refers to him as "the Word" (Gk. *logos*). John's readers would have recognized in this term *logos* a dual reference, both to the powerful, creative Word of God in the Old Testament by which the heavens and earth were created (Ps. 33:6) and to the organizing or unifying principle of the universe, the thing that held it together and allowed it to make sense, in Greek thinking.[21] John is identifying Jesus with both of these ideas and saying that he is not only the powerful, creative Word of God and the organizing or unifying force in the universe, but also that he became man: "The Word became flesh and dwelt among us, full of grace and truth; we have beheld his glory, glory as of the only Son from the Father" (John 1:14). Here is another strong claim to deity coupled with an explicit statement that Jesus also became man and moved among us as a man.

Further evidence of claims to deity can be found in the fact that Jesus calls himself "*the* Son of man." This title is used eighty-four times in the four gospels but only by Jesus and only to speak of himself (note, e.g., Matt. 16:13 with Luke 9:18). In the rest of the New Testament, the phrase "*the* Son of man" (with the definite article "the") is used only once, in Acts 7:56, where Stephen refers to Christ as the Son of Man. This unique term has as its background the vision in Daniel 7 where Daniel saw one like a "Son of Man" who "came to the Ancient of Days" and was given "dominion and glory and kingdom, *that all peoples, nations, and languages should serve him; his dominion is an everlasting dominion,* which shall not pass away" (Dan. 7:13–14). It is striking that this "son of man" came "with the clouds of heaven" (Dan. 7:13). This passage clearly speaks of someone who had heavenly origin and who was given *eternal rule* over the *whole world.* The high priests did not miss the point of this passage when Jesus said, "Hereafter you will see the Son of man *seated at the right hand of Power, and coming on the clouds of heaven*" (Matt. 26:64). The reference to Daniel 7:13–14 was unmistakable, and the high priest and his council knew that Jesus was claiming to be the eternal world ruler of heavenly origin spoken of in Daniel's vision. Immediately they said, "He has uttered blasphemy. . . . He deserves death" (Matt. 26:65–66). Here Jesus finally made explicit the strong claims to eternal world rule that were earlier hinted at in his frequent use of the title "the Son of man" to apply to himself.

Though the title "Son of God" can sometimes be used simply to refer to Israel (Matt. 2:15), or to man as created by God (Luke 2:38), or to redeemed man generally (Rom. 8:14, 19, 23), there are nevertheless instances in which the phrase "Son of God" refers to Jesus as the heavenly, eternal Son who is equal to God himself (see Matt. 11:25–30; 17:5; 1 Cor. 15:28; Heb. 1:1–3, 5, 8). This is especially true in John's gospel where Jesus is seen as a unique Son from the Father (John 1:14, 18, 34, 49) who fully reveals the Father (John 8:19; 14:9). As Son he is so great that we can trust in him for eternal life (something that could be said of no created being: John 3:16, 36; 20:31). He is also the one who has all authority from the Father to give life, pronounce eternal judgment, and rule over all (John 3:36; 5:20–22, 25; 10:17; 16:15). As Son he has been sent by the Father, and therefore he existed before he came into the world (John 3:17; 5:23; 10:36).

---

[21]See Guthrie, *New Testament Theology,* esp. p. 326.

The first three verses of Hebrews are emphatic in saying that the Son is the one whom God "appointed the heir of all things, through whom also he created the world" (Heb. 1:2). This Son, says the writer, "reflects the glory of God and bears the very stamp [lit., is the 'exact duplicate,' Gk. *charaktēr*) of his nature, upholding the universe by his word of power" (Heb. 1:3). Jesus is the exact duplicate of the "nature" (or being, Gk. *hypostasis*) of God, making him exactly equal to God in every attribute. Moreover, he continually upholds the universe "by his word of power," something that only God could do.

These passages combine to indicate that the title "Son of God" *when applied to Christ* strongly affirms his deity as the eternal Son in the Trinity, one equal to God the Father in all his attributes.

2. Evidence That Jesus Possessed Attributes of Deity. In addition to the specific affirmations of Jesus' deity seen in the many passages quoted above, we see many examples of actions in Jesus' lifetime that point to his divine character.

Jesus demonstrated his *omnipotence* when he stilled the storm at sea with a word (Matt. 8:26–27), multiplied the loaves and fish (Matt. 14:19), and changed water into wine (John 2:1–11). Some might object that these miracles just showed the power of the Holy Spirit working through him, just as the Holy Spirit could work through any other human being, and therefore these do not demonstrate Jesus' own deity. But the contextual explanations of these events often point not to what they demonstrate about the power of the Holy Spirit but to what they demonstrate about Jesus himself. For instance, after Jesus turned water into wine, John tells us, "This, the first of his miraculous signs, Jesus did at Cana in Galilee, and *manifested his glory;* and his disciples believed in him" (John 2:11). It was not the glory of the Holy Spirit that was manifested but the glory of Jesus himself, as his divine power worked to change water into wine. Similarly, after Jesus stilled the storm on the Sea of Galilee, the disciples did not say, "How great is the power of the Holy Spirit working through this prophet," but rather, "What sort of man is this, that even winds and sea *obey him?*" (Matt. 8:27). It was the authority of Jesus himself to which the winds and the waves were subject, and this could only be the authority of God who rules over the seas and has power to still the waves (cf. Ps. 65:7; 89:9; 107:29).[22]

Jesus asserts his *eternity* when he says, "Before Abraham was, I am" (John 8:58, see discussion above), or, "I am the Alpha and the Omega" (Rev. 22:13).

The *omniscience* of Jesus is demonstrated in his knowing people's thoughts (Mark 2:8) and seeing Nathaniel under the fig tree from far away (John 1:48), and knowing "from the first who those were that did not believe, and who it was that would betray him" (John 6:64). Of course, the revelation of individual, specific events or facts is something that God could give to anyone who had a gift of prophecy in the Old or New Testaments. But Jesus' knowledge was much more extensive than that. He knew "who those were that did not believe," thus implying that he knew the belief or unbelief that was in the hearts of all men. In fact, John says explicitly that Jesus "*knew all men* and needed no one to bear witness of man" (John 2:25). The disciples could later say to him, "Now we know that *you*

---

[22]I recognize that other passages attribute some of Christ's miracles to the Holy Spirit—see Matt. 12:28; Luke 4:14, 18, 40.

know all things" (John 16:30). These statements say much more than what could be said of any great prophet or apostle of the Old Testament or New Testament, for they imply omniscience on the part of Jesus.[23]

Finally, after his resurrection, when Jesus asked Peter if he loved him, Peter answered, "Lord, *you know everything;* you know that I love you" (John 21:17). Here Peter is saying much more than that Jesus knows his heart and knows that he loves him. He is rather making a general statement ("You know everything") and from it he is drawing a specific conclusion ("You know that I love you"). Peter is confident that Jesus knows what is in the heart of every person, and therefore he is sure that Jesus knows his own heart.

The divine attribute of *omnipresence* is not directly affirmed to be true of Jesus during his earthly ministry. However, while looking forward to the time that the church would be established, Jesus could say, "Where two or three are gathered in my name, *there am I* in the midst of them" (Matt. 18:20). Moreover, before he left the earth, he told his disciples, "I am with you always, to the close of the age" (Matt. 28:20).[24]

That Jesus possessed divine *sovereignty,* a kind of authority possessed by God alone, is seen in the fact that he could forgive sins (Mark 2:5–7). Unlike the Old Testament prophets who declared, "Thus says the Lord," he could preface his statements with the phrase, "But *I say to you*" (Matt. 5:22, 28, 32, 34, 39, 44)—an amazing claim to his own authority. He could speak with the authority of God himself because he was himself fully God. He had "all things" delivered into his hands by the Father and the authority to reveal the Father to whomever he chose (Matt. 11:25–27). Such is his authority that the future eternal state of everyone in the universe depends on whether they believe in him or reject him (John 3:36).

Jesus also possessed the divine attribute of *immortality,* the inability to die. We see this indicated near the beginning of John's gospel, when Jesus says to the Jews, "Destroy this temple, and in three days *I will raise it up*" (John 2:19). John explains that he was not speaking about the temple made with stones in Jerusalem, "but he spoke of the temple of *his body.* When therefore he was raised from the dead, his disciples remembered that he had said this; and they believed the scripture and the word which Jesus had spoken" (John 2:21–22). We must insist of course that Jesus really did die: this very passage speaks of the time when "he was raised from the dead." But it is also significant that Jesus predicts that he will have an active role in his own resurrection: "*I will raise it up.*" Although other Scripture passages tell us that God the Father was active in raising Christ from the dead, here he says that he himself will be active in his resurrection.

Jesus claims the power to lay down his life and take it up again in another passage in John's gospel: "For this reason the Father loves me, because I lay down my life, that I may take it again. No one takes it from me, but I lay it down on my own accord. I have power to lay it down, and I have power to take it again; this charge I have received from my Father" (John 10:17–18). Here Jesus speaks of a power no other

---

[23]See below, pp. 65–68, on Mark 13:32, and on the question of how omniscience can be consistent with Christ's learning things as a man.

[24]I do not mean to imply that these verses show that Jesus' human nature was omnipresent. Jesus' human nature,

including his physical body, was never more than one place at one time. It is probably best to understand these verses to refer to Jesus' divine nature (see below, pp. 61–66, for discussion of the distinction between Christ's two natures). See also Matt. 8:13.

human being has had—the power to lay down his own life *and* the power to take it up again. Once again, this is an indication that Jesus possessed the divine attribute of immortality. Similarly, the author of Hebrews says that Jesus "has become a priest, not according to a legal requirement concerning bodily descent but by the power of *an indestructible life*" (Heb. 7:16). (The fact that immortality is a unique characteristic of God alone is seen in 1 Tim. 6:16, which speaks of God as the one "who alone has immortality.")

Another clear attestation to the deity of Christ is the fact that he is counted *worthy to be worshiped,* something that is true of no other creature, including angels (see Rev. 19:10), but only God alone. Yet Scripture says of Christ that "God has highly exalted him and bestowed on him the name which is above every name, that at the name of Jesus every knee should bow, in heaven and on earth and under the earth, and every tongue confess that Jesus Christ is Lord, to the glory of God the Father" (Phil. 2:9–11). Similarly, God commands the angels to worship Christ, for we read, "When he brings the first-born into the world, he says, 'Let all God's angels worship him'" (Heb. 1:6).

John is allowed a glimpse of the worship that occurs in heaven, for he sees thousands and thousands of angels and heavenly creatures around God's throne saying, "Worthy is the Lamb who was slain, to receive power and wealth and wisdom and might and honor and glory and blessing!" (Rev. 5:12). Then he hears *every creature* in heaven and on earth and under the earth and in the sea, and all therein, saying, 'To him who sits upon the throne *and to the Lamb* be blessing and honor and glory and might for ever and ever!'" (Rev. 5:13). Christ is here called "the Lamb who was slain," and he is accorded the universal worship offered to God the Father, thus clearly demonstrating his equality in deity.[25]

3. Did Jesus Give Up Some of His Divine Attributes While on Earth? (The Kenosis Theory). Paul writes to the Philippians,

> Have this mind among yourselves, which is yours in Christ Jesus, who, though he was in the form of God, did not count equality with God a thing to be grasped, but *emptied himself,* taking the form of a servant, being born in the likeness of men. (Phil. 2:5–7)

Beginning with this text, several theologians in Germany (from about 1860–1880) and in England (from about 1890–1910) advocated a view of the incarnation that had not been advocated before in the history of the church. This new view was called the "kenosis theory," and the overall position it represented was called "kenotic theology." The *kenosis theory* holds that Christ gave up some of his divine attributes while he was on earth as a man. (The word *kenosis* is taken from the Greek verb *kenoō,* which generally means "to empty," and is translated "emptied himself" in Phil. 2:7.) According to the theory Christ "emptied himself" of some of his divine attributes, such as omniscience, omnipresence, and omnipotence, while he was on earth as a man. This was viewed as

---

[25]See also Matt. 28:17 where Jesus accepted worship from his disciples after his resurrection.

a voluntary self-limitation on Christ's part, which he carried out in order to fulfill his work of redemption.[26]

But does Philippians 2:7 teach that Christ emptied himself of some of his divine attributes, and does the rest of the New Testament confirm this? The evidence of Scripture points to a negative answer to both questions. We must first realize that no recognized teacher in the first 1,800 years of church history, including those who were native speakers of Greek, thought that "emptied himself" in Philippians 2:7 meant that the Son of God gave up some of his divine attributes. Second, we must recognize that the text does not say that Christ "emptied himself of some powers" or "emptied himself of divine attributes" or anything like that. Third, the text *does* describe what Jesus did in this "emptying": he did not do it by giving up any of his attributes but rather by "taking the form of a servant," that is, by coming to live as a man, and "being found in human form he humbled himself and became obedient unto death, even death on a cross" (Phil. 2:8). Thus, the context itself interprets this "emptying" as equivalent to "humbling himself" and taking on a lowly status and position. Thus, the NIV, instead of translating the phrase, "He *emptied* himself," translates it, "but *made himself nothing*" (Phil. 2:7 NIV). The emptying includes change of role and status, not essential attributes or nature.

A fourth reason for this interpretation is seen in Paul's purpose in this context. His purpose has been to persuade the Philippians that they should "do nothing from selfishness or conceit, but in humility count others better than yourselves" (Phil. 2:3), and he continues by telling them, "Let each of you look not only to his own interests, but also to the interests of others" (Phil. 2:4). To persuade them to be humble and to put the interests of others first, he then holds up the example of Christ: "Have this mind among yourselves, which is yours in Christ Jesus, who, though he was in the form of God, did not count equality with God a thing to be grasped, but emptied himself, taking the form of a servant . . ." (Phil. 2:5–7).

Now in holding up Christ as an example, he wants the Philippians to imitate Christ. But certainly he is not asking the Philippian Christians to "give up" or "lay aside" any of their essential attributes or abilities! He is not asking them to "give up" their intelligence or strength or skill and become a diminished version of what they were. Rather, he is asking them to put the interests of others first: "Let each of you look not only to his own interests, but also to the interests of others" (Phil. 2:4). And because that is his goal, it fits the context to understand that he is using Christ as the supreme example of one who did just that: he put the interests of others first and was willing to give up some of the privilege and status that was his as God.

Therefore, the best understanding of this passage is that it talks about Jesus giving up the *status* and *privilege* that was his in heaven: he "did not count equality with God a thing to be grasped" (or "clung to for his own advantage"), but "emptied himself" or "humbled himself" for our sake, and came to live as a man. Jesus speaks elsewhere of the "glory" he had with the Father "before the world was made" (John 17:5), a glory

---

[26]A very clear overview of the history of kenotic theology is found in the article "Kenosis, a Kenotic Theology" by S. M. Smith, in *EDT*, pp. 600–602. Surprisingly (for the volume in which his essay appears), Smith ends up endorsing kenotic theology as a valid form of orthodox, biblical faith (p. 602)!

that he had given up and was going to receive again when he returned to heaven. And Paul could speak of Christ who, "though he was rich, yet for your sake he became poor" (2 Cor. 8:9), once again speaking of the privilege and honor that he deserved but temporarily gave up for us.

The fifth and final reason why the "kenosis" view of Philippians 2:7 must be rejected is the larger context of the teaching of the New Testament and the doctrinal teaching of the entire Bible. If it were true that such a momentous event as this happened, that the eternal Son of God ceased for a time to have all the attributes of God—ceased, for a time, to be omniscient, omnipotent, and omnipresent, for example—then we would expect that such an incredible event would be taught clearly and repeatedly in the New Testament, not found in the very doubtful interpretation of one word in one epistle. But we find the opposite of that: we do not find it stated anywhere else that the Son of God ceased to have some of the attributes of God that he had possessed from eternity. In fact, if the kenosis theory were true (and this is a foundational objection against it), then we could no longer affirm Jesus was fully God while he was here on earth.[27] The kenosis theory ultimately denies the full deity of Jesus Christ and makes him something less than fully God. S. M. Smith admits, "All forms of classical orthodoxy either explicitly reject or reject in principle kenotic theology."[28]

It is important to realize that the major force persuading people to accept kenotic theory was not that they had discovered a better understanding of Philippians 2:7 or any other passage of the New Testament, but rather the increasing discomfort people were feeling with the formulations of the doctrine of Christ in historic, classical orthodoxy. It just seemed too incredible for modern rational and "scientific" people to believe that Jesus Christ could be truly human and fully, absolutely God at the same time.[29] The kenosis theory began to sound more and more like an acceptable way to say that (in some sense) Jesus was God, but a kind of God who had for a time given up some of his Godlike qualities, those that were most difficult for people to accept in the modern world.

[27]Sometimes the word *kenosis* is used in a weaker sense not to apply to the kenosis theory in its full sense, but simply to refer to a more orthodox understanding of Phil. 2:7, in which it means simply that Jesus gave up his glory and privilege for a time while he was on earth. (This is essentially the view we have advocated in this text.) But it does not seem at all wise to use the term "kenosis" to refer to such a traditional understanding of Phil. 2:7, for it is too easily confused with the full-blown kenosis doctrine that essentially denies the full deity of Christ. To take a term that formally applies to a false doctrinal teaching and then use it to apply to a scripturally sound position is just confusing to most people.

[28]S. M. Smith, "Kenosis, A Kenotic Theology," p. 601.

[29]Smith points out that one of the primary influences leading some to adopt kenotic theology was the growth of modern psychology in the nineteenth century: "The age was learning to think in terms of the categories of psychology. Consciousness was a central category. If at our 'center' is our consciousness, and if Jesus was both omniscient God and limited man, then he had two centers and was thus fundamentally not one of us. Christology was becoming inconceivable for some" (ibid., pp. 600–601). In other words, pressures of modern psychological study were making belief in the combination of full deity and full humanity in the one person of Christ difficult to explain or even intellectually embarrassing: how could someone be so different from us and still be truly a man?

Yet we might respond that modern psychology is inherently limited in that its only object of study is simple human beings. No modern psychologist has ever studied anyone who was perfectly free from sin (as Christ was) and who was both fully God and fully man (as Christ was). If we limit our understanding to what modern psychology tells us is "possible" or "conceivable," then we will have neither a sinless Christ nor a divine Christ. In this as in many other points of doctrine, our understanding of what is "possible" must be determined not by modern empirical study of a finite, fallen world, but by the teachings of Scripture itself.

4. Conclusion: Christ Is Fully Divine. The New Testament, in hundreds of explicit verses that call Jesus "God" and "Lord" and use a number of other titles of deity to refer to him, and in many passages that attribute actions or words to him that could only be true of God himself, affirms again and again the full, absolute deity of Jesus Christ. "In him *all the fulness of God* was pleased to dwell" (Col. 1:19), and "in him the whole fulness of deity dwells bodily" (Col. 2:9). In an earlier section we argued that Jesus is truly and fully man. Now we conclude that he is truly and fully God as well. His name is rightly called "Emmanuel," that is, "God with us" (Matt. 1:23).

5. Is the Doctrine of the Incarnation "Unintelligible" Today? Throughout history there have been objections to the New Testament teaching on the full deity of Christ. One recent attack on this doctrine deserves mention here because it created a large controversy, since the contributors to the volume were all recognized church leaders in England. The book was called *The Myth of God Incarnate*, edited by John Hick (London: SCM, 1977). The title gives away the thesis of the book: the idea that Jesus was "God incarnate" or "God come in the flesh" is a "myth" — a helpful story, perhaps, for the faith of earlier generations, but not one that can really be believed by us today.

The argument of the book begins with some foundational assumptions: (1) the Bible does not have absolute divine authority for us today (p. i), and (2) Christianity, like all human life and thought, is evolving and changing over time (p. ii). The basic claims of the book are laid out in the first two chapters. In chapter 1, Maurice Wiles argues that it is possible to have Christianity without the doctrine of the incarnation. The church has given up earlier doctrines, such as the "real presence" of Christ in the Lord's Supper, the inerrancy of Scripture, and the virgin birth; therefore, it is possible to give up the traditional doctrine of the incarnation and still keep the Christian faith as well (pp. 2–3). Moreover, the doctrine of the incarnation is not directly presented in Scripture but originated in a setting where belief in the supernatural was credible; nevertheless, it has never been a coherent or intelligible doctrine through the history of the church (pp. 3–5).

Regarding the New Testament teaching, Francis Young, in chapter 2, argues that the New Testament contains the writings of many diverse witnesses who tell of their own understanding of Christ, but that no single or unified view of Christ can be gained from the entire New Testament; the early church's understanding of the person of Christ was developing in various directions over time. Young concludes that the situation is similar today: within the Christian church many diverse *personal responses* to the story of Jesus Christ are acceptable for us as well, and that would certainly include the response that sees Christ as a man in whom God was uniquely at work but not by any means a man who was also fully God.[30]

From the standpoint of evangelical theology, it is significant to note that this forthright rejection of Jesus' deity could only be advocated upon a prior assumption that the New Testament is not to be accepted as an absolute divine authority for us, truthful at

---

[30]The book was quickly answered by another series of essays, *The Truth of God Incarnate,* ed. Michael Green (Sevenoaks, Kent, U.K.: Hodder and Stoughton, and Grand Rapids: Eerdmans, 1977). Later the authors of *The Myth of God Incar-* *nate* and several of their critics published the proceedings of a three-day meeting in a third book: Michael Golder, ed., *Incarnation and Myth: The Debate Continued* (London: SCM, 1979).

every point. This question of authority is, in many cases, the great dividing line in conclusions about the person of Christ. Second, much of the criticism of the doctrine of the incarnation focused on the claim that it was not "coherent" or "intelligible." Yet at root this is simply an indication that the authors are unwilling to accept anything that does not appear to fit in with their "scientific" worldview in which the natural universe is a closed system not open to such divine intrusions as miracles and the incarnation. The assertion that "Jesus was fully God and fully man in one person," though not a contradiction, is a paradox that we cannot fully understand in this age and perhaps not for all eternity, but this does not give us the right to label it "incoherent" or "unintelligible." The doctrine of the incarnation as understood by the church throughout history has indeed been coherent and intelligible, though no one maintains that it provides us with an exhaustive explanation of how Jesus is both fully God and fully man. Our proper response is not to reject the clear and central teaching of Scripture about the incarnation, but simply to recognize that it will remain a paradox, that this is all that God has chosen to reveal to us about it, and that it is true. If we are to submit ourselves to God and to his words in Scripture, then we must believe it.

6. Why Was Jesus' Deity Necessary? In the previous section we listed several reasons why it was necessary for Jesus to be fully man in order to earn our redemption. Here it is appropriate to recognize that it is crucially important to insist on the full deity of Christ as well, not only because it is clearly taught in Scripture, but also because (1) only someone who is infinite God could bear the full penalty for all the sins of all those who would believe in him—any finite creature would have been incapable of bearing that penalty; (2) salvation is from the Lord (Jonah 2:9 NASB), and the whole message of Scripture is designed to show that no human being, no creature, could ever save man—only God himself could; and (3) only someone who was truly and fully God could be the one mediator between God and man (1 Tim. 2:5), both to bring us back to God and also to reveal God most fully to us (John 14:9).

Thus, if Jesus is not fully God, we have no salvation and ultimately no Christianity. It is no accident that throughout history those groups that have given up belief in the full deity of Christ have not remained long within the Christian faith but have soon drifted toward the kind of religion represented by Unitarianism in the United States and elsewhere. "No one who denies the Son has the Father" (1 John 2:23). "Any one who goes ahead and does not abide in the doctrine of Christ does not have God; he who abides in the doctrine has both the Father and the Son" (2 John 9).

C. The Incarnation: Deity and Humanity in the One Person of Christ

The biblical teaching about the full deity and full humanity of Christ is so extensive that both have been believed from the earliest times in the history of the church. But a precise understanding of how full deity and full humanity could be combined together in one person was formulated only gradually in the church and did not reach the final form until the Chalcedonian Definition in A.D. 451. Before that point, several inadequate views of the person of Christ were proposed and then rejected. One view, Arianism, held that Jesus was not fully divine. But three other views that were eventually rejected as heretical should be mentioned at this point.

1. Three Inadequate Views of the Person of Christ.

a. Apollinarianism: Apollinaris, who became bishop in Laodicea about A.D. 361, taught that the one person of Christ had a human body but not a human mind or spirit, and that the mind and spirit of Christ were from the divine nature of the Son of God. This view may be represented as in figure 2.1.

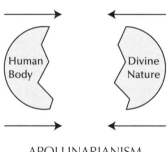

APOLLINARIANISM
Figure 2.1

But the views of Apollinaris were rejected by the leaders of the church at that time, who realized that it was not just our human body that needed salvation and needed to be represented by Christ in his redemptive work, but our human minds and spirits (or souls) as well: Christ had to be fully and truly man if he was to save us (Heb. 2:17). Apollinarianism was rejected by several church councils, from the Council of Alexandria in A.D. 362 to the Council of Constantinople in A.D. 381.

b. Nestorianism: Nestorianism is the doctrine that there were two separate persons in Christ, a human person and a divine person, a teaching that is distinct from the biblical view that sees Jesus as one person. Nestorianism may be diagramed as in figure 2.2.

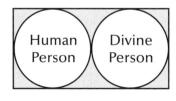

NESTORIANISM
Figure 2.2

Nestorius was a popular preacher at Antioch, and from A.D. 428 was bishop of Constantinople. Although Nestorius himself probably never taught the heretical view that goes by his name (the idea that Christ was two persons in one body, rather than one person), through a combination of several personal conflicts and a good deal of ecclesiastical politics, he was removed from his office of bishop and his teachings were condemned.[31]

It is important to understand why the church could not accept the view that Christ was two distinct persons. Nowhere in Scripture do we have an indication that the human nature of Christ, for example, is an independent person, deciding to do something contrary to the divine nature of Christ. Nowhere do we have an indication of the human and divine natures talking to each other or struggling within Christ, or any such thing. Rather, we have a consistent picture of a single person acting in wholeness and unity. Jesus always speaks as "I," not as "we,"[32] though he can refer to himself and the Father together as "we" (John 14:23). The Bible always speaks of Jesus as "he," not as "they." And, though we can sometimes distinguish actions of his divine nature and actions of his human nature in order to help us understand some of the statements and actions recorded in Scripture, the Bible itself does not say "Jesus' human nature did this" or "Jesus' divine nature did that," as though they were separate persons, but always talks about what the *person* of Christ did. Therefore, the church continued to insist that Jesus was one person, although possessing both a human nature and a divine nature.

c. Monophysitism (Eutychianism): A third inadequate view is called *monophysitism,* the view that Christ had one nature only (Gk. *monos,* "one," and *physis,* "nature"). The primary advocate of this view in the early church was Eutyches (c. A.D. 378–454), who was the leader of a monastery at Constantinople. Eutyches taught the opposite error from Nestorianism, for he denied that the human nature and divine nature in Christ remained fully human and fully divine. He held rather that the human nature of Christ was taken up and absorbed into the divine nature, so that both natures were changed somewhat and *a third kind of nature* resulted.[33] An analogy to Eutychianism can be seen if we put a drop of ink in a glass of water: the mixture resulting is neither pure ink nor pure water, but some kind of third substance, a mixture of the two in which both the ink and the water are changed. Similarly, Eutyches taught that Jesus was a mixture of divine and human elements in which both were somewhat modified to form one new nature. This may be represented as in figure 2.3.

---

[31]Harold O. J. Brown says, "Nestorius' incarnate person was a single person, not two as his critics thought, but he could not convince others that it was so. Consequently he has gone down in history as a great heretic although what he actually believed was reaffirmed at Chalcedon" (*Heresies: The Image of Christ in the Mirror of Heresy and Orthodoxy from the Apostles to the Present* (Garden City, New York: Doubleday, 1984), p. 176). Brown's extensive discussion of Nestorianism and related issues on pp. 172–84 is very helpful.

[32]There is an unusual usage in John 3:11, where Jesus suddenly shifts to the plural, "Truly, truly, I say to you, *we* speak of what we know, and bear witness to what we have seen." Jesus may have been referring to himself and some disciples with

him who are not mentioned, in contrast with the "we" of the Jewish rulers that Nicodemus alluded to when he opened the conversation: "Rabbi, *we* know that you are a teacher come from God" (John 3:2). Or Jesus may have been speaking of himself together with the witness of the Holy Spirit, whose work is the subject of the conversation (vv. 5–9). In any case, Jesus is not referring to himself as "we," but calls himself "I" in that very sentence. See discussion in Leon Morris, *The Gospel According to John* (Grand Rapids: Eerdmans, 1971), pp. 221–22.

[33]A variant form of Eutychianism held that the human nature was simply lost in the divine, so that the resulting single nature was the divine nature only.

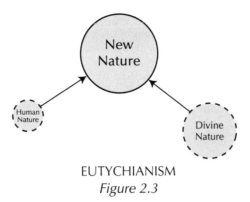

EUTYCHIANISM
Figure 2.3

Monophysitism also rightly caused great concern in the church, because, by this doctrine, Christ was neither truly God nor truly man. And if that was so, he could not truly represent us as a man nor could he be true God and able to earn our salvation.

2. The Solution to the Controversy: The Chalcedonian Definition of A.D. 451. In order to attempt to solve the problems raised by the controversies over the person of Christ, a large church council was convened in the city of Chalcedon near Constantinople (modern Istanbul), from October 8 to November 1, A.D. 451. The resulting statement, called the Chalcedonian Definition, guarded against Apollinarianism, Nestorianism, and Eutychianism. It has been taken as the standard, orthodox definition of the biblical teaching on the person of Christ since that day by Catholic, Protestant, and Orthodox branches of Christianity alike.[34]

The statement is not long, and we may quote it in its entirety:[35]

> We, then, following the holy Fathers, all with one consent, teach men to confess one and the same Son, our Lord Jesus Christ, the same perfect in Godhead and also perfect in manhood; truly God and truly man, of a reasonable [rational] soul and body; *consubstantial [coessential] with the Father according to the Godhead, and consubstantial with us according to the Manhood;* in all things like unto us, without sin; begotten before all ages of the Father according to the Godhead, and in these latter days, for us and for our salvation, born of the Virgin Mary, the Mother of God, according to the Manhood; one and the same Christ, Son, Lord, Only-begotten, to be acknowledged in *two natures, inconfusedly, unchangeably, indivisibly, inseparably;* the distinction of natures being by no means taken away by the union, but rather *the property of each nature being preserved,* and concurring in *one Person* and one Subsistence, not parted or divided into two persons, but one and the same Son, and only begotten, God, the Word, the Lord Jesus

---

[34]However, it should be noted that three localized groups of ancient churches rejected the Chalcedonian definition and still endorse monophysitism to this day: the Ethiopian Orthodox church, the Coptic Orthodox church (in Egypt), and the Syrian Jacobite church. See H. D. McDonald, "Monophysitism," in *NDT*, pp. 442–43.

[35]English translation taken from Philip Schaff, *Creeds of Christendom*, 3 vols. (Grand Rapids: Baker, 1983 reprint of 1931 edition), 2:62–63.

Christ, as the prophets from the beginning [have declared] concerning him, and the Lord Jesus Christ himself has taught us, and the Creed of the holy Fathers has been handed down to us.

Against the view of Apollinaris that Christ did not have a human mind or soul, we have the statement that he was "*truly man*, of a *reasonable soul* and body . . . *consubstantial with us* according to the Manhood; in all things like unto us." (The word *consubstantial* means "having the same nature or substance.")

In opposition to the view of Nestorianism that Christ was two persons united in one body, we have the words "*indivisibly, inseparably* . . . concurring in *one Person* and one Subsistence, not parted or divided into two persons."

Against the view of Monophysitism that Christ had only one nature, and that his human nature was lost in the union with the divine nature, we have the words "to be acknowledged in *two natures, inconfusedly, unchangeably* . . . the distinction of natures being by no means taken away by the union, but rather *the property of each nature being preserved*." The human and the divine natures were not confused or changed when Christ became man, but the human nature remained a truly human nature, and the divine nature remained a truly divine nature.

Figure 2.4 may be helpful in showing this, in contrast to the earlier diagrams. It indicates that the eternal Son of God took to himself a truly human nature, and that Christ's divine and human natures remain distinct and retain their own properties, yet they are eternally and inseparably united together in one person.

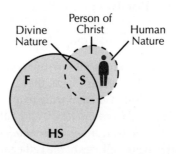

CHALCEDONIAN CHRISTOLOGY
Figure 2.4

Some have said that the Chalcedonian Definition really did not define for us in any positive way what the person of Christ actually *is,* but simply told us several things that it *is not.* In this way some have said that it is not a very helpful definition. But such an accusation is misleading and inaccurate. The definition actually did a great deal to help us understand the biblical teaching correctly. It taught that Christ definitely has two natures, a human nature and a divine nature. It taught that his divine nature is exactly the same as that of the Father ("consubstantial with the Father according to the Godhead"). And it maintained that the human nature is exactly like our human nature, yet without sin ("consubstantial with us according to the Manhood; in all things like unto us, without sin"). Moreover, it affirmed that in the person of Christ the human nature retains its distinctive characteristics and the divine nature retains its distinctive characteristics ("the distinction of natures being by no means taken away by the union, but rather *the property of each nature being preserved"*). Finally, it affirmed that, whether we can understand it or not, these two natures are united together in the one person of Christ.

When the Chalcedonian Definition says that the two natures of Christ occur together "in one Person and one *Subsistence,"* the Greek word translated as "Subsistence" is the word *hypostasis,* "being." Hence the union of Christ's human and divine natures in one person is sometimes called the *hypostatic union.* This phrase simply means the union of Christ's human and divine natures in one being.

3. Combining Specific Biblical Texts on Christ's Deity and Humanity. When we examine the New Testament, as we did above in the sections on Jesus' humanity and deity, there are several passages that seem difficult to fit together (How could Jesus be omnipotent and yet weak? How could he leave the world and yet be present everywhere? How could he learn things and yet be omniscient?). As the church struggled to understand these teachings, it finally came up with the Chalcedonian Definition, which spoke of two distinct natures in Christ that retain their own properties yet remain together in one person. This distinction, which helps us in our understanding of the biblical passages mentioned earlier, also seems to be demanded by those passages.

a. One Nature Does Some Things That the Other Nature Does Not Do: Evangelical theologians in previous generations have not hesitated to distinguish between things done by Christ's human nature but not by his divine nature, or by his divine nature but not by his human nature. It seems that we have to do this if we are willing to affirm the Chalcedonian statement about "the *property of each nature* being preserved." But few recent theologians have been willing to make such distinctions, perhaps because of a hesitancy to affirm something we cannot understand.

When we are talking about Jesus' human nature, we can say that he ascended to heaven and is no longer in the world (John 16:28; 17:11; Acts 1:9–11).[36] But with respect to his divine nature, we can say that Jesus is everywhere present: "Where two or three are gathered in my name, *there am I* in the midst of them" (Matt. 18:20); "I am with you always, to the close of the age" (Matt. 28:20); "If a man loves me, he will keep my word, and my Father will love him, and *we* will come to him and make our home with him" (John 14:23). So we can say that both things are true about the *person* of Christ—he has returned to heaven, *and* he is also present with us.

Similarly, we can say that Jesus was about thirty years old (Luke 3:23), if we are speaking with respect to his human nature, but we can say that he eternally existed (John 1:1–2; 8:58) if we are speaking of his divine nature.

In his human nature, Jesus was weak and tired (Matt. 4:2; 8:24; Mark 15:21; John 4:6), but in his divine nature he was omnipotent (Matt. 8:26–27; Col. 1:17; Heb. 1:3). Particularly striking is the scene on the Sea of Galilee where Jesus was asleep in the stern

---

[36]Lutheran theologians, following Martin Luther, have sometimes claimed that Jesus' human nature, even his human body, is also everywhere present or "ubiquitous." But this position has not been adopted by any other segment of the Christian church, and it seems to have been a position that Luther himself took mainly in an attempt to justify his view that Christ's body was actually present in the Lord's Supper (not in the elements themselves, but with them).

of the boat, presumably because he was weary (Matt. 8:24). But he was able to arise from his sleep and calm the wind and sea with a word (Matt. 8:26–27)! Tired yet omnipotent! Here Jesus' weak human nature completely hid his omnipotence until that omnipotence broke forth in a sovereign word from the Lord of heaven and earth.

If someone asks whether Jesus, when he was asleep in the boat, was also "continually carrying along all things by his word of power" (Heb. 1:3, author's translation), and whether all things in the universe were being held together by him at that time (see Col. 1:17), the answer must be yes, for those activities have always been and will always be the particular responsibility of the second person of the Trinity, the eternal Son of God. Those who find the doctrine of the incarnation "inconceivable" have sometimes asked whether Jesus, when he was a baby in the manger at Bethlehem, was also "upholding the universe." To this question the answer must also be yes: Jesus was not just potentially God or someone in whom God uniquely worked, but was *truly and fully God,* with all the attributes of God. He was "a Savior, who is Christ *the Lord*" (Luke 2:11). Those who reject this as impossible simply have a different definition of what is "possible" than God has, as revealed in Scripture.[37] To say that we cannot understand this is appropriate humility. But to say that it is not possible seems more like intellectual arrogance.

In a similar way, we can understand that in his human nature, Jesus died (Luke 23:46; 1 Cor. 15:3). But with respect to his divine nature, he did not die, but was able to raise himself from the dead (John 2:19; 10:17–18; Heb. 7:16). Yet here we must give a note of caution: it is true that when Jesus died his physical body died and his human soul (or spirit) was separated from his body and passed into the presence of God the Father in heaven (Luke 23:43, 46). In this way he experienced a death that is like the one we as believers experience if we die before Christ returns. And it is not correct to say that Jesus' divine nature died, or could die, if "die" means a cessation of activity, a cessation of consciousness, or a diminution of power. Nevertheless, by virtue of union with Jesus' human nature, his divine nature somehow tasted something of what it was like to go through death. The *person* of Christ experienced death. Moreover, it seems difficult to understand how Jesus' human nature alone could have borne the wrath of God against the sins of millions of people. It seems that Jesus' divine nature had somehow to participate in the bearing of wrath against sin that was due to us (though Scripture nowhere explicitly affirms this). Therefore, even though Jesus' divine nature did not actually

---

[37]A. N. S. Lane explicitly denies the Chalcedonian view of Christ on the ground that it cannot be: "Omniscience and ignorance, omnipotence and impotence cannot coexist. The former swamps the latter" ("Christology Beyond Chalcedon," in *Christ the Lord: Studies in Christology Presented to Donald Guthrie,* edited by Harold H. Rowden (Leicester and Downers Grove, Ill.: InterVarsity Press, 1982), p. 270. He says that Christ "explicitly denied his omniscience (Mt. 24:36 = Mk. 13:32) but even the clear words of Christ have not sufficed to counter the pull of docetism. . . . The affirmation of the omniscience of the historical Jesus has no biblical basis and indeed runs counter to the clear teaching of the Gospels. . . . It has serious theological implications in that it undermines his true humanity as taught in Scripture" (p. 271).

But (see pp. 65–68, below) Matt. 24:36 and Mark 13:32 are certainly capable of being understood to refer to Jesus' knowledge in his human nature. And when Lane says that omniscience and ignorance "cannot coexist" he is simply pitting one part of a biblical paradox against another and then asserting that one part is impossible. On what grounds are we justified in saying that an omniscient divine nature and a human nature with limited knowledge "cannot coexist,"? Or that an omnipotent divine nature and a weak human nature "cannot coexist"? Such assertions fundamentally deny that infinite deity and finite humanity can exist together in the same person—in other words, they deny that Jesus could be *fully* God and *fully* man at the same time. In this way, they deny the essence of the incarnation.

die, Jesus went through the experience of death as a whole person, and both human and divine natures somehow shared in that experience. Beyond that, Scripture does not enable us to say more.

The distinction between Jesus' human and divine natures also helps us understand Jesus' temptations. With respect to his human nature, he certainly was tempted in every way as we are, yet without sin (Heb. 4:15). Yet with respect to his divine nature, he was not tempted, because God cannot be tempted with evil (James 1:13).

At this point it seems necessary to say that Jesus had two distinct wills, a human will and a divine will, and that the wills belong to the two distinct natures of Christ, not to the person. In fact, there was a position, called the *monothelite* view, which held that Jesus had only "one will," but that was certainly a minority view in the church, and it was rejected as heretical at a church council in Constantinople in A.D. 681. Since then the view that Christ had two wills (a human will and a divine will) has been generally, but not universally, held through the church. In fact, Charles Hodge says:

> The decision against Nestorius, in which the unity of Christ's person was asserted; that against Eutyches, affirming the distinction of natures; and that against the Monothelites, declaring that the possession of a human nature involves of necessity the possession of a human will, have been received as the true faith by the Church universal, the Greek, Latin, and Protestant.[38]

Hodge explains that the church thought that "to deny Christ a human will, was to deny he had a human nature, or was truly a man. Besides, it precluded the possibility of his having been tempted, and therefore contradicted the Scriptures, and separated him so far from his people he could not sympathize with them in their temptations."[39] Moreover, Hodge notes that along with the idea that Christ had two wills is the related idea that he had two centers of consciousness or intelligence: "As there are two distinct natures, human and divine, there are of necessity two intelligences and two wills, the one fallible and finite, the other immutable and infinite."[40]

This distinction of two wills and two centers of consciousness helps us understand how Jesus could learn things and yet know all things. On the one hand, with respect to his human nature, he had limited knowledge (Mark 13:32; Luke 2:52). On the other hand, Jesus clearly knew all things (John 2:25; 16:30; 21:17). Now this is only understandable if Jesus learned things and had limited knowledge with respect to his human nature but was always omniscient with respect to his divine nature, and therefore he was able any time to "call to mind" whatever information would be needed for his ministry. In this way we can understand Jesus' statement concerning the time of his return: "But of that day or that hour no one knows, not even the angels in heaven, nor the Son, but only the Father" (Mark 13:32). This ignorance of the time of his return was true of Jesus' human nature and human consciousness only, for in his divine nature he was certainly omniscient and certainly knew the time when he would return to the earth.[41]

---

[38]Charles Hodge, *Systematic Theology,* 3 vols. (1871–73; reprint, Grand Rapids: Eerdmans, 1970), 2:405.

[39]Ibid., pp. 404–5.

[40]Ibid., p. 405.

[41]In commenting on Mark 13:32, John Calvin, H. B. Swete, an Anglican commentator (*The Gospel According to St. Mark* [London: Macmillan, 1913], p. 316), and R. C. H. Lenski, a Lutheran commentator (*The Interpretation of St. Mark's*

At this point someone may object that if we say that Jesus had two centers of consciousness and two wills, that *requires* that he was two distinct persons, and we have really fallen into the error of "Nestorianism." But in response, it must simply be affirmed that two wills and two centers of consciousness *do not* require that Jesus be two distinct persons. It is mere assertion without proof to say that they do. If someone responds that he or she *does not understand* how Jesus could have two centers of consciousness and still be one person, then that fact may certainly be admitted by all. But failing to understand something does not mean that it is impossible, only that our understanding is limited. The great majority of the church throughout its history has said that Jesus had two wills and centers of consciousness, yet he remained one person. Such a formulation is not impossible, merely a mystery that we do not now fully understand. To adopt any other solution would create a far greater problem: it would require that we give up either the full deity or the full humanity of Christ, and that we cannot do.[42]

b. Anything Either Nature Does, the Person of Christ Does: In the previous section we mentioned a number of things that were done by one nature but not the other in the person of Christ. Now we must affirm that anything that is true of the human or the divine nature is true of the person of Christ. Thus Jesus can say, "Before Abraham was, I am" (John 8:58). He does not say, "Before Abraham was, my divine nature existed," because he is free to talk about anything done by his divine nature alone or his human nature alone as something that *he* did.

In the human sphere, this is certainly true of our conversation as well. If I type a letter, even though my feet and toes had nothing to do with typing the letter, I do not tell people, "My fingers typed a letter and my toes had nothing to do with it" (though that is true). Rather, I tell people, "*I* typed a letter." That is true because anything that is done by one part of me is done by *me*.

Thus, "*Christ* died for our sins" (1 Cor. 15:3). Even though actually only his human body ceased living and ceased functioning, it was nonetheless *Christ* as a person who died for our sin. This is simply a means of affirming that whatever can be said of one nature or the other can be said of the *person* of Christ.

Therefore it is correct for Jesus to say, "I am leaving the world" (John 16:28), or "I am no more in the world" (John 17:11), but at the same time to say, "I am with you always" (Matt. 28:20). Anything that is done by one nature or the other is done by the *person* of Christ.

Gospel [Minneapolis: Augsburg, 1961 (reprint)], p. 590), all attribute this ignorance of Jesus to his human nature only, not to his divine nature.

[42]At this point an analogy from our human experience may be somewhat helpful. Anyone who has run in a race knows that near the end of the race there are conflicting desires within. On the one hand, the runner's lungs and legs and arms seem to be crying out, "Stop! Stop!" There is a clear desire to stop because of the physical pain. On the other hand, something in the runner's mind says, "Go on! Go on! I want to win!" We have all known similar instances of conflicting desires within.

Now if we, being ordinary human beings, can have differing or distinct desires within us and yet be one person, how much more possible is that for one who was both man and God at the same time? If we say we do not understand how that could be, we simply admit our ignorance of the situation, for none of us has ever experienced what it is like to be both God and man at the same time, nor will we ever have such an experience ourselves. We should not say it is impossible, but, if we are convinced that New Testament texts lead us to this conclusion, we should accept it and agree with it.

c. Titles That Remind Us of One Nature Can Be Used of the Person Even When the Action Is Done by the Other Nature: The New Testament authors sometimes use titles that remind us of either the human nature or the divine nature in order to speak of the person of Christ, even though the action mentioned may be done only by the other nature than the one we might think of from the title. For example, Paul says that if the rulers of this world had understood the wisdom of God, "they would not have crucified *the Lord of glory*" (1 Cor. 2:8). Now when we see the phrase "the Lord of glory" it reminds us specifically of Jesus' divine nature. But Paul uses this title (probably intentionally to show the horrible evil of the crucifixion) to say that Jesus was "crucified." Even though Jesus' divine nature was not crucified, it was true of Jesus as a *person* that he was crucified, and Paul affirms that about him even though he uses the title "the Lord of glory."

Similarly, when Elizabeth calls Mary "the mother of *my Lord*" (Luke 1:43), the name "my Lord" is a title that reminds us of Christ's divine nature. Yet Mary of course is not the mother of Jesus' divine nature, which has always existed. Mary is simply the mother of the human nature of Christ. Nevertheless, Elizabeth can call her "the mother of my Lord" because she is using the title "Lord" to refer to the person of Christ. A similar expression occurs in Luke 2:11: "For to you *is born* this day in the city of David a Savior, who is Christ *the Lord.*"

In this way, we can understand Mark 13:32, where Jesus says no one knows the time of his return, "not even the angels in heaven, *nor the Son,* but only the Father." Though the term "the Son" specifically reminds us of Jesus' heavenly, eternal sonship with God the Father, it is really used here not to speak specifically of his divine nature, but to speak generally of him as a person, and to affirm something that is in fact true of his human nature only.[43] And it is true that in one important sense (that is, with respect to his human nature) Jesus did not know the time when he would return.

d. Brief Summary Sentence: Sometimes in the study of systematic theology, the following sentence has been used to summarize the incarnation: "Remaining what he was, he became what he was not." In other words, while Jesus continued "remaining" what he was (that is, fully divine) he also became what he previously had not been (that is, fully human as well). Jesus did not give up any of his deity when he became man, but he did take on humanity that was not his before.

e. "Communication" of Attributes: Once we have decided that Jesus was fully man and fully God, and that his human nature remained *fully* human and his divine nature remained *fully* divine, we can still ask whether there were some qualities or abilities that were given (or "communicated") from one nature to the other. It seems there were.

(1) From the Divine Nature to the Human Nature: Although Jesus' human nature did not change its essential character, because it was united with the divine nature in the

---

[43]Similar usage is perhaps seen in John 3:13 and Acts 20:28 (in this latter verse some manuscripts read "with his own blood").

one person of Christ, Jesus' human nature gained (a) a worthiness to be worshiped and (b) an inability to sin, both of which did not belong to human beings otherwise.[44]

(2) From the Human Nature to the Divine Nature: Jesus' human nature gave him (a) an ability to experience suffering and death; (b) an ability to understand by experience what we are experiencing; and (c) an ability to be our substitute sacrifice, which Jesus as God alone could not have done.

f. Conclusion: At the end of this long discussion, it may be easy for us to lose sight of what is actually taught in Scripture. It is by far the most amazing miracle of the entire Bible—far more amazing than the resurrection and more amazing even than the creation of the universe. The fact that the infinite, omnipotent, eternal Son of God could become man and join himself to a human nature forever, so that infinite God became one person with finite man, will remain for eternity the most profound miracle and the most profound mystery in all the universe.

QUESTIONS FOR PERSONAL APPLICATION

1. After reading this chapter, are there specific ways in which you now think of Jesus as being more like you than you did before? What are these? How can a clearer understanding of Jesus' humanity help you face temptations? How can it help you to pray? What are the most difficult situations in your life right now? Can you think of any similar situations that Jesus might have faced? Does that encourage you to pray confidently to him? Can you picture what it would have been like if you had been present when Jesus said, "Before Abraham was, I am"? What would you have felt? Honestly, what would your response have been? Now try visualizing yourself as present when Jesus made some of the other "I am" statements recorded in John's gospel.[45]

2. After reading this chapter, is there anything that you understand more fully about the deity of Jesus? Can you describe (and perhaps identify with) what the disciples must have felt as they came to a growing realization of who Jesus actually was? Do you think Jesus is the one person you would be able to trust with your life for all eternity? Will you be happy to join with thousands of others in worshiping around his throne in heaven? Do you delight in worshiping him now?

---

[44]See above, note 36, on the Lutheran view that ubiquity was also communicated from the divine nature to the human.

[45]See the list of "I am" statements at note 20, above.

SPECIAL TERMS

Apollinarianism	kenosis theory
Arianism	Logos
Chalcedonian Definition	Lord
communication of attributes	monophysitism
docetism	monothelite view
Eutychianism	Nestorianism
God	Son of God
hypostatic union	Son of Man
impeccability	virgin birth
incarnation	

BIBLIOGRAPHY

Anselm. "The Incarnation of the Word." In *Anselm of Canterbury*. Vol. 3. Toronto: Edwin Mellen, 1976.

_____. *Why God Became Man: and The Virgin Conception and Original Sin.* Trans. by Joseph M. Colleran. Albany, N.Y.: Magi, 1969.

Athanasius. *On the Incarnation.* Translated by a religious of C.S.M.V. New York: Macmillan, 1946.

Berkouwer, G. C. *The Person of Christ.* Trans. by John Vriend. Grand Rapids: Eerdmans, 1954.

Bray, G. L. *Creeds, Councils and Christ.* Leicester: Inter-Varsity Press, 1984.

_____. "Christology." In *NDT*, pp. 137–40.

Brown, Harold O. J. *Heresies: The Image of Christ in the Mirror of Heresy and Orthodoxy From the Apostles to the Present.* Garden City, N.Y.: Doubleday, 1984.

Bruce, F. F. *Jesus: Lord and Savior.* The Jesus Library, ed. by Michael Green. Downers Grove, Ill.: InterVarsity Press, 1986.

Erickson, Millard. *The Word Became Flesh: A Contemporary Incarnational Christology.* Grand Rapids: Baker, 1991.

Guthrie, Donald. *Jesus the Messiah.* Grand Rapids: Zondervan, 1972.

_____. *New Testament Theology.* Leicester and Downers Grove, Ill.: InterVarsity Press, 1981, pp. 219–365.

Harris, Murray J. *Jesus As God.* Grand Rapids: Baker, 1992.

Hughes, Philip Edgcumbe. *The True Image: The Origin and Destiny of Man in Christ.* Grand Rapids: Eerdmans, and Leicester: Inter-Varsity Press, 1989, pp. 211–414.

Longenecker, Richard. *The Christology of Early Jewish Christianity.* London: SCM, 1970.

Marshall, I. Howard. *I Believe in the Historical Jesus.* Grand Rapids: Eerdmans, 1977.

McGrath, Alister E. *Understanding Jesus: Who He Is and Why He Matters.* Grand Rapids: Zondervan, 1987.

Moule, C. F. D. *The Origin of Christology.* Cambridge: Cambridge University Press, 1977.

Payne, Philip B. "Jesus' Implicit Claim to Deity in His Parables." *TrinJ*, vol. 2, n.s., no. 1 (Spring 1981), pp. 3–23.

Reymond, Robert L. *Jesus, Divine Messiah*. Phillipsburg, N.J.: Presbyterian and Reformed, 1990.

Runia, Klaas. *The Present-Day Christological Debate*. Leicester: Inter-Varsity Press, 1984.

Sproul, R. C. *The Glory of Christ*. Wheaton, Ill.: Tyndale, 1990.

Stein, R. H. "Jesus Christ." In *EDT*, pp. 582–85.

Wallace, R. S. "Christology." In *EDT*, pp. 221–27.

Walvoord, John F. *Jesus Christ Our Lord*. Chicago: Moody, 1969.

Wells, David F. *The Person of Christ: A Biblical and Historical Analysis of the Incarnation*. Westchester, Ill.: Crossway, 1984.

SCRIPTURE MEMORY PASSAGE

John 1:14: *And the Word became flesh and dwelt among us, full of grace and truth; we have beheld his glory, glory as of the only Son from the Father.*

HYMN

"Fairest Lord Jesus"

Fairest Lord Jesus, ruler of all nature,
Son of God and Son of Man!
Thee will I cherish, thee will I honor,
Thou, my soul's glory, joy, and crown.

Fair are the meadows, fair are the woodlands,
Robed in the blooming garb of spring:
Jesus is fairer, Jesus is purer,
Who makes the woeful heart to sing.

Fair is the sunshine, fair is the moonlight,
And all the twinkling, starry host:
Jesus shines brighter, Jesus shines purer
Than all the angels heav'n can boast.

Beautiful Savior! Lord of the nations!
Son of God and Son of Man!
Glory and honor, praise, adoration,
Now and forever more be thine.

FROM *MÜNSTER GESANGBUCH*, 1677, TRANSLATED 1850, 1873

THE ATONEMENT

Was it necessary for Christ to die? Did Christ's entire earthly life earn any saving benefits for us? The cause and nature of the atonement. Did Christ descend into hell?

EXPLANATION AND SCRIPTURAL BASIS

We may define the atonement as follows: *The atonement is the work Christ did in his life and death to earn our salvation.* This definition indicates that we are using the word *atonement* in a broader sense than it is sometimes used. Sometimes it is used to refer only to Jesus' dying and paying for our sins on the cross. But, as will be seen below, since saving benefits also come to us from Christ's life, we have included that in our definition as well.[1]

A. The Cause of the Atonement

What was the ultimate cause that led to Christ's coming to earth and dying for our sins? To find this we must trace the question back to something in the character of God himself. And here Scripture points to two things: the *love* and *justice* of God.

The love of God as a cause of the atonement is seen in the most familiar passage in the Bible: "For God *so loved the world* that he gave his only Son, that whoever believes in him should not perish but have eternal life" (John 3:16). But the justice of God also required that God find a way that the penalty due to us for our sins would be paid (for he could not accept us into fellowship with himself unless the penalty was paid). Paul explains that this was why God sent Christ to be a "propitiation" (Rom. 3:25 NASB) (that is, a sacrifice

---

[1]Of course, there are also saving benefits that come to us from Christ's resurrection and ascension, from his continuing high priestly work of intercession for us, and from his second coming. For the sake of clarity, I have here included under the title "atonement" only those things that Christ did for our salvation during his earthly life and in his death.

that bears God's wrath so that God becomes "propitious" or favorably disposed toward us): it was "*to show God's righteousness,* because in his divine forbearance he had passed over former sins" (Rom. 3:25). Here Paul says that God had been forgiving sins in the Old Testament but no penalty had been paid—a fact that would make people wonder whether God was indeed just and ask how he could forgive sins without a penalty. No God who was truly just could do that, could he? Yet when God sent Christ to die and pay the penalty for our sins, "it was to prove at the present time that he himself is righteous and that he justifies him who has faith in Jesus" (Rom. 3:26).

Therefore both the love and the justice of God were the ultimate cause of the atonement. It is not helpful for us to ask which is more important, however, because without the love of God, he would never have taken any steps to redeem us, yet without the justice of God, the specific requirement that Christ should earn our salvation by dying for our sins would not have been met. Both the love and the justice of God were equally important.

B. The Necessity of the Atonement

Was there any other way for God to save human beings than by sending his Son to die in our place?

Before answering this question, it is important to realize that it was not necessary for God to save any people at all. When we appreciate that "God did not spare the angels when they sinned, but cast them into hell and committed them to pits of nether gloom to be kept until the judgment" (2 Peter 2:4), then we realize that God could also have chosen with perfect justice to have left us in our sins awaiting judgment: he could have chosen to save no one, just as he did with the sinful angels. So in this sense the atonement was not absolutely necessary.

But once God, in his love, decided to save some human beings, then several passages in Scripture indicate that there was no other way for God to do this than through the death of his Son. Therefore, the atonement was not absolutely necessary, but, as a "consequence" of God's decision to save some human beings, the atonement was absolutely necessary. This is sometimes called the "consequent absolute necessity" view of the atonement.

In the Garden of Gethsemane Jesus prays, "*If it be possible,* let this cup pass from me; nevertheless, not as I will, but as you will" (Matt. 26:39). We may be confident that Jesus always prayed according to the will of the Father, and that he always prayed with fullness of faith. Thus it seems that this prayer, which Matthew takes pains to record for us, shows that it was *not possible* for Jesus to avoid the death on the cross which was soon to come to him (the "cup" of suffering that he had said would be his). If he was going to accomplish the work that the Father sent him to do, and if people were going to be redeemed for God, then it was necessary for him to die on the cross.

He said something similar after his resurrection, when he was talking with two disciples on the road to Emmaus. They were sad that Jesus had died, but his response was, "O foolish men, and slow of heart to believe all that the prophets have spoken! Was it not *necessary* that the Christ should suffer these things and enter into his glory?" (Luke 24:25–26). Jesus understood that God's plan of redemption (which he explained for the disciples from many Old Testament Scriptures, Luke 24:27) made it necessary for the Messiah to die for the sins of his people.

As we saw above, Paul in Romans 3 also shows that if God were to be righteous, and still save people, he had to send Christ to pay the penalty for sins: "It was to prove at the present time that he himself is righteous and that he justifies him who has faith in Jesus" (Rom. 3:26). The epistle to the Hebrews emphasizes that Christ had to suffer for our sins: "He *had to* be made like his brethren in every respect, so that he might become a merciful and faithful high priest in the service of God, to make expiation [lit. 'propitiation'] for the sins of the people" (Heb. 2:17). The author of Hebrews also argues that since "it is impossible that the blood of bulls and goats should take away sins" (Heb. 10:4), a better sacrifice is required (Heb. 9:23). Only the blood of Christ, that is, his death, would be able really to take away sins (Heb. 9:25–26). There was no other way for God to save us than for Christ to die in our place.

C. The Nature of the Atonement

In this section we consider two aspects of Christ's work: (1) Christ's obedience for us, in which he obeyed the requirements of the law in our place and was perfectly obedient to the will of God the Father as our representative, and (2) Christ's sufferings for us, in which he took the penalty due for our sins and as a result died for our sins.

It is important to notice that in both of these categories the primary emphasis and the primary influence of Christ's work of redemption is not on us, but on God the Father. Jesus obeyed the Father in our place and perfectly met the demands of the law. And he suffered in our place, receiving in himself the penalty that God the Father would have visited upon us. In both cases, the atonement is viewed as objective; that is, something that has primary influence directly on God himself. Only secondarily does it have application to us, and this is only because there was a definite event in the relationship between God the Father and God the Son that secured our salvation.

1. Christ's Obedience for Us (Sometimes Called His "Active Obedience"). If Christ had only earned forgiveness of sins for us, then we would not merit heaven. Our guilt would have been removed, but we would simply be in the position of Adam and Eve before they had done anything good or bad and before they had passed a time of probation successfully. To be established in righteousness forever and to have their fellowship with God made sure forever, Adam and Eve had to obey God perfectly over a period of time. Then God would have looked on their faithful obedience with pleasure and delight, and they would have lived with him in fellowship forever.

For this reason, Christ had to live a life of perfect obedience to God in order to earn righteousness for us. He had to obey the law for his whole life on our behalf so that the positive merits of his perfect obedience would be counted for us. Sometimes this is called Christ's "active obedience," while his suffering and dying for our sins is called his "passive obedience."[2] Paul says his goal is that he may be found in Christ, "*not having*

---

[2]Some have objected that this "active" and "passive" terminology is not entirely satisfactory, because even in paying for our sins Christ was in one sense actively accepting the suffering given him by the Father and was even active in laying down his own life (John 10:18). Moreover, both aspects of Christ's obedience continued through his whole life: his active obedience included faithful obedience from birth up to and including the point of his death; and his suffering on our behalf, which found

a righteousness of [his] own, based on law, but *that which is through faith in Christ,* the righteousness from God that depends on faith" (Phil. 3:9). It is not just moral neutrality that Paul knows he needs from Christ (that is, a clean slate with sins forgiven), but a positive moral righteousness. And he knows that that cannot come from himself, but must come through faith in Christ. Similarly, Paul says that Christ has been made *"our righteousness"* (1 Cor. 1:30). And he quite explicitly says, "For as by one man's disobedience many were made sinners, so by one man's obedience many will be *made righteous"* (Rom. 5:19).

Some theologians have not taught that Christ needed to achieve a lifelong record of perfect obedience for us. They have simply emphasized that Christ had to die and thereby pay the penalty for our sins.[3] But such a position does not adequately explain why Christ did more than just die for us; he also became our "righteousness" before God. Jesus said to John the Baptist, before he was baptized by him, "It is fitting for us *to fulfil all righteousness"* (Matt. 3:15).

It might be argued that Christ had to live a life of perfect righteousness for his own sake, not for ours, before he could be a sinless sacrifice for us. But Jesus had no need to live a life of perfect obedience for his own sake—he had shared love and fellowship with the Father for all eternity and was in his own character eternally worthy of the Father's good pleasure and delight. He rather had to "fulfill all righteousness" for our sake; that is, for the sake of the people whom he was representing as their head. Unless he had done this for us, we would have no record of obedience by which we would merit God's favor and merit eternal life with him. Moreover, if Jesus had needed only sinlessness and not also a life of perfect obedience, he could have died for us when he was a young child rather than when he was thirty-three years old.

By way of application, we ought to ask ourselves whose lifelong record of obedience we would rather rely on for our standing before God, Christ's or our own? As we think about the life of Christ, we ought to ask ourselves, was it good enough to deserve God's approval? And are we willing to rely on his record of obedience for our eternal destiny?

2. Christ's Sufferings for Us (Sometimes Called His "Passive Obedience"). In addition to obeying the law perfectly for his whole life on our behalf, Christ also took on himself the sufferings necessary to pay the penalty for our sins.

a. Suffering for His Whole Life: In a broad sense the penalty Christ bore in paying for our sins was suffering in both his body and soul throughout his life. Though Christ's sufferings culminated in his death on the cross (see below), his whole life in a fallen world involved suffering. For example, Jesus endured tremendous suffering during the

---

its climax in the crucifixion, continued through his whole life (see discussion below). Nevertheless, the distinction between active and passive obedience is still useful because it helps us appreciate the two aspects of Christ's work for us. (See the discussion in John Murray, *Redemption Accomplished and Applied* [Grand Rapids: Eerdmans, 1955], pp. 20–24.) R. L. Reymond prefers the terms *preceptive* (for active) and *penal*

(for passive), in his article "Obedience of Christ," *EDT,* p. 785.

[3] For example, I could find no discussion of the active obedience of Christ in the seven-volume *Systematic Theology* by Lewis Sperry Chafer (Dallas: Dallas Seminary Press, 1947–48) or in Millard Erickson's *Christian Theology* (Grand Rapids: Baker, 1985), pp. 761–800.

temptation in the wilderness (Matt. 4:1 – 11), when he was assaulted for forty days by the attacks of Satan.[4] He also suffered in growing to maturity, "Although he was a Son, he learned obedience through what he *suffered*" (Heb. 5:8). He knew suffering in the intense opposition he faced from Jewish leaders throughout much of his earthly ministry (see Heb. 12:3 – 4). We may suppose too that he experienced suffering and grief at the death of his earthly father,[5] and certainly he experienced grief at the death of his close friend Lazarus (John 11:35). In predicting the coming of the Messiah, Isaiah said he would be "a *man of sorrows,* and acquainted with grief" (Isa. 53:3).

b. The Pain of the Cross: The sufferings of Jesus intensified as he drew near to the cross. He told his disciples of something of the agony he was going through when he said, "My soul is very sorrowful, even to death" (Matt. 26:38). It was especially on the cross that Jesus' sufferings for us reached their climax, for it was there that he bore the penalty for our sin and died in our place. Scripture teaches us that there were four different aspects of the pain that Jesus experienced:

(1)Physical Pain and Death: We do not need to hold that Jesus suffered more physical pain than any human being has ever suffered, for the Bible nowhere makes such a claim. But we still must not forget that death by crucifixion was one of the most horrible forms of execution ever devised by man.

Many readers of the Gospels in the ancient world would have witnessed crucifixions and thus would have had a painfully vivid mental picture upon reading the simple words "And they crucified him" (Mark 15:24). A criminal who was crucified was essentially forced to inflict upon himself a very slow death by suffocation. When the criminal's arms were outstretched and fastened by nails to the cross, he had to support most of the weight of his body with his arms. The chest cavity would be pulled upward and outward, making it difficult to exhale in order to be able to draw a fresh breath. But when the victim's longing for oxygen became unbearable, he would have to push himself up with his feet, thus giving more natural support to the weight of his body, releasing some of the weight from his arms, and enabling his chest cavity to contract more normally. By pushing himself upward in this way the criminal could fend off suffocation, but it was extremely painful because it required putting the body's weight on the nails holding the feet, and bending the elbows and pulling upward on the nails driven through the wrists.[6] The criminal's back, which had been torn open repeatedly by a previous flogging, would scrape against the wooden cross with each breath. Thus Seneca (first century A.D.) spoke of a crucified man "drawing the breath of life amid long-drawn-out agony" (Epistle 101, to Lucilius, section 14).

A physician writing in the *Journal of the American Medical Association* in 1986 explained the pain that would have been experienced in death by crucifixion:

---

[4]In Mark 1:13 the present participle *peirazomenos*, "being tempted," modifies the imperfect main verb of the clause (*ēn*, "was"), indicating that Jesus was continually being tempted throughout the forty days in which he was in the wilderness.

[5]Although Scripture does not explicitly say that Joseph died during Jesus' life, we hear nothing of him after Jesus is twelve years old: see discussion in chapter 2, n. 7.

[6]The Greek word usually translated "hand" (*cheir:* Luke 24:39 – 40; John 20:20) can sometimes refer to the arm (BAGD, p. 880; LSJ, p. 1983, 2). A nail through the hands would not have been able to support the weight of the body, for the hands would have torn.

Adequate exhalation required lifting the body by pushing up on the feet and by flexing the elbows. . . . However, this maneuver would place the entire weight of the body on the tarsals and would produce searing pain. Furthermore, flexion of the elbows would cause rotation of the wrists about the iron nails and cause fiery pain along the damaged median nerves. . . . Muscle cramps and paresthesias of the outstretched and uplifted arms would add to the discomfort. As a result, each respiratory effort would become agonizing and tiring and lead eventually to asphyxia.[7]

In some cases, crucified men would survive for several days, nearly suffocating but not quite dying. This was why the executioners would sometimes break the legs of a criminal, so that death would come quickly, as we see in John 19:31–33:

Since it was the day of Preparation, in order to prevent the bodies from remaining on the cross on the sabbath (for that sabbath was a high day), the Jews asked Pilate that their legs might be broken, and that they might be taken away. So the soldiers came and broke the legs of the first, and of the other who had been crucified with him; but when they came to Jesus and saw that he was already dead, they did not break his legs.

(2) The Pain of Bearing Sin: More awful than the pain of physical suffering that Jesus endured was the psychological pain of bearing the guilt for our sin. In our own experience as Christians we know something of the anguish we feel when we know we have sinned. The weight of guilt is heavy on our hearts, and there is a bitter sense of separation from all that is right in the universe, an awareness of something that in a very deep sense ought not to be. In fact, the more we grow in holiness as God's children, the more intensely we feel this instinctive revulsion against evil.

Now Jesus was perfectly holy. He hated sin with his entire being. The thought of evil, of sin, contradicted everything in his character. Far more than we do, Jesus instinctively rebelled against evil. Yet in obedience to the Father, and out of love for us, Jesus took on himself all the sins of those who would someday be saved. Taking on himself all the evil against which his soul rebelled created deep revulsion in the center of his being. All that he hated most deeply was poured out fully upon him.

Scripture frequently says that our sins were put on Christ: "The LORD has laid on him the iniquity of us all" (Isa. 53:6), and "He *bore the sin* of many" (Isa. 53:12). John the Baptist calls Jesus "the Lamb of God, who takes away the sin of the world" (John 1:29). Paul declares that God made Christ *"to be sin"* (2 Cor. 5:21) and that Christ became "a curse for us" (Gal. 3:13). The author of Hebrews says that Christ was "offered once to bear the sins of many" (Heb. 9:28). And Peter says, "He himself *bore our sins* in his body on the tree" (1 Peter 2:24).[8]

---

[7]William Edwards, M.D., et al., *JAMA* vol. 255, no. 11 (March 21, 1986), p. 1461.

[8]See Wayne Grudem, *1 Peter,* TNTC (Leicester: Inter-Varsity Press, and Grand Rapids: Eerdmans, 1988), pp. 133–34, for a detailed answer to Deissmann's view that 1 Peter 2:24 means that Christ "carried our sins up to the cross" but did not himself bear the guilt for our sins on the cross. Influenced by Deissmann, BAGD, p. 63, 3, surprisingly deny that the verb *anapherō,* which is used in 1 Peter 2:24 can mean "bear," but Polybius 1.36.3 and Thucydides 3.38.3 provide extrabiblical examples of that meaning, and it certainly has that meaning in the LXX of Isa. 53:4, 11, 12, and in the quotation of Isa. 53:12 in Heb. 9:28; cf. LSJ, p. 125, 3.

The passage from 2 Corinthians quoted above, together with the verses from Isaiah, indicate that it was God the Father who put our sins on Christ. How could that be? In the same way in which Adam's sins were imputed to us, so God *imputed* our sins to Christ; that is, he *thought of them as belonging to Christ,* and, since God is the ultimate judge and definer of what really is in the universe, when God thought of our sins as belonging to Christ then in fact they actually did belong to Christ. This does not mean that God thought that Christ had himself committed the sins, or that Christ himself actually had a sinful nature, but rather that the guilt for our sins (that is, the liability to punishment) was thought of by God as belonging to Christ rather than to us.

Some have objected that it was not fair for God to do this, to transfer the guilt of sin from us to an innocent person, Christ. Yet we must remember that Christ voluntarily took on himself the guilt for our sins, so this objection loses much of its force. Moreover, God himself (Father, Son, and Holy Spirit) is the ultimate standard of what is just and fair in the universe, and he decreed that the atonement would take place in this way, and that it did in fact satisfy the demands of his own righteousness and justice.

(3) Abandonment: The physical pain of crucifixion and the pain of taking on himself the absolute evil of our sins were aggravated by the fact that Jesus faced this pain alone. In the Garden of Gethsemane, when Jesus took with him Peter, James and John, he confided something of his agony to them: "My soul is very sorrowful, even to death; remain here, and watch" (Mark 14:34). This is the kind of confidence one would disclose to a close friend, and it implies a request for support in his hour of greatest trial. Yet as soon as Jesus was arrested, "all the disciples forsook him and fled" (Matt. 26:56).

Here also there is a very faint analogy in our experience, for we cannot live long without tasting the inward ache of rejection, whether it be rejection by a close friend, by a parent or child, or by a wife or husband. Yet in all those cases there is at least a sense that we could have done something differently, that at least in small part we may be at fault. It was not so with Jesus and the disciples, for, "having loved his own who were in the world, he loved them to the end" (John 13:1). He had done nothing but love them; in return, they all abandoned him.

But far worse than desertion by even the closest of human friends was the fact that Jesus was deprived of the closeness to the Father that had been the deepest joy of his heart for all his earthly life. When Jesus cried out "Eli, Eli, lama sabach-thani?" that is, "My God, my God, why have you forsaken me?" (Matt. 27:46), he showed that he was finally cut off from the sweet fellowship with his heavenly Father that had been the unfailing source of his inward strength and the element of greatest joy in a life filled with sorrow. As Jesus bore our sins on the cross, he was abandoned by his heavenly Father, who is "of purer eyes than to behold evil" (Hab. 1:13). He faced the weight of the guilt of millions of sins alone.

(4) Bearing the Wrath of God: Yet more difficult than these three previous aspects of Jesus' pain was the pain of bearing the wrath of God upon himself. As Jesus bore the guilt of our sins alone, God the Father, the mighty Creator, the Lord of the universe, poured out on Jesus the fury of his wrath: Jesus became the object of the intense hatred of sin and vengeance against sin which God had patiently stored up since the beginning of the world.

Romans 3:25 tells us that God put forward Christ as a *"propitiation"* (NASB) a word that means "a sacrifice that bears God's wrath to the end and in so doing changes God's wrath toward us into favor." Paul tells us that "This was to show God's righteousness, because in his divine forbearance he had passed over former sins; it was to prove at the present time that he himself is righteous and that he justifies him who has faith in Jesus" (Rom. 3:25–26). God had not simply forgiven sin and forgotten about the punishment in generations past. He had forgiven sins and stored up his righteous anger against those sins. But at the cross the fury of all that stored-up wrath against sin was unleashed against God's own Son.

Many theologians outside the evangelical world have strongly objected to the idea that Jesus bore the wrath of God against sin.[9] Their basic assumption is that since God is a God of love, it would be inconsistent with his character to show wrath against the human beings he has created and for whom he is a loving Father. But evangelical scholars have convincingly argued that the idea of the wrath of God is solidly rooted in both the Old and New Testaments: "The whole of the argument of the opening part of Romans is that all men, Gentiles and Jews alike, are sinners, and that they come under the wrath and the condemnation of God."[10]

Three other crucial passages in the New Testament refer to Jesus' death as a "propitiation": Hebrews 2:17; 1 John 2:2; and 4:10. The Greek terms (the verb *hilaskomai*, "to make propitiation" and the noun *hilasmos*, "a sacrifice of propitiation") used in these passages have the sense of "a sacrifice that turns away the wrath of God—and thereby makes God propitious (or favorable) toward us."[11] This is the consistent meaning of these words outside the Bible where they were well understood in reference to pagan Greek religions. These verses simply mean that Jesus bore the wrath of God against sin.

It is important to insist on this fact, because it is the heart of the doctrine of the atonement. It means that there is an eternal, unchangeable requirement in the holiness and justice of God that sin be paid for. Furthermore, before the atonement ever could have an effect on our subjective consciousness, it first had an effect on God and his relation to the sinners he planned to redeem. Apart from this central truth, the death of Christ really cannot be adequately understood (see discussion of other views of the atonement below).

Although we must be cautious in suggesting any analogies to the experience Christ went through (for his experience was and always will be without precedent or comparison), nonetheless, all our understanding of Jesus' suffering comes in some sense by way of analogous experiences in our life—for that is how God teaches us in Scripture. Once again our human experience provides a very faint analogy that helps us understand what it means to bear the wrath of God. Perhaps as children we have faced the wrath of a human father

---

[9]See the detailed linguistic argument of C. H. Dodd, *The Bible and the Greeks* (London: Hodder and Stoughton, 1935), pp. 82–95. Dodd argues that the idea of propitiation was common in pagan religions but foreign to the thought of Old Testament and New Testament writers.

[10]Leon Morris, "Propitiation," *EDT*, p. 888 (includes brief bibliography). Morris's own work has represented the best of evangelical scholarship on this question: see his *The Apostolic Preaching of the Cross*, 3d ed. (London: Tyndale Press, 1965), pp. 144–213.

[11]Under the influence of scholars who denied that the idea of propitiation was in the New Testament, the RSV translated *hilasmos* as "expiation," a word that means "an action that cleanses from sin" but includes no concept of appeasing God's wrath.

when we have done wrong, or perhaps as adults we have known the anger of an employer because of a mistake we have made. We are inwardly shaken, disturbed by the crashing of another personality, filled with displeasure, into our very selves, and we tremble. We can hardly imagine the personal disintegration that would threaten if the outpouring of wrath came not from some finite human being but from Almighty God. If even the presence of God when he does not manifest wrath arouses fear and trembling in people (cf. Heb. 12:21, 28–29), how terrible it must be to face the presence of a wrathful God (Heb. 10:31).

With this in mind, we are now better able to understand Jesus' cry of desolation, "My God, my God, why have you forsaken me?" (Matt. 27:46b). The question does not mean, "Why have you left me forever?" for Jesus knew that he was leaving the world, that he was going to the Father (John 14:28; 16:10, 17). Jesus knew that he would rise again (John 2:19; Luke 18:33; Mark 9:31, et al.). It was "for the joy that was set before him" that Jesus "endured the cross, despising the shame, and is seated at the right hand of the throne of God" (Heb. 12:2). Jesus knew that he could still call God "my God." This cry of desolation is not a cry of total despair. Furthermore, "Why have you forsaken me?" does not imply that Jesus wondered why he was dying. He had said, "The Son of man also came not to be served but to serve, and to give his life as a ransom for many" (Mark 10:45). Jesus knew that he was dying for our sins.

Jesus' cry is a quotation from Psalm 22:1, a psalm in which the psalmist asks why God is so far from helping him, why God delays in rescuing him:

> My God, my God, why have you forsaken me?
> Why are you so far from helping me, from the words of my
>   groaning?
> O my God, I cry by day, but you do not answer;
>   and by night, but find no rest. (Ps. 22:1–2)

Yet the psalmist was eventually rescued by God, and his cry of desolation turned into a hymn of praise (vv. 22–31). Jesus, who knew the words of Scripture as his own, knew well the context of Psalm 22. In quoting this psalm, he is quoting a cry of desolation that also has implicit in its context an unremitting faith in the God who will ultimately deliver him. Nevertheless, it remains a very real cry of anguish because the suffering has gone on so long and no release is in sight.

With this context for the quotation it is better to understand the question "Why have you forsaken me?" as meaning, "Why have you left me *for so long?*" This is the sense it has in Psalm 22. Jesus, in his human nature, knew he would have to bear our sins, to suffer and to die. But, in his human consciousness, he probably did not know how long this suffering would take. Yet to bear the guilt of millions of sins even for a moment would cause the greatest anguish of soul. To face the deep and furious wrath of an infinite God even for an instant would cause the most profound fear. But Jesus' suffering was not over in a minute—or two—or ten. When would it end? Could there be yet more weight of sin? Yet more wrath of God? Hour after hour it went on—the dark weight of sin and the deep wrath of God poured over Jesus in wave after wave. Jesus at last cried out, "My God, my God, why have you forsaken me?" Why must this suffering go on so long? Oh God, my God, will you ever bring it to an end?

Then at last Jesus knew his suffering was nearing completion. He knew he had consciously borne all the wrath of the Father against our sins, for God's anger had abated and the awful heaviness of sin was being removed. He knew that all that remained was to yield up his spirit to his heavenly Father and die. With a shout of victory Jesus cried out, "It is finished!" (John 19:30). Then with a loud voice he once more cried out, "Father, into your hands I commit my spirit!" (Luke 23:46). And then he voluntarily gave up the life that no one could take from him (John 10:17–18), and he died. As Isaiah had predicted, "he poured out his soul to death" and "bore the sin of many" (Isa. 53:12). God the Father saw "the fruit of the travail of his soul" and was "satisfied" (Isa. 53:11).

c. Further Understanding of the Death of Christ:

(1) The Penalty Was Inflicted by God the Father: If we ask, "Who required Christ to pay the penalty for our sins?" the answer given by Scripture is that the penalty was inflicted by God the Father as he represented the interests of the Trinity in redemption. It was God's justice that required that sin be paid for, and, among the members of the Trinity, it was God the Father whose role was to require that payment. God the Son voluntarily took upon himself the role of bearing the penalty for sin. Referring to God the Father, Paul says, "For our sake he made him to be sin who knew no sin [that is, Christ], so that in him we might become the righteousness of God" (2 Cor. 5:21). Isaiah said, "The LORD has laid on him the iniquity of us all" (Isa. 53:6). He goes on to describe the sufferings of Christ: "Yet it was the will of the LORD to bruise him; he has put him to grief" (Isa. 53:10).

Herein we see something of the amazing love of both God the Father and God the Son in redemption. Not only did Jesus know that he would bear the incredible pain of the cross, but God the Father also knew that he would have to inflict this pain on his own deeply loved Son. "God shows his love for us in that while we were yet sinners Christ died for us" (Rom. 5:8).

(2) Not Eternal Suffering but Complete Payment: If we had to pay the penalty for our own sins, we would have to suffer eternally in separation from God. However, Jesus did not suffer eternally. There are two reasons for this difference: (a) If we suffered for our own sins, we would never be able to make ourselves right with God again. There would be no hope because there would be no way to live again and earn perfect righteousness before God, and there would be no way to undo our sinful nature and make it right before God. Moreover, we would continue to exist as sinners who would not suffer with pure hearts of righteousness before God, but would suffer with resentment and bitterness against God, thus continually compounding our sin. (b) Jesus was able to bear all the wrath of God against our sin and to bear it to the end. No mere man could ever have done this, but by virtue of the union of divine and human natures in himself, Jesus was able to bear all the wrath of God against sin and bear it to the end. Isaiah predicted that God "shall see the fruit of the travail of his soul *and be satisfied*" (Isa. 53:11). When Jesus knew that he had paid the full penalty for our sin, he said, *"It is finished"* (John 19:30). If Christ had not paid the full penalty, there would still be condemnation left for us. But since he has paid the full penalty that is due to us, "There is therefore now no condemnation for those who are in Christ Jesus" (Rom. 8:1).

It should help us at this point to realize that nothing in the eternal character of God and nothing in the laws God had given for mankind required that there be eternal suffering to pay for man's sins. In fact, if there is eternal suffering, it simply shows that the penalty has never been fully paid, and that the evildoer continues to be a sinner by nature. But when Christ's sufferings at last came to an end on the cross, it showed that he had borne the full measure of God's wrath against sin and there was no penalty left to pay. It also showed that he was himself righteous before God. In this way the fact that Christ suffered for a limited time rather than eternally shows that his suffering was a sufficient payment for sins. The author of Hebrews repeats this theme again and again, emphasizing the completion and the finality of Christ's redemptive work:

> Nor was it to offer himself repeatedly, as the high priest enters the Holy Place yearly with blood not his own; for then he would have had to suffer repeatedly since the foundation of the world. But as it is, he has appeared once for all at the end of the age to put away sin by the sacrifice of himself. . . . Christ, having been offered once *to bear the sins of many,* will appear a second time, not to deal with sin but to save those who are eagerly waiting for him. (Heb. 9:25–28)

This New Testament emphasis on the completion and finality of Christ's sacrificial death stands in contrast to the Roman Catholic teaching that in the mass there is a repetition of the sacrifice of Christ.[12] Because of this official teaching of the Roman Catholic Church, many Protestants since the Reformation, and still today, are convinced that they cannot in good conscience actually participate in the Roman Catholic mass, because it would seem to be an endorsement of the Catholic view that the sacrifice of Christ is repeated every time the mass is offered.

The New Testament emphasis on the completion and finality of Christ's sacrifice of himself for us has much practical application, because it assures us that there is no more penalty for sin left for us to pay. The penalty has entirely been paid by Christ, and we should have no remaining fear of condemnation or punishment.

(3) The Meaning of the Blood of Christ: The New Testament frequently connects the blood of Christ with our redemption. For example, Peter says, "You know that you were ransomed from the futile ways inherited from your fathers, not with perishable things such as silver or gold, but with the precious blood of Christ, like that of a lamb without blemish or spot" (1 Peter 1:18–19).

The blood of Christ is the clear outward evidence that his life blood was poured out when he died a sacrificial death to pay for our redemption — "the blood of Christ"

---

[12]Ludwig Ott, *Fundamentals of Catholic Dogma,* trans. Patrick Lynch (Rockford, Ill.: TAN, 1960), p. 408, says, "In the Sacrifice of the Mass and in the Sacrifice of the Cross the Sacrificial Gift and the Primary Sacrificing Priest are identical; only the nature and the mode of the offering are different. . . . according to the Thomistic view, *in every Mass Christ also performs an actual immediate sacrificial activity,* which, however, must not be conceived as a totality of many successive acts but as one single uninterrupted sacrificial act of the Transfigured Christ. The purpose of the Sacrifice is the same in the Sacrifice of the Mass as in the Sacrifice of the Cross; primarily the glorification of God, secondarily atonement, thanksgiving and appeal."

means his death in its saving aspects.[13] Although we may think that Christ's blood (as evidence that his life had been given) would have exclusive reference to the removal of our judicial guilt before God—for this is its primary reference—the New Testament authors also attribute to it several other effects. By the blood of Christ our consciences are cleansed (Heb. 9:14), we gain bold access to God in worship and prayer (Heb. 10:19), we are progressively cleansed from remaining sin (1 John 1:7; cf. Rev. 1:5b), we are able to conquer the accuser of the brethren (Rev. 12:10–11), and we are rescued out of a sinful way of life (1 Peter 1:18–19).[14]

Scripture speaks so much about the blood of Christ because its shedding was very clear evidence that his life was being given in judicial execution (that is, he was condemned to death and died paying a penalty imposed both by an earthly human judge and by God himself in heaven). Scripture's emphasis on the blood of Christ also shows the clear connection between Christ's death and the many sacrifices in the Old Testament that involved the pouring out of the life blood of the sacrificial animal. These sacrifices all pointed forward to and prefigured the death of Christ.

(4) Christ's Death as "Penal Substitution": The view of Christ's death presented here has frequently been called the theory of *"penal substitution."* Christ's death was "penal" in that he bore a penalty when he died. His death was also a "substitution" in that he was a substitute for us when he died. This has been the orthodox understanding of the atonement held by evangelical theologians, in contrast to other views that attempt to explain the atonement apart from the idea of the wrath of God or payment of the penalty for sin (see below).

This view of the atonement is sometimes called the theory of *vicarious atonement*. A "vicar" is someone who stands in the place of another or who represents another. Christ's death was therefore "vicarious" because he stood in our place and represented us. As our representative, he took the penalty that we deserve.

d. New Testament Terms Describing Different Aspects of the Atonement: The atoning work of Christ is a complex event that has several effects on us. It can therefore be viewed from several different aspects. The New Testament uses different words to describe these; we shall examine four of the more important terms.

The four terms show how Christ's death met the four needs that we have as sinners:

1. We deserve to *die* as the penalty for sin.
2. We deserve to *bear God's wrath* against sin.
3. We are *separated* from God by our sins.
4. We are in *bondage to sin* and to the kingdom of Satan.

These four needs are met by Christ's death in the following ways:

(1) Sacrifice: To pay the penalty of death that we deserved because of our sins, Christ died as a sacrifice for us. "He has appeared once for all at the end of the age to put away sin by the sacrifice of himself" (Heb. 9:26).

---

[13]So Leon Morris, *The Apostolic Preaching of the Cross,* pp. 112–26.

[14]This paragraph has been taken from Grudem, *1 Peter,* p. 84.

(2) Propitiation: To remove us from the wrath of God that we deserved, Christ died as a propitiation for our sins. "In this is love, not that we loved God, but that He loved us and sent His Son to be the propitiation for our sins" (1 John 4:10 NASB).

(3) Reconciliation: To overcome our separation from God, we needed someone to provide reconciliation and thereby bring us back into fellowship with God. Paul says that God "through Christ reconciled us to himself and gave us the ministry of reconciliation; that is, in Christ God was reconciling the world to himself" (2 Cor. 5:18–19).

(4) Redemption: Because we as sinners are in bondage to sin and to Satan, we need someone to provide redemption and thereby "redeem" us out of that bondage. When we speak of redemption, the idea of a "ransom" comes into view. A ransom is the price paid to redeem someone from bondage or captivity. Jesus said of himself, "For the Son of man also came not to be served but to serve, and to give his life *as a ransom for many*" (Mark 10:45). If we ask to whom the ransom was paid, we realize that the human analogy of a ransom payment does not fit the atonement of Christ in every detail. Though we were in bondage to sin and to Satan, there was no "ransom" paid either to "sin" or to Satan himself, for they did not have power to demand such payment, nor was Satan the one whose holiness was offended by sin and who required a penalty to be paid for sin. As we saw earlier, the penalty for sin was paid by Christ and received and accepted by God the Father. But we hesitate to speak of paying a "ransom" to God the Father, because it was not he who held us in bondage but Satan and our own sins. Therefore at this point the idea of a ransom payment cannot be pressed in every detail. It is sufficient to note that a price was paid (the death of Christ) and the result was that we were "redeemed" from bondage.

We were redeemed from bondage to Satan because "the whole world is in the power of the evil one" (1 John 5:19), and when Christ came he died to "deliver all those who through fear of death were subject to lifelong bondage" (Heb. 2:15). In fact, God the Father "has delivered us from the dominion of darkness and transferred us to the kingdom of his beloved Son" (Col. 1:13).

As for deliverance from bondage to sin, Paul says, "So you also must consider yourselves dead to sin and alive to God in Christ Jesus. . . . For sin will have no dominion over you, since you are not under law but under grace" (Rom. 6:11, 14). We have been delivered from bondage to the guilt of sin and from bondage to its ruling power in our lives.

e. Other Views of the Atonement: In contrast to the penal substitution view of the atonement presented in this chapter, several other views have been advocated in the history of the church.

(1) The Ransom to Satan Theory: This view was held by Origen (c. A.D. 185–c. 254), a theologian from Alexandria and later Caesarea, and after him by some others in the early history of the church. According to this view, the ransom Christ paid to redeem us was paid to Satan, in whose kingdom all people were by virtue of sin.

This theory finds no direct confirmation in Scripture and has few supporters in the history of the church. It falsely thinks of Satan rather than God as the one who required that a payment be made for sin and thus completely neglects the demands of God's justice with respect to sin. It views Satan as having much more power than he actually does, namely, power to demand whatever he wants from God, rather than as one who has been cast down from heaven and has no right to demand anything of God. Nowhere does Scripture say that we as sinners owe anything to Satan, but it repeatedly says that God requires of us a payment for our sins. This view also fails to deal with the texts that speak of Christ's death as a propitiation offered to God the Father for our sins, or with the fact that God the Father represented the Trinity in accepting the payment for sins from Christ (see discussion above).

(2) The Moral Influence Theory: First advocated by Peter Abelard (1079–1142), a French theologian, the moral influence theory of the atonement holds that God did not require the payment of a penalty for sin, but that Christ's death was simply a way in which God showed how much he loved human beings by identifying with their sufferings, even to the point of death. Christ's death therefore becomes a great teaching example that shows God's love to us and draws from us a grateful response, so that in loving him we are forgiven.

The great difficulty with this viewpoint is that it is contrary to so many passages of Scripture that speak of Christ dying for sin, bearing our sin, or dying as a propitiation. Moreover, it robs the atonement of its objective character, because it holds that the atonement had no effect on God himself. Finally, it has no way of dealing with our guilt—if Christ did not die to pay for our sins, we have no right to trust in him for forgiveness of sins.

(3) The Example Theory: The example theory of the atonement was taught by the Socinians, the followers of Faustus Socinus (1539–1604), an Italian theologian who settled in Poland in 1578 and attracted a wide following.[15] The example theory, like the moral influence theory, also denies that God's justice requires payment for sin; it says that Christ's death simply provides us with an example of how we should trust and obey God perfectly, even if that trust and obedience leads to a horrible death. Whereas the moral influence theory says that Christ's death teaches us how much God loves us, the example theory says that Christ's death teaches us how we should live. Support for this view could be found in 1 Peter 2:21, "For to this you have been called, because Christ also suffered for you, leaving you an example, that you should follow in his steps."

While it is true that Christ is an example for us even in his death, the question is whether this fact is the complete explanation of the atonement. The example theory fails to account for the many Scriptures that focus on Christ's death as a payment for sin, the fact that Christ bore our sins, and the fact that he was the propitiation for our sins. These considerations alone mean that the theory must be rejected. Moreover, this view really

---

[15]The Socinians were anti-trinitarian since they denied the deity of Christ; their thought led to modern Unitarianism.

ends up arguing that man can save himself by following Christ's example and by trusting and obeying God just as Christ did. Thus it fails to show how the guilt of our sin can be removed, because it does not hold that Christ actually paid the penalty for our sins or made provision for our guilt when he died.

(4) The Governmental Theory: The governmental theory of the atonement was first taught by a Dutch theologian and jurist, Hugo Grotius (1583–1645). This theory holds that God did not actually have to require payment for sin, but, since he was omnipotent God, he could have set aside that requirement and simply forgiven sins without the payment of a penalty. Then what was the purpose of Christ's death? It was God's demonstration of the fact that his laws had been broken, that he is the moral lawgiver and governor of the universe, and that some kind of penalty would be required whenever his laws were broken. Thus Christ did not exactly pay the penalty for the actual sins of any people, but simply suffered to show that when God's laws are broken there must be some penalty paid.

The problem with this view again is that it fails to account adequately for all the Scriptures that speak of Christ bearing our sins on the cross, of God laying on Christ the iniquity of us all, of Christ dying specifically for our sins, and of Christ being the propitiation for our sins. Moreover, it takes away the objective character of the atonement by making its purpose not the satisfaction of God's justice but simply that of influencing us to realize that God has laws that must be kept. This view also implies that we cannot rightly trust in Christ's completed work for forgiveness of sin, because he has not actually made payment for those sins. Moreover, it makes the actual earning of forgiveness for us something that happened in God's own mind apart from the death of Christ on the cross—he had already decided to forgive us without requiring any penalty from us and then punished Christ only to demonstrate that he was still the moral governor of the universe. But this means that Christ (in this view) did not actually earn forgiveness or salvation for us, and thus the value of his redemptive work is greatly minimized. Finally, this theory fails to take adequate account of the unchangeableness of God and the infinite purity of his justice. To say that God can forgive sins without requiring any penalty (in spite of the fact that throughout Scripture sin always requires the payment of a penalty) is seriously to underestimate the absolute character of the justice of God.

f. Did Christ Descend into Hell?[16] It is sometimes argued that Christ descended into hell after he died. The phrase "he descended into hell" does not occur in the Bible. But the widely used Apostles' Creed reads, "was crucified, dead, and buried, he descended into hell; the third day he rose again from the dead." Does this mean that Christ endured further suffering after his death on the cross? As we shall see below, an examination of the biblical evidence indicates that he did not. But before looking at the relevant biblical texts, it is appropriate to examine the phrase "he descended into hell" in the Apostles' Creed.

(1) The Origin of the Phrase, "He Descended into Hell": A murky background lies behind much of the history of the phrase itself. Its origins, where they can be found, are

---

[16]The following section is taken from Wayne Grudem, "He Did Not Descend Into Hell: A Plea for Following Scripture Instead of the Apostles' Creed," *JETS* vol. 34, no. 1 (March, 1991), pp. 103–13.

THE GRADUAL FORMATION OF THE APOSTLES' CREED

CREDO (I believe)			
Art. III			
Ultimate Text of the Western Creed	*Qui Conceptus est*	*De Spirita Sancto*	*Natus*	*Ex Maria Virgine*
Pirminius, A.D. 750	Who was conceived	By the Holy Ghost	Born	Of the Virgin Mary
I. St. Irenaeus, A.D. 200	τὸν σαρκ-ωθέντα ὑπὲρ τῆς ἡμετέρας σωτηρίας (ἄνθρωπος ἐγένετο)		(Generationum)	τὴν ἐκ παρθέ-νου γέννησιν (ex Virgine)
II. Tertullian, A.D. 220	(missum a Petre in Virginem)	(EX SPIRITU Patris Dei et virtute)	NATUM (carnem factum et ex ea natum)	EX VIRGINE MARIA
III. St. Cyprian, A.D. 250				
IV. Novatian, A.D. 260				
V. Marcellus, A.D. 341		ἐκ πνεύματος ἁγίου	γεννηθέντα	καὶ Μαρίας τῆς παρθένου
VI. Rufinus, A.D. 390 Aquileja	QUI	de Spiritu SANCTO	natus est	ex Maria Virgine
VII. Rufinus, Rome, A.D. 390	qui	de Spiritu Sancto	natus est	ex Maria Virgine
VIII. St. Augustine, A.D. 400	qui	de Spiritu Santo *also* [per Sp. Sanct.]	natus est	ex Maria Virgine *also* [et]
IX. St. Nicetas, A.D. 450	qui	ex Spiritu Sancto	natus est	et Virgine Maria
X. Eusebius Gallus, A.D. 550 (?)	qui	de Spiritu Sancto	natus est	ex Maria Virgine
XI. Sacramentarium Gallicanum. A.D. 650	qui conceptus est	de Spiritu Sancto	natus est	ex Maria Virgine

THE GRADUAL FORMATION OF THE APOSTLES' CREED

Art. III				
Passus	*Sub Pontio Pilato*	*Crucifixus*	*Mortuus*	*Et Sepultus*
Suffered	Under Pontius Pilate	Was crucified	Dead	And buried
καὶ τὸ πάθος	(SUB PONTIO PILATO)			
CRUCIFIXUM (passum)	sub Pontio Pilato		(MORTUUM)	(ET SEPULTUM secundum Scripturas)
	τὸν ἐπὶ ποντίου πιλάτου	σταυρωθέντα		καὶ ταφέντα
	sub Pontio Pilate	crucifixus		et sepultus
	sub Pontio Pilate	crucifixus		et sepultus
passus	sub Pontio Pilate	crucifixus		et sepultus
passus	sub Pontio Pilate			
			mortuus	et sepultus
passus	sub Pontio Pilate	crucifixus	mortuus	et sepultus

THE GRADUAL FORMATION OF THE APOSTLES' CREED

	Art. V			Art. VI	
Descendit ad Inferna	Tertia die	Resurrexit	a mortuis	Ascendit ad coelos	Sedet ad dexteram
He descended into hell	The third day	He rose again	From the dead	He ascended into heaven	And sitteth at the right hand
		καὶ τὴν ἔγερσιν (et resurgens)	ἐκ νεκρῶν	εἰς τοὺς οὐρανοὺς ἀνάλημψιν (et in claritate receptus)	
	TERTIA DIE	resuscitatum (a Patre) (resurrexisse)	E MORTUIS	receptum in coelis (in coelos resumptum) (in coelos ereptum)	SEDENTEM nunc AD DEXTERAM
	καὶ τῇ τρίτῃ ἡμέρα	ἀναστάντα	ἐκ τῶν νεκρῶν	ἀναβάντα εἰς τοὺς οὐρανούς	καὶ καθημένον ἐν δεξιὰ
DESCENDIT in INFERNA	tertia die	RESURREXIT	A mortuis	ASCENDIT in COELOS	SEDET ad dexteram
	tertia die	resurrexit	a mortuis	ascendit in coelos	SEDET ad dexteram
	tertio die	resurrexit	a mortuis	ascendit in coelos	sedet ad dexteram
	tertio die	resurrexit	vivus a mortuis	ascendit in coelos	sedet ad dexteram
	tertia die	resurrexit	a mortuis	ascendit AD coelos	sedet ad dexteram
Descendit AD Inferna	tertia die	resurrexit	a mortuis	ascendit ad coelos	sedet ad dexteram

far from praiseworthy. The great church historian Philip Schaff has summarized the development of the Apostles' Creed in an extensive chart, part of which is reproduced in part on pages 86–88.[17]

This chart shows that, unlike the Nicene Creed and the Chalcedonian Definition, the Apostles' Creed was not written or approved by a single church council at one specific time. Rather, it gradually took shape from about A.D. 200 to 750.

It is surprising to find that the phrase "he descended into hell" was not found in any of the early versions of the Creed (in the versions used in Rome, in the rest of Italy, and in Africa) until it appeared in one of two versions from Rufinus in A.D. 390. Then it was not included again in any version of the Creed until A.D. 650. Moreover, Rufinus, the only person who included it before A.D. 650, did not think that it meant that Christ descended into hell, but understood the phrase simply to mean that Christ was "buried."[18] In other words, he took it to mean that Christ "descended into the grave." (The Greek form has *hadēs,* which can mean just "grave," not *geenna,* "hell, place of punishment."). We should also note that the phrase only appears in one of the two versions of the Creed that we have from Rufinus: it was not in the Roman form of the Creed that he preserved.

This means, therefore, that until A.D. 650 no version of the Creed included this phrase with the intention of saying that Christ "descended into hell" — the only version to include the phrase before A.D. 650 gives it a different meaning. At this point one wonders if the term *apostolic* can in any sense be applied to this phrase, or if it really has a rightful place in a creed whose title claims for itself descent from the earliest apostles of Christ.

This survey of the historical development of the phrase also raises the possibility that when the phrase first began to be more commonly used, it may have been in other versions (now lost to us) that did not have the expression "and buried." If so, it probably would have meant to others just what it meant to Rufinus: "descended into the grave." But later when the phrase was incorporated into different versions of the Creed that already had the phrase "and buried," some other explanation had to be given to it. This mistaken insertion of the phrase after the words "and buried" — apparently done by someone around A.D. 650 — led to all sorts of attempts to explain "he descended into hell" in some way that did not contradict the rest of Scripture.

Some have taken it to mean that Christ suffered the pains of hell while on the cross. Calvin, for example, says that "Christ's descent into hell" refers to the fact that he not only died a bodily death but that "it was expedient at the same time for him to undergo the severity of God's vengeance, to appease his wrath and satisfy his just judgment."[19]

---

[17]This chart is taken from *The Creeds of Christendom,* 3 vols. (Grand Rapids: Baker, 1983 reprint of 1931 edition), 2:52–55.

[18]See Schaff, *Creeds,* 1.21, n. 6; see also 46, n. 2. Schaff notes that the phrase was found somewhat earlier (around A.D. 360), but then it was not in any orthodox creeds or any versions of the Apostles' Creed but in some creeds of the Arians — people who denied the full deity of Christ, holding that the Son was created by the Father (see Schaff, *Creeds,* 2.46, n. 2). (Schaff does not give documentation for this reference to Arian creeds.)

It should be noted that Schaff throughout his *Creeds of Christendom* has several editorial comments defending an actual descent of Christ into hell after his death on the cross. Thus, for example, he says that "Rufinus himself, however, misunderstood it by making it to mean the same as buried" (1.21, n. 6) — thus Schaff assumes that to understand the phrase to mean "he descended into the grave" is to *misunderstand* it (see also 2.46, n. 2; 3.321, n. 1).

[19]John Calvin, *Institutes of the Christian Religion,* 1.515 (2.16.10).

Similarly, the Heidelberg Catechism, Question 44, asks,

> Why is it added: He descended into Hades?
>
> Answer: That in my greatest temptations I may be assured that Christ, my Lord, by his inexpressible anguish, pains, and terrors which he suffered in his soul on the cross and before, has redeemed me from the anguish and torment of hell.[20]

But is this a satisfactory explanation of the phrase, "he descended into hell"? While it is true that Christ suffered the outpouring of God's wrath on the cross, this explanation does not really fit the phrase in the Apostles' Creed—"descended" hardly represents this idea, and the placement of the phrase after "was crucified, dead, and buried" makes this an artificial and unconvincing interpretation.

Others have understood it to mean that Christ continued in the "state of death" until his resurrection. The Westminster Larger Catechism, Question 50, says,

> Christ's humiliation after his death consisted in his being buried, and continuing in the state of the dead, and under the power of death till the third day; which hath been otherwise expressed in these words, He descended into hell.

Though it is true that Christ continued in the state of death until the third day, once again it is a strained and unpersuasive explanation of "he descended into hell," for the placement of the phrase would then give the awkward sense, "he was crucified, dead, and buried; he descended to being dead." This interpretation does not explain what the words first meant in this sequence but is rather an unconvincing attempt to salvage some theologically acceptable sense out of them.

Moreover, the English word "hell" has no such sense as simply "being dead" (though the Greek word *hadēs* can mean this), so this becomes a doubly artificial explanation for English-speaking people.

Finally, some have argued that the phrase means just what it appears to mean on first reading: that Christ actually did descend into hell after his death on the cross. It is easy to understand the Apostles' Creed to mean just this (indeed, that is certainly the natural sense), but then another question arises: Can this idea be supported from Scripture?

(2) Possible Biblical Support for a Descent into Hell: Support for the idea that Christ descended into hell has been found primarily in five passages: Acts 2:27; Romans 10:6–7; Ephesians 4:8–9; 1 Peter 3:18–20; and 1 Peter 4:6. (A few other passages have been appealed to, but less convincingly.)[21] On closer inspection, do any of those passages clearly establish this teaching?

(a) Acts 2:27. This is part of Peter's sermon on the Day of Pentecost, where he is quoting Psalm 16:10. In the King James Version the verse reads: "because thou wilt not *leave my soul in hell,* neither wilt thou suffer thine Holy One to see corruption."

---

[20]Schaff, *Creeds,* 3.321.

[21]For example, Matt. 12:40, which says that Christ will be three days and nights "in the heart of the earth," simply refers to the fact that he was in the grave between his death and resurrection (cf., in the LXX, Ps. 45[46]:2 with Jonah 2:3).

Does this mean that Christ entered hell after he died? Not necessarily, because another sense is certainly possible for these verses. The word "hell" here represents a New Testament Greek term (*hades*) and an Old Testament Hebrew term (שְׁאוֹל *'ôl*, popularly translated as sheol) that can mean simply "the grave" or "death" (the state of being dead). Thus, the NIV translates: "Because you will not *abandon me to the grave*, nor will you let your Holy One see decay" (Acts 2:27). This sense is preferable because the context emphasizes that Christ's body rose from the grave, unlike David's, which remained in the grave. The reasoning is: "My body also will live in hope" (v. 26), "because you will not abandon me to the grave" (v. 27). Peter is using David's psalm to show that Christ's body did not decay—he is therefore unlike David, who "died and was buried, and his tomb is here to this day" (v. 29 NIV). Therefore this passage about Christ's resurrection from the grave does not convincingly support the idea that Christ descended into hell.

(b) Romans 10:6–7. These verses contain two rhetorical questions, again Old Testament quotations (from Deut. 30:13): "Do not say in your heart, 'Who will ascend into heaven?' (that is, to bring Christ down) or 'Who will descend into the abyss?' (that is, to bring Christ up from the dead)." But this passage hardly teaches that Christ descended into hell. The point of the passage is that Paul is telling people not to ask these questions, because Christ is not far away—he is near—and faith in him is as near as confessing with our mouth and believing in our heart (v. 9). These prohibited questions are questions of unbelief, not assertions of what Scripture teaches. However, some may object that Paul would not have anticipated that his readers would ask such questions unless it was widely known that Christ did in fact descend "into the abyss." However, even if this were true, Scripture would not be saying or implying that Christ went into "hell" (in the sense of a place of punishment for the dead, ordinarily expressed by Gk. *geenna*), but rather that he went into "the abyss" (Gk. *abyssos*, a term which often in the LXX is used of the depths of the ocean [Gen. 1:2; 7:11; 8:2; Deut. 8:7; Ps. 106(107):26], but it can also apparently refer just to the realm of the dead [Ps. 70(71):20]).[22]

Paul here uses the word "deep" (*abyssos*) as a contrast to "heaven" in order to give the sense of a place that is unreachable, inaccessible to human beings. The contrast is not, "Who shall go to find Christ in a place of great blessing (heaven) or a place of great punishment (hell)?" but rather, "Who shall go to find Christ in a place that is inaccessibly high (heaven) or in a place that is inaccessibly low (the deep, or the realm of death)?" No clear affirmation or denial of a "descent into hell" can be found in this passage.

(c) Ephesians 4:8–9. Here Paul writes, "In saying, 'He ascended,' what does it mean but that he had also descended into the lower parts of the earth?"

Does this mean that Christ "descended" to hell? It is at first unclear what is meant by "the lower parts of the earth," but another translation seems to give the best sense: "What does 'he ascended' mean except that he also descended to the *lower, earthly regions?*" (NIV). Here

---

[22]1 Clem. 28:3 uses *abyssos* instead of the Septuagint's *hades* to translate Ps. 139:8, "If I make my bed in Sheol, thou art there!" In the New Testament, the term is used only in Luke 8:31; Rom. 10:7; and seven times in Revelation (there it refers to the "bottomless pit"). Therefore, although the term can refer to the abode of condemned demons (as in Revelation), this is not its common sense in the LXX or a necessary sense in its New Testa-ment usage. The primary force of the term is a place that is deep, unfathomable to human beings, ordinarily unable to be reached by them. (C. E. B. Cranfield, *A Critical and Exegetical Commentary on the Epistle to the Romans*, ICC (Edinburgh: T. & T. Clark, 1975), 2.525, notes that *abyssos* is the ordinary LXX translation for Hebrew *tehōm*, and that *tehōm* is used in the Mishnah [Pesahim 7:7; Nazir 9:2] to refer to a grave that had been unknown.)

the NIV takes "descended" to refer to Christ's coming to earth as a baby (the Incarnation). The last four words are an acceptable understanding of the Greek text, taking the phrase "the lower regions *of* the earth" to mean "lower regions *which are* the earth" (the grammatical form in Greek would then be called a genitive of apposition). We do the same thing in English—for example, in the phrase "the city of Chicago," we mean "the city which is Chicago."

The NIV rendering is preferable in this context because Paul is saying that the Christ who went up to heaven (in his ascension) is the same one who earlier came down from heaven (v. 10). That "descent" from heaven occurred, of course, when Christ came to be born as a man. So the verse speaks of the incarnation, not of a descent into hell.[23]

(d) 1 Peter 3:18–20. For many people this is the most puzzling passage on this entire subject. Peter tells us that Christ was "put to death in the flesh but made alive in the spirit; *in which he went and preached to the spirits in prison,* who formerly did not obey, when God's patience waited in the days of Noah, during the building of the ark" (RSV).

Does this refer to Christ preaching in hell?

Some have taken "he went and preached to the spirits in prison" to mean that Christ went into hell and preached to the spirits who were there—either proclaiming the gospel and offering a second chance to repent, or just proclaiming that he had triumphed over them and that they were eternally condemned.

But these interpretations fail to explain adequately either the passage itself or its setting in this context. Peter does not say that Christ preached to spirits generally, but only to those "who formerly did not obey . . . *during the building of the ark.*" Such a limited audience—those who disobeyed during the building of the ark—would be a strange group for Christ to travel to hell and preach to. If Christ proclaimed his triumph, why only to these sinners and not to all? And if he offered a second chance for salvation, why only to these sinners and not to all? Even more difficult for this view is the fact that Scripture elsewhere indicates that there is no opportunity for repentance after death (Luke 16:26; Heb. 10:26–27).

Moreover, the context of 1 Peter 3 makes "preaching in hell" unlikely. Peter is encouraging his readers to witness boldly to hostile unbelievers around them. He just told them to "always be prepared to give an answer to everyone who asks you" (1 Peter 3:15 NIV). This evangelistic motif would lose its urgency if Peter were teaching a second chance for salvation after death. And it would not fit at all with a "preaching" of condemnation.

Does it refer to Christ preaching to fallen angels?

To give a better explanation for these difficulties, several commentators have proposed taking "spirits in prison" to mean demonic spirits, the spirits of fallen angels, and have said that Christ proclaimed condemnation to these demons. This (it is claimed) would comfort Peter's readers by showing them that the demonic forces oppressing them would also be defeated by Christ.

However, Peter's readers would have to go through an incredibly complicated reasoning process to draw this conclusion when Peter does not explicitly teach it. They would have to reason from (1) some demons who sinned long ago were condemned, to (2) other

---

[23]Referring to Eph. 4:9, H. Bietenhard says, "In modern exposition the reference of this passage to the *descensus ad* *inferos* ("he descended into hell" in the Apostles' Creed) is almost without exception rejected" (*NIDNTT*, 2:210).

demons are now inciting your human persecutors, to (3) those demons will likewise be condemned someday, to (4) therefore your persecutors will finally be judged as well. Finally Peter's readers would get to Peter's point: (5) Therefore don't fear your persecutors.

Those who hold this "preaching to fallen angels" view must assume that Peter's readers would "read between the lines" and conclude all this (points 2–5) from the simple statement that Christ "preached to the spirits in prison, who formerly did not obey" (1 Peter 3:19–20). But does it not seem too farfetched to say that Peter knew his readers would read all this into the text?

Moreover, Peter emphasizes hostile *persons*, not demons, in the context (1 Peter 3:14, 16). And where would Peter's readers get the idea that angels sinned "during the building of the ark"? There is nothing of that in the Genesis story about the building of the ark. And (in spite of what some have claimed), if we look at all the traditions of Jewish interpretation of the flood story, we find no mention of angels sinning specifically "during the building of the ark."[24] Therefore the view that Peter is speaking of Christ's proclamation of judgment to fallen angels is really not persuasive either.

Does it refer to Christ's proclaiming release to Old Testament saints?

Another explanation is that Christ, after his death, went and proclaimed release to Old Testament believers who had been unable to enter heaven until the completion of Christ's redemptive work.

But again we may question whether this view adequately accounts for what the text actually says. It does not say that Christ preached to those who were believers or faithful to God, but to those "who formerly *did not obey*"—the emphasis is on their disobedience. Moreover, Peter does not specify Old Testament believers generally, but only those who were disobedient "in the days of Noah, during the building of the ark" (1 Peter 3:20).

Finally, Scripture gives us no clear evidence to make us think that full access to the blessings of being in God's presence in heaven were withheld from Old Testament believers when they died—indeed, several passages suggest that believers who died before Christ's death did enter into the presence of God at once because their sins were forgiven by trusting in the Messiah who was to come (Gen. 5:24; 2 Sam. 12:23; Pss. 16:11; 17:15; 23:6; Eccl. 12:7; Matt. 22:31–32; Luke 16:22; Rom. 4:1–8; Heb. 11:5).

A more satisfying explanation.

The most satisfactory explanation of 1 Peter 3:19–20 seems rather to be one proposed (but not really defended) long ago by Augustine: the passage refers not to something Christ did between his death and resurrection, but to what he did "in the spiritual realm of existence" (or "through the Spirit") *at the time of Noah*. When Noah was building the ark, Christ "in spirit" was preaching through Noah to the hostile unbelievers around him.[25]

This view gains support from two other statements of Peter. In 1 Peter 1:11, he says that the "Spirit of Christ" was speaking in the Old Testament prophets. This suggests that Peter could readily have thought that the "Spirit of Christ" was speaking through Noah

---

[24]For an extensive discussion of Jewish interpretations of the sin of the "sons of God" in Gen. 6:2, 4, and of the identity of those who sinned while the ark was being built, see "Christ Preaching Through Noah: 1 Peter 3:19–20 in the Light of Dominant Themes in Jewish Literature," in Grudem, *1 Peter,* pp. 203–39. (This appendix has a lengthy discussion of 1 Peter 3:19–20, which I have only briefly summarized here.)

[25]This section is a brief summary of a more extensive discussion of this passage in Wayne Grudem, *The First Epistle of Peter,* pp. 157–62 and 203–39.

as well. Then in 2 Peter 2:5, he calls Noah a *"preacher* of righteousness" (NIV), using the noun (*kēryx*) that comes from the same root as the verb "preached" (*ekēryxen*) in 1 Peter 3:19. So it seems likely that when Christ "preached to the spirits in prison" he did so through Noah in the days before the flood.

The people to whom Christ preached through Noah were unbelievers on the earth at the time of Noah, but Peter calls them "spirits in prison" because they are now in the prison of hell—even though they were not just "spirits" but persons on earth when the preaching was done. (The NASB says Christ preached "to the spirits now in prison.") We can speak the same way in English: "I knew President Clinton when he was a college student" is an appropriate statement, even though he was not president when he was in college. The sentence means, "I knew the man who is now President Clinton when he was still a student in college." So "Christ preached to the spirits in prison" means "Christ preached to people who are now spirits in prison when they were still persons on earth."[26]

This interpretation is very appropriate to the larger context of 1 Peter 3:13–22. The parallel between the situation of Noah and the situation of Peter's readers is clear at several points:

Noah	Peter's readers
Righteous minority	Righteous minority
Surrounded by hostile unbelievers	Surrounded by hostile unbelievers
God's judgment was near	God's judgment may come soon (1 Peter 4:5, 7; 2 Peter 3:10)
Noah witnessed boldly (by Christ's power)	They should witness boldly by Christ's power (1 Peter 3:14, 16–17; 3:15; 4:11)
Noah was finally saved	They will finally be saved (1 Peter 3:13–14; 4:13; 5:10)

Such an understanding of the text seems to be by far the most likely solution to a puzzling passage. Yet this means that our fourth possible support for a descent of Christ into hell also turns up negative—the text speaks rather of something Christ did on earth at the time of Noah.

(e) 1 Peter 4:6. This fifth and final passage says, "For this is why the gospel was preached even to the dead, that though judged in the flesh like men, they might live in the spirit like God."

Does this verse mean that Christ went to hell and preached the gospel to those who had died? If so, it would be the only passage in the Bible that taught a "second chance" for salvation after death and would contradict passages such as Luke 16:19–31 and Hebrews 9:27,

---

[26]My student Tet-Lim Yee has called my attention to another very similar expression elsewhere in Scripture: Naomi speaks of how kindly Ruth and Orpah "have dealt with the dead" (Ruth 1:8), referring to their treatment of their husbands while the husbands were still alive.

which clearly seem to deny this possibility. Moreover, the passage does not explicitly say that Christ preached to people after they had died, and could rather mean that the gospel in general was preached (this verse does not even say that Christ preached) to people who are now dead, but that it was preached to them while they were still alive on earth.

This is a common explanation, and it seems to fit this verse much better. It finds support in the second word of the verse, "this," which refers back to the final judgment mentioned at the end of verse 5. Peter is saying that it was because of the final judgment that the gospel was preached to the dead.

This would comfort the readers concerning their Christian friends who had already died. They may have wondered, "Did the gospel benefit them, since it didn't save them from death?" Peter answers that the reason the gospel was preached to those who had died was not to save them from physical death (they were "judged in the flesh like men") but to save them from final judgment (they will "live in the spirit like God"). Therefore, the fact that they had died did not indicate that the gospel had failed in its purpose—for they would surely live forever in the spiritual realm.

Thus, "the dead" are people who have died and are now dead, even though they were alive and on earth when the gospel was preached to them. (The NIV translates, "For this is the reason the gospel was preached even to *those who are now dead*," and NASB has "those who are dead.") This avoids the doctrinal problem of a "second chance" of salvation after death and fits both the wording and the context of the verse.

We conclude, therefore, that this last passage, when viewed in its context, turns out to provide no convincing support for the doctrine of a descent of Christ into hell.

At this point, people on all sides of the question of whether Christ actually descended into hell should be able to agree at least that the idea of Christ's "descent into hell" is not taught clearly or explicitly in any passage of Scripture. And many people (including the present author) will conclude that this idea is not taught in Scripture at all. But beyond the question of whether any passage positively teaches this idea, we must ask whether it is contrary to any passages of Scripture.

(3) Biblical Opposition to a "Descent into Hell": In addition to the fact that there is little if any biblical support for a descent of Christ into hell, there are some New Testament texts that argue against the possibility of Christ's going to hell after his death.

Jesus' words to the thief on the cross, "Today you will be with me in Paradise" (Luke 23:43), imply that after Jesus died his soul (or spirit) went immediately to the presence of the Father in heaven, even though his body remained on earth and was buried. Some people deny this by arguing that "Paradise" is a place distinct from heaven, but in both of the other New Testament uses the word clearly means "heaven": in 2 Corinthians 12:4 it is the place to which Paul was caught up in his revelation of heaven, and in Revelation 2:7 it is the place where we find the tree of life—which is clearly heaven in Revelation 22:2 and 14.[27]

---

[27]Further support for this idea is found in the fact that though the word *paradeisos*, "paradise," could simply mean "pleasant garden" (esp. used in the LXX of the Garden of Eden), it also frequently meant "heaven" or "a place of blessedness in the presence of God": see Isa. 51:3; Ezek. 28:13; 31:8–9; T. Levi 18:10; 1 Enoch 20:7; 32:3; Sib. Or. 3:48. This was increasingly the sense of the term in intertestamental Jewish literature (for several more references see Joachim Jeremias, *paradeisos*, *TDNT* 5 [1967], pp. 765–73, esp. 767, nn. 16–23).

In addition, the cry of Jesus, "It is finished" (John 19:30) strongly suggests that Christ's suffering was finished at that moment and so was his alienation from the Father because of bearing our sin. This implies that he would not descend into hell, but would go at once into the Father's presence.

Finally, the cry, "Father, into your hands I commit my spirit" (Luke 23:46), also suggests that Christ expected (correctly) the immediate end of his suffering and estrangement and the welcoming of his spirit into heaven by God the Father (note Stephen's similar cry in Acts 7:59).

These texts indicate, then, that Christ in his death experienced the same things believers in this present age experience when they die: his dead body remained on earth and was buried (as ours will be), but his spirit (or soul) passed immediately into the presence of God in heaven (just as ours will). Then on the first Easter morning, Christ's spirit was reunited with his body and he was raised from the dead—just as Christians who have died will (when Christ returns) be reunited to their bodies and raised in their perfect resurrection bodies to new life.[28]

This fact has pastoral encouragement for us: we need not fear death, not only because eternal life lies on the other side, but also because we know that our Savior himself has gone through exactly the same experience we will go through—he has prepared, even sanctified the way, and we follow him with confidence each step of that way. This is much greater comfort regarding death than could ever be given by any view of a descent into hell.

(4) Conclusion Regarding the Apostles' Creed and the Question of Christ's Possible Descent into Hell: Does the phrase "he descended into hell" deserve to be retained in the Apostles' Creed alongside the great doctrines of the faith on which all can agree? The single argument in its favor seems to be the fact that it has been around so long. But an old mistake is still a mistake—and as long as it has been around there has been confusion and disagreement over its meaning.

On the other side, there are several compelling reasons against keeping the phrase. It has no clear warrant from Scripture and indeed seems to be contradicted by some passages in Scripture. It has no claim to being "apostolic" and no support (in the sense of a "descent into hell") from the first six centuries of the church. It was not in the earliest versions of the Creed and was only included in it later because of an apparent misunderstanding about its meaning. Unlike every other phrase in the Creed, it represents not some major doctrine on which all Christians agree, but rather a statement about which most Christians seem to disagree.[29] It is at best confusing and in most cases mis-

---

[28]John 20:17 ("Do not hold me, for I have not yet ascended to the Father") is best understood to mean that Jesus in his new resurrected state, with a resurrection body, had not yet ascended back to heaven; therefore, Mary should not try to hold on to Jesus' body. The perfect tense of *anabebēka*, "ascended," gives the sense, "I have not yet ascended and remained in the place where I ascended" or "I am not yet in the ascended state" (the latter phrase is from D. A. Carson, *The Gospel According to John*

[Leicester: Inter-Varsity Press, and Grand Rapids: Eerdmans, 1991], p. 644).

[29]Randall E. Otto adopts a similar recommendation: "To include such a mysterious article in the creed, which is supposed to be a summary of the basic and vital tenets of the faith, seems very unwise" ("*Descendit in Inferna*: A Reformed Review of a Doctrinal Conundrum," *WTJ* 52 [1990], p. 150).

leading for modern Christians. My own judgment is that there would be all gain and no loss if it were dropped from the Creed once for all.

Concerning the doctrinal question of whether Christ did descend into hell after he died, the answer from several passages of Scripture seems clearly to be no.

D. The Extent of the Atonement

One of the differences between Reformed theologians and other Catholic and Protestant theologians has been the question of the extent of the atonement. The question may be put this way: when Christ died on the cross, did he pay for the sins of the entire human race or only for the sins of those who he knew would ultimately be saved?

Non-Reformed people argue that the gospel offer in Scripture is repeatedly made to all people, and for this offer to be genuine, the payment for sins must have already been made and must be actually available for all people. They also say that if the people whose sins Christ paid for are limited, then the free offer of the gospel also is limited, and the offer of the gospel cannot be made to all mankind without exception.

On the other hand, Reformed people argue that if Christ's death actually paid for the sins of every person who ever lived, then there is no penalty left for *anyone* to pay, and it necessarily follows that all people will be saved, without exception. For God could not condemn to eternal punishment anyone whose sins are already paid for: that would be demanding double payment, and it would therefore be unjust. In answer to the objection that this compromises the free offer of the gospel to every person, Reformed people answer that we do not know who they are who will come to trust in Christ, for only God knows that. As far as we are concerned, the free offer of the gospel is to be made to everybody without exception. We also know that everyone who repents and believes in Christ will be saved, so all are called to repentance (cf. Acts 17:30). The fact that God foreknew who would be saved, and that he accepted Christ's death as payment for their sins only, does not inhibit the free offer of the gospel, for who will respond to it is hidden in the secret counsels of God. That we do not know who will respond no more constitutes a reason for not offering the gospel to all than not knowing the extent of the harvest prevents the farmer from sowing seed in his fields.

Finally, Reformed people argue that God's purposes in redemption are agreed upon within the Trinity and they are certainly accomplished. Those whom God planned to save are the same people for whom Christ also came to die, and to those same people the Holy Spirit will certainly apply the benefits of Christ's redemptive work, even awakening their faith (John 1:12; Phil. 1:29; cf. Eph. 2:2) and calling them to trust in him. What God the Father purposed, God the Son and the Holy Spirit agreed to and surely carried out.

1. Scripture Passages Used to Support the Reformed View. Several Scripture passages speak of the fact that Christ died for his people. "The good shepherd lays down his life *for the sheep*" (John 10:11). "I lay down my life for the sheep" (John 10:15). Paul speaks of "the church of God which he obtained with the blood of his own Son" (Acts 20:28). He also says, "He who did not spare his own Son but gave him up for us all, will he not also give us all things with him?" (Rom. 8:32). This passage indicates a connection between God's purpose in giving up his Son "for us all" and giving us "all things" that pertain to salvation as well. In the next sentence Paul clearly limits the application of this to those who will be saved because he says, "Who shall bring any charge against God's elect?" (Rom. 8:33) and in the next verse mentions Christ's death as a reason why no one shall bring a charge against the elect (8:34). In another passage, Paul says, "Husbands, love your wives, as Christ loved the church and gave himself up *for her*" (Eph. 5:25).

Moreover, Christ during his earthly ministry is aware of a group of people whom the Father has given to him. "All that the Father gives me will come to me; and him who comes to me I will not cast out . . . this is the will of him who sent me, that I should lose nothing of all that he has given me, but raise it up at the last day" (John 6:37–39). He also says, "I am not praying for the world but for those whom you have given me, for they are yours" (John 17:9). He then goes on from this specific reference to the disciples to say, "I do not pray for these only, but also for those who believe in me through their word" (John 17:20).

Finally, some passages speak of a definite transaction between the Father and the Son when Christ died, a transaction that had specific reference to those who would believe. For example, Paul says, "God shows his love for us in that while we were yet sinners Christ died *for us*" (Rom. 5:8). He adds, "For if while we were enemies *we were reconciled to God by the death of his Son,* much more, now that we are reconciled, shall we be saved by his life" (Rom. 5:10). This reconciliation to God occurred with respect to the specific people who would be saved, and it occurred "while we were enemies." Similarly, Paul says, "*For our sake* he made him to be sin who knew no sin, so that in him we might become the righteousness of God" (2 Cor. 5:21; cf. Gal. 1:4; Eph. 1:7). And "Christ redeemed *us* from the curse of the law, having become a curse *for us*" (Gal. 3:13).

Further support for the Reformed view is found in the consideration that all the blessings of salvation, including faith, repentance, and all of the works of the Holy Spirit in applying redemption, were also secured by Christ's redemptive work specifically for his people. Those for whom he earned forgiveness also have had those other benefits earned for them (cf. Eph. 1:3–4; 2:8; Phil. 1:29).[30]

What I have called "the Reformed view" in this section is commonly referred to as "limited atonement."[31] However, most theologians who hold this position today do not

[30]I am not aware of any Arminians who hold what I have called the "Reformed view," the view that is commonly called "particular redemption" or "limited atonement." But it does not seem logically impossible for someone to hold a traditional Arminian position (that God foreknew who would believe and predestined them on the basis of that foreknowledge) coupled with the belief that Christ's death actually paid the penalty for the sins of those who God knew would believe and not for any others. This is just to say that, while "limited atonement" is necessarily part of a Reformed viewpoint because it logically follows from the overall sovereignty of God in the entire work of redemption, one could (in theory at least) hold to "limited atonement" and not adopt a Reformed position on other points concerning God's sovereignty in life generally or in salvation in particular.

[31]Thus, it is the "L" in the acronym "TULIP," which represents the so-called "five points of Calvinism," five doctrinal positions that distinguish Calvinists or Reformed theologians from many other Protestants. The five points represented by the word are: Total depravity, Unconditional election, Limited atonement, Irresistible grace, and Perseverance of the saints. (Whenever this book advocates these five doctrinal points, it attempts to point out the arguments in favor of an opposing position and provide an appropriate bibliography representing both views.)

prefer the term "limited atonement" because it is so easily subject to misunderstanding, as if this view somehow held that Christ's atoning work was deficient in some way. The term that is usually preferred is *particular redemption,* since this view holds that Christ died for particular people (specifically, those who would be saved and whom he came to redeem), that he foreknew each one of them individually (cf. Eph. 1:3–5) and had them individually in mind in his atoning work.[32]

The opposite position, that Christ's death actually paid for the sins of all people who ever lived, is called "general redemption" or "unlimited atonement."

2. Scripture Passages Used to Support the Non-Reformed View (General Redemption or Unlimited Atonement). A number of Scripture passages indicate that in some sense Christ died for the whole world. John the Baptist said, "Behold, the Lamb of God, who takes away the sin *of the world!*" (John 1:29). And John 3:16 tells us that "God so loved the world that he gave his only Son, that whoever believes in him should not perish but have eternal life." Jesus said, "The bread which I shall give for the life of the world is my flesh" (John 6:51). Paul says that in Christ "God was reconciling *the world* to himself" (2 Cor. 5:19). We read of Christ that "he is the expiation [lit. 'propitiation'] for our sins, and not for ours only but also for the sins of *the whole world*" (1 John 2:2). Paul writes that Christ Jesus "gave himself as a ransom *for all*" (1 Tim. 2:6). And the author of Hebrews says that Jesus was for a little while made lower than the angels "so that by the grace of God he might taste death for every one" (Heb. 2:9).

Other passages appear to speak of Christ dying for those who will not be saved. Paul says, "Do not let what you eat cause the ruin of one for whom Christ died" (Rom. 14:15). In a similar context he tells the Corinthians not to eat publicly at an idol's temple because they might encourage those who are weak in their faith to violate their consciences and eat food offered to idols. He then says, "And so by your knowledge this weak man is destroyed, the brother *for whom Christ died*" (1 Cor. 8:11). Peter writes about false teachers as follows: "But false prophets also arose among the people, just as there will be false teachers among you, who will secretly bring in destructive heresies, *even denying the Master who bought them,* bringing upon themselves swift destruction" (2 Peter 2:1; cf. Heb. 10:29).

3. Some Points of Agreement and Some Conclusions about Disputed Texts. It would be helpful first to list the points on which both sides agree:

1. Not all will be saved.

2. A free offer of the gospel can rightly be made to every person ever born. It is completely true that "whoever will" may come to Christ for salvation, and no one who comes to him will be turned away. This free offer of the gospel is extended in good faith to every person.

3. All agree that Christ's death in itself, because he is the infinite Son of God, has infinite merit and is in itself sufficient to pay the penalty of the sins of as many or as few as

---

[32]Reformed people argue that it is the other view that really limits the power of the atonement because on that view the atonement does not actually guarantee salvation for God's people but only makes salvation possible for all people. In other words, if the atonement is not limited with respect to the number of people to which it applies, then it must be limited with respect to what it actually accomplishes.

the Father and the Son decreed. The question is not about the intrinsic merits of Christ's sufferings and death, but about the number of people for whom the Father and the Son thought Christ's death to be sufficient payment at the time Christ died.

Beyond these points of agreement, however, a difference remains concerning the following question: "When Christ died, did he *actually pay the penalty* only for the sins of those who would believe in him, or for the sins of every person who ever lived?" On this question it seems that those who hold to particular redemption have stronger arguments on their side. First, an important point that is not generally answered by advocates of the general redemption view is that people who are eternally condemned to hell suffer the penalty for all of their own sins, and therefore their penalty could not have been fully taken by Christ. Those who hold the general redemption view sometimes answer that people suffer in hell because of the sin of rejecting Christ, even though their other sins were paid for. But this is hardly a satisfactory position, for (1) some have never rejected Christ because they have never heard of him, and (2) the emphasis of Scripture when it speaks of eternal punishment is not on the fact that the people suffer because they have rejected Christ, but on the fact that they suffer because of their own sins in this life (see Rom. 5:6–8, 13–16, et al.). This significant point seems to tip the argument decisively in favor of the particular redemption position.

Another significant point in favor of particular redemption is the fact that Christ completely earned our salvation, paying the penalty for all our sins. He did not just redeem us potentially, but actually redeemed us as individuals whom he loved. A third weighty point in favor of particular redemption is that there is eternal unity in the counsels and plans of God and in the work of the Father, Son, and Holy Spirit in accomplishing their plans (see Rom. 8:28–30).

With regard to Scripture passages used to support general redemption, the following may be said: Several passages that speak about "the world" simply mean that sinners generally will be saved, without implying that every single individual in the world will be saved. So the fact that Christ is the Lamb of God who takes away the sin of the world (John 1:29) does not mean (on anybody's interpretation) that Christ actually removes the sins of every single person in the world, for both sides agree that not all are saved. Similarly, the fact that God was in Christ reconciling the world to himself (2 Cor. 5:19) does not mean that every single person in the world was reconciled to God, but that sinners generally were reconciled to God. Another way of putting these two passages would be to say that Jesus was the Lamb of God who takes away the sin of sinners, or that God was in Christ reconciling sinners to himself. This does not mean that all sinners will be saved or were reconciled, but simply that these groups in general, but not necessarily every single person in them, were the objects of God's redeeming work: it essentially means that "God so loved sinners that he gave his only Son . . ." without implying that every sinner in the whole world will be saved.

The passages that speak about Christ dying "for" the whole world are best understood to refer to the free offer of the gospel that is made to all people. When Jesus says, "The bread which I shall give *for the life of the world* is my flesh" (John 6:51), it is in the context of speaking of himself as the Bread that came down from heaven, which is offered to people and which they may, if they are willing, receive for themselves. Earlier in the same discussion Jesus said that "the bread of God is that which comes down from heaven, and gives life to the world" (John 6:33). This may be understood in the sense of bringing redeeming life into the world but not meaning that every single person in the world will have that redeeming life. Jesus then speaks of himself as inviting others to come and take up this living bread: "He who comes to me shall not hunger, and he who believes in me shall never thirst. . . . This is the bread which comes down from heaven, that a man may eat of it and not die. I am the living bread which came down from heaven; if any one eats of this bread, he will live for ever; and the bread which I shall give for the life of the world is my flesh" (John 6:35, 50–51). Jesus gives his flesh to bring life into the world and to offer life to the world, but to say that Jesus came to offer eternal life to the world (a point on which both sides agree) is not to say that he actually paid the penalty for the sins of everyone who would ever live, for that is a separate question.

When John says that Christ "is the propitiation for our sins, and not for ours only but also for the sins of the whole world" (1 John 2:2, author's translation), he may simply be understood to mean that Christ is the atoning sacrifice that the gospel now *makes available for* the sins of everyone in the world. The preposition "for" (Gk. *peri* plus genitive) is ambiguous with respect to the specific sense in which Christ is the propitiation "for" the sins of the world. *Peri* simply means "concerning" or "with respect to" but is not specific enough to define the exact way in which Christ is the sacrifice with respect to the sins of the world. It would be entirely consistent with the language of the verse to think that John is simply saying that Christ is the atoning sacrifice who is available to pay for the sins of anyone in the world.[33] Likewise, when Paul says that Christ "gave himself as a ransom *for all*" (1 Tim. 2:6), we are to understand this to mean a ransom available for all people, without exception.[34]

When the author of Hebrews says that Christ was made lower than the angels "so that by the grace of God he might taste death for every one" (Heb. 2:9), the passage is best understood to refer to every one of Christ's people, every one who is redeemed. It does not say everyone "in the whole world" or any such expression, and in the immediate context the author is certainly speaking of those who are redeemed (see "bringing many sons to glory" [v. 10]; "those who are sanctified" [v. 11]; and "the children God has given me" [v. 13]). The Greek word *pas*, here translated "every one," is also used in a similar sense to mean "all of God's people" in Hebrews 8:11, "for *all* shall know me," and in Hebrews 12:8, "If you are left without discipline, in which *all* have participated, then you are illegitimate children and not sons." In both cases the "all" is not explicitly restricted by a specific

---

[33]Compare a similar sense for the phrase "for sins" (Gk. *peri harmartiōn*) in Heb. 10:26 where the author says that if someone continues on sinning deliberately after receiving the knowledge of the truth "there no longer remains a sacrifice for sins." This does not mean that Christ's sacrifice no longer exists, but it is no longer available for that person who has willfully spurned it and put himself beyond the realm of willing repentance. Here "sacrifice for sins" means "a sacrifice available to be claimed for the payment of sins." In the same way 1 John 2:2 can mean "the propitiation *available for* the sins of the whole world [esp. with reference to Gentiles as well as Jews]."

[34]When Paul says that God "is the Savior of all men, especially of those who believe" (1 Tim. 4:10), he is referring to God the Father, not to Christ, and probably uses the word "Savior" in the sense of "one who preserves people's lives and rescues them from danger" rather than the sense of "one who forgives their sins," for surely Paul does not mean that every single person will be saved. However, another possible meaning is that God "is the Savior of all sorts of people—that is, of people who believe" (for a defense of this view see George W. Knight III, *The Pastoral Epistles*, NIGTC [Grand Rapids: Eerdmans, 1992], pp. 203–4).

phrase such as "all of God's people," but this is clearly the sense in the overall context. Of course, in other contexts, the same word "all" can mean "all people without exception," but this must be determined from the individual context in each case.

When Paul speaks in Romans 14:15 and 1 Corinthians 8:11 about the possibility of destroying one for whom Christ died, it seems best here as well to think of the word "for" in the sense that Christ died *"to make salvation available for"* these people or "to bring the free offer of the gospel to" these people who are associated with the fellowship of the church. He does not seem to have in mind the specific question of the inter-trinitarian decision regarding whose sins the Father counted Christ's death as a payment for. Rather, he is speaking of those to whom the gospel has been offered. In another passage, when Paul calls the weak man a "brother for whom Christ died" in 1 Corinthians 8:11, he is not necessarily pronouncing on the inward spiritual condition of a person's heart, but is probably just speaking according to what is often called the "judgment of charity" by which people who are participating in the fellowship of the church can rightly be referred to as brothers and sisters.[35]

When Peter speaks of false teachers who bring in destructive heresies, "even denying the Master who bought them" (2 Peter 2:1), it is unclear whether the word "Master" (Gk. *despotēs*) refers to Christ (as in Jude 4) or to God the Father (as in Luke 2:29; Acts 4:24; Rev. 6:10). In either case, the Old Testament allusion is probably to Deuteronomy 32:6, where Moses says to the rebellious people who have turned away from God, "Is not he your Father *who has bought you?"* (author's translation).[36] Peter is drawing an analogy between the past false prophets who arose among the Jews and those who will be false teachers within the churches to which he writes: "But false prophets also arose among the people, just as there will be false teachers among you, who will secretly bring in destructive heresies, even denying the Master who bought them" (2 Peter 2:1). In line with this clear reference to false prophets in the Old Testament, Peter also alludes to the fact that the rebellious Jews turned away from God who "bought" them out of Egypt in the exodus. From the time of the exodus onward, any Jewish person would have considered himself or herself one who was "bought" by God in the exodus and therefore a person of God's own possession. In this sense, the false teachers arising among the people were denying God their Father, to whom they rightfully belonged.[37] So the text means not that Christ had redeemed these

---

[35]Another possible interpretation of these two passages is that "destroy" means ruin the ministry or Christian growth of someone who will nonetheless remain a believer but whose principles will be compromised. That sense would certainly fit the context well in both cases, but one argument against it is that the Greek word *apollymi*, "destroy," which is used in both cases, seems a stronger word than would be appropriate if that were Paul's intention. The same word is used often of eternal destruction (see John 3:16; Rom. 2:12; 1 Cor. 1:18; 15:18; 2 Cor. 2:15; 4:3; 2 Peter 3:9). However, the context of 1 Cor. 8:11 may indicate a different sense than these other passages, for this verse does not talk about God "destroying" someone but about other human beings doing something to "destroy" another—which suggests a weaker sense for the term here.

[36]Though the Septuagint does not use Peter's term *agora-zō* but rather *kataomai*, the words are synonymous in many cases, and both can mean "buy, purchase"; the Hebrew term in Deut. 32:6 is *qānāh*, which frequently means "purchase, buy" in the Old Testament.

[37]This is the view taken by John Gill, *The Cause of God and Truth* (Grand Rapids: Baker, 1980; repr. of 1855 ed.; first published 1735), p. 61. Gill discusses other possible interpretations of the passage, but this seems most persuasive. We should realize that in both of his epistles, Peter very frequently portrays the churches to which he is writing in terms of the rich imagery of the people of God in the Old Testament: see W. Grudem, *The First Epistle of Peter*, p. 113.

false prophets, but simply that they were rebellious Jewish people (or church attenders in the same position as the rebellious Jews) who were rightly owned by God because they had been brought out of the land of Egypt (or their forefathers had), but they were ungrateful to him. Christ's specific redemptive work on the cross is not in view in this verse.[38]

With regard to the verses that talk of Christ's dying for his sheep, his church, or his people, non-Reformed people may answer that these passages do not deny that he died to pay the penalty for others as well. In response, while it is true that they do not explicitly deny that Christ died for others as well, their frequent reference to his death for his people would at least strongly suggest that this is a correct inference. Even if they do not absolutely imply such a particularizing of redemption, these verses do at least seem to be most naturally interpreted in this way.

In conclusion, it seems to me that the Reformed position of "particular redemption" is most consistent with the overall teaching of Scripture. But once that has been said, several points of caution need to be raised.

4. Points of Clarification and Caution Regarding This Doctrine. It is important to state some points of clarification and also some areas in which we can rightly object to the way in which some advocates of particular redemption have expressed their arguments. It is also important to ask what the pastoral implications are for this teaching.

1. It seems to be a mistake to state the question as Berkhof does[39] and focus on the purpose of the Father and the Son, rather than on what actually happened in the atonement. If we confine the discussion to the purpose of the atonement, then this is just another form of the larger dispute between Calvinists and Arminians over whether God's purpose is (a) to save all people, a purpose that is frustrated by man's will to rebel—the Arminian position—or whether God's purpose is (b) to save those whom he has chosen—the Calvinist position. This question will not be decided at the narrow point of the question of the extent of the atonement, for the specific scriptural texts on that point are too few and can hardly be said to be conclusive on either side. One's decisions on these passages will tend to be determined by one's view of the larger question as to what Scripture as a whole teaches about the nature of the atonement and about the broader issues of God's providence, sovereignty, and the doctrine of election. Whatever decisions are made on those larger topics will apply specifically to this point, and people will come to their conclusions accordingly.

Rather than focusing on the purpose of the atonement, therefore, the question is rightfully asked about the atonement itself: Did Christ pay for the sins of all unbelievers who will be eternally condemned, and did he pay for their sins fully and completely on the cross? It seems that we have to answer no to that question.

2. The statements "Christ died for his people only" and "Christ died for all people" are both true in some senses, and too often the argument over this issue has been confused because of various senses that can be given to the word "for" in these two statements.

---

[38]The Greek word *despotēs,* "Master," is elsewhere used of God in contexts that emphasize his role as Creator and Ruler of the world (Acts 4:24; Rev. 6:10).

[39]Berkhof says, "The question does relate to the design of the atonement. Did the Father in sending Christ, and did Christ in coming into the world, to make atonement for sin, do this with the design or for the purpose of saving only the elect or all men? That is the question, and that only is the question" (*Systematic Theology,* [Grand Rapids: Eerdmans, 1939, 1941], p. 394).

The statement "Christ died for his people only" can be understood to mean that "Christ died to actually pay the penalty for all the sins of his people only." In that sense it is true. But when non-Reformed people hear the sentence "Christ died for his people only," they often hear in it, "Christ died so that he could make the gospel available only to a chosen few," and they are troubled over what they see as a real threat to the free offer of the gospel to every person. Reformed people who hold to particular redemption should recognize the potential for misunderstanding that arises with the sentence "Christ died for his people only," and, out of concern for the truth and out of pastoral concern to affirm the free offer of the gospel and to avoid misunderstanding in the body of Christ, they should be more precise in saying exactly what they mean. The simple sentence, "Christ died for his people only," while true in the sense explained above, is seldom understood in that way when people unfamiliar with Reformed doctrine hear it, and it therefore is better not to use such an ambiguous sentence at all.

On the other hand, the sentence, "Christ died for all people," is true if it means, "Christ died to make salvation available to all people" or if it means, "Christ died to bring the free offer of the gospel to all people." In fact, this is the kind of language Scripture itself uses in passages like John 6:51; 1 Timothy 2:6; and 1 John 2:2.[40] It really seems to be only nit-picking that creates controversies and useless disputes when Reformed people insist on being such purists in their speech that they object any time someone says that "Christ died for all people." There are certainly acceptable ways of understanding that sentence that are consistent with the speech of the scriptural authors themselves.

Similarly, I do not think we should rush to criticize an evangelist who tells an audience of unbelievers, "Christ died for your sins," if it is made clear in the context that it is necessary to trust in Christ before one can receive the benefits of the gospel offer. In that sense the sentence is simply understood to mean "Christ died to offer you forgiveness for your sins" or "Christ died to make available forgiveness for your sins." The important point here is that sinners realize that salvation is available for everyone and that payment of sins is available for everyone.

At this point some Reformed theologians will object and will warn us that if we say to unbelievers, "Christ died for your sins," the unbelievers will draw the conclusion, "Therefore I am saved no matter what I do." But this does not seem to be a problem in actual fact, for whenever evangelicals (Reformed or non-Reformed) speak about the gospel to unbelievers, they are always very clear on the fact that the death of Christ has no benefit for a person unless that person believes in Christ. Therefore, the problem seems to be more something that Reformed people *think* unbelievers should believe (if they were consistent in reasoning back into the secret counsels of God and the relationship between the Father and Son in the counsels of the Trinity at the point of Christ's propitiatory sacrifice on the cross). But unbelievers simply do not reason that way: they know that they must exercise faith in Christ before they will experience any benefits from his saving work. Moreover, it is far more likely that people will understand the sentence "Christ died for your sins" in the doctrinally correct sense that "Christ died

---

[40]Berkhof says that 1 Tim. 2:1 refers to "the revealed will of God that both Jews and Gentiles should be saved" (ibid., p. 396).

in order to offer you forgiveness for your sins" rather than in the doctrinally incorrect sense, "Christ died and completely paid the penalty already for all your sins."[41]

3. In terms of the practical, pastoral effects of our words, both those who hold to particular redemption and those who hold to general redemption agree at several key points:

a. Both sincerely want to avoid implying that people will be saved whether they believe in Christ or not. Non-Reformed people sometimes accuse Reformed people of saying that the elect will be saved irrespective of responding to the gospel, but this is clearly a misrepresentation of the Reformed position. On the other hand, Reformed people think that those who hold to general redemption are in danger of implying that everybody will be saved whether they believe in Christ or not. But this is not a position that non-Reformed people actually hold, and it is always precarious to criticize people for a position that they do not say they hold, just because you think that they should hold that position if they were consistent with their other views.

b. Both sides want to avoid implying that there might be some people who come to Christ for salvation but are turned away because Christ did not die for them. No one wants to say or imply to an unbeliever, "Christ might have died for your sins (and then again he might not have!)." Both sides want to clearly affirm that all who come to Christ for salvation will in fact be saved. "Him who comes to me I will not cast out" (John 6:37).

c. Both sides want to avoid implying that God is hypocritical or insincere when he makes the free offer of the gospel. It is a genuine offer, and it is always true that all who wish to come to Christ for salvation and who do actually come to him will be saved.

d. Finally, we may ask why this matter is so important after all. Although Reformed people have sometimes made belief in particular redemption a test of doctrinal orthodoxy, it would be healthy to realize that Scripture itself never singles this out as a doctrine of major importance, nor does it once make it the subject of any explicit theological discussion. Our knowledge of the issue comes only from incidental references to it in passages whose concern is with other doctrinal or practical matters. In fact, this is really a question that probes into the inner counsels of the Trinity and does so in an area in which there is very little direct scriptural testimony—a fact that should cause us to be cautious. A balanced pastoral perspective would seem to be to say that this teaching of particular redemption *seems* to us to be true, that it gives logical consistency to our theological system, and that it can be helpful in assuring people of Christ's love for them individually and of the completeness of his redemptive work for them; but that it also is a subject that almost inevitably leads to some confusion, some misunderstanding, and often some wrongful argumentativeness and divisiveness among God's people—all of which are negative pastoral considerations. Perhaps that is why the apostles such as John and Peter and Paul, in their wisdom, placed almost no emphasis on this question at all. And perhaps we would do well to ponder their example.

---

[41]I am not here arguing that we should be careless in our language; I am arguing that we should not rush to criticize when other Christians unreflectively use ambiguous language without intending to contradict any teaching of Scripture.

QUESTIONS FOR PERSONAL APPLICATION

1. In what ways has this chapter enabled you to appreciate Christ's death more than you did before? Has it given you more or less confidence in the fact that your sins have actually been paid for by Christ?

2. If the ultimate cause of the atonement is found in the love and justice of God, then was there anything in you that required God to love you or to take steps to save you (when he looked forward and thought of you as a sinner in rebellion against him)? Does your answer to this question help you to appreciate the character of God's love for you as a person who did not at all deserve that love? How does that realization make you feel in your relationship to God?

3. Do you think that Christ's sufferings were enough to pay for your sins? Are you willing to rely on his work to pay for all your sins? Do you think he is a sufficient Savior, worthy of your trust? When he invites you, "Come to me . . . and I will give you rest" (Matt. 11:28), do you now trust him? Will you now and always rely on him with your whole heart for complete salvation?

4. If Christ bore all the guilt for our sins, all the wrath of God against sin, and all the penalty of the death that we deserved, then will God ever turn his wrath against you as a believer (see Rom. 8:31–39)? Can any of the hardships or sufferings that you experience in life be due to the wrath of God against you? If not, then why do we as Christians experience difficulties and sufferings in this life (see Rom. 8:28; Heb. 12:3–11)?

5. Do you think Christ's life was good enough to deserve God's approval? Are you willing to rely on it for your eternal destiny? Is Jesus Christ a reliable enough and good enough Savior for you to trust him? Which would you rather trust in for your eternal standing before God: your own life or Christ's?

6. If Christ has indeed redeemed you from bondage to sin and to the kingdom of Satan, are there areas of your life in which you could more fully realize this to be true? Could this realization give you more encouragement in your Christian life?

7. Do you think it was fair for Christ to be your substitute and to pay your penalty? When you think about him acting as your substitute and dying for you, what attitude and emotion is called forth in your heart?

SPECIAL TERMS

active obedience	particular redemption
atonement	passive obedience
blood of Christ	penal substitution
consequent absolute necessity	propitiation
example theory	ransom to Satan theory
general redemption	reconciliation

governmental theory

impute

limited atonement

moral influence theory

redemption

sacrifice

unlimited atonement

vicarious atonement

BIBLIOGRAPHY

Bauckham, Richard J. "Descent into Hell." In *NDT,* pp. 194–95.

Berkouwer, G. C. *The Work of Christ.* Trans. by Cornelius Lambregtse. Grand Rapids: Eerdmans, 1965.

Brown, John. *The Sufferings and Glories of the Messiah.* Evanston, Ind.: Sovereign Grace Publishers, 1959 (reprint of 1852 edition).

Campbell, John McLeod. *The Nature of the Atonement.* 6th ed. London and New York: Macmillan, 1886 (first published in 1856).

Elwell, Walter. "Atonement, Extent of the." In *EDT,* pp. 98–100.

Green, Michael. *The Empty Cross of Jesus.* The Jesus Library, ed. by Michael Green. Downers Grove, Ill.: InterVarsity Press, 1984.

Grensted, L. W. *A Short History of the Doctrine of the Atonement.* Manchester: University Press, and London: Longmans, 1962.

Hodge, Archibald A. *The Atonement.* London: T. Nelson, 1868.

McDonald, H. D. *The Atonement of the Death of Christ.* Grand Rapids: Baker, 1985.

McGrath, Alister E. *Luther's Theology of the Cross: Martin Luther's Theological Breakthrough.* Oxford: Basil Blackwell, 1985.

_____. *The Mystery of the Cross.* Grand Rapids: Zondervan, 1988.

_____. *What Was God Doing on the Cross?* Grand Rapids: Zondervan, 1993.

Martin, Hugh. *The Atonement: In Its Relations to the Covenant, the Priesthood, the Intercession of Our Lord.* Philadelphia: Smith and English, 1871.

Morey, Robert A. *Studies in the Atonement.* Southbridge, Mass.: Crowne, 1989.

Morris, Leon. *The Apostolic Preaching of the Cross.* 3d ed. Grand Rapids: Eerdmans, 1965.

_____. "Atonement." In *EDT,* p. 97.

_____. *The Atonement: Its Meaning and Significance.* Leicester and Downers Grove, Ill: InterVarsity Press, 1983.

_____. "Atonement, Theories of the." In *EDT,* pp. 100–102.

_____. *The Cross in the New Testament.* Grand Rapids: Eerdmans, 1965.

_____. *The Cross of Jesus.* Grand Rapids: Eerdmans, and Exeter: Paternoster, 1988.

Murray, John. *Redemption Accomplished and Applied.* Grand Rapids: Eerdmans, 1955, pp. 9–78.

Owen, John. *The Death of Death in the Death of Christ.* Carlisle, Pa.: Banner of Truth, 1959 (includes excellent introductory essay by J. I. Packer).

Smeaton, George. *The Doctrine of the Atonement as Taught by Christ Himself.* Grand Rapids: Zondervan, 1953 (reprint of 1871 edition).

Smeaton, George. *The Apostles' Doctrine of the Atonement.* Grand Rapids: Zondervan, 1957 (reprint of 1870 edition).

Stott, John R. W. *The Cross of Christ.* Leicester and Downers Grove, Ill.: InterVarsity Press, 1986.

Turretin, Francis. *The Atonement of Christ.* Trans. by James R. Willson. Grand Rapids: Baker, 1978 (reprint of 1859 edition; first published in Latin in 1674).

Wallace, Ronald S. *The Atoning Death of Christ.* Westchester, Ill.: Crossway, 1981.

SCRIPTURE MEMORY PASSAGE

Romans 3:23–26: *Since all have sinned and fall short of the glory of God, they are justified by his grace as a gift, through the redemption which is in Christ Jesus, whom God put forward as an expiation [lit. 'propitiation'] by his blood, to be received by faith. This was to show God's righteousness, because in his divine forbearance he had passed over former sins; it was to prove at the present time that he himself is righteous and that he justifies him who has faith in Jesus.*

HYMN

"When I Survey the Wondrous Cross"

When I survey the wondrous cross
    On which the Prince of Glory died,
My richest gain I count but loss,
    And pour contempt on all my pride.

Forbid it, Lord, that I should boast,
    Save in the death of Christ my God:
All the vain things that charm me most,
    I sacrifice them to his blood.

See, from his head, his hands, his feet,
    Sorrow and love flow mingled down:
Did e'er such love and sorrow meet,
    Or thorns compose so rich a crown?

His dying crimson, like a robe,
    Spread o'er his body on the tree;
Then am I dead to all the globe,
    And all the globe is dead to me.

Were the whole realm of nature mine,
    That were a present far too small;
Love so amazing, so divine,
    Demands my soul, my life, my all.

AUTHOR: ISAAC WATTS, 1707

Chapter 4

RESURRECTION AND ASCENSION

What was Christ's resurrection body like?
What is its significance for us? What happened
to Christ when he ascended into heaven?
What is meant by the states of Jesus Christ?

EXPLANATION AND SCRIPTURAL BASIS

A. Resurrection

1. New Testament Evidence. The Gospels contain abundant testimony to the resurrection of Christ (see Matt. 28:1–20; Mark 16:1–8; Luke 24:1–53; John 20:1–21:25). In addition to these detailed narratives in the four gospels, the book of Acts is a story of the apostles' proclamation of the resurrection of Christ and of continued prayer to Christ and trust in him as the one who is alive and reigning in heaven. The Epistles depend entirely on the assumption that Jesus is a living, reigning Savior who is now the exalted head of the church, who is to be trusted, worshiped, and adored, and who will some day return in power and great glory to reign as King over the earth. The book of Revelation repeatedly shows the risen Christ reigning in heaven and predicts his return to conquer his enemies and reign in glory. Thus the entire New Testament bears witness to the resurrection of Christ.[1]

---

[1]The historical arguments for the resurrection of Christ are substantial and have persuaded many skeptics who started to examine the evidence for the purpose of disproving the resurrection. The best-known account of such a change from skepticism to belief is Frank Morison, *Who Moved the Stone?* (London: Faber and Faber, 1930; reprint, Grand Rapids: Zondervan, 1958). A widely used booklet summarizing the arguments is J. N. D. Anderson, *The Evidence for the Resurrection* (London and Downers Grove, Ill.: InterVarsity Press, 1966). (Both Morison and Anderson were trained as lawyers.) More recent and detailed presentations are found in William Lane Craig, *The Son Rises: The Historical Evidence for the Resurrection of Jesus* (Chicago: Moody, 1981); Gary Habermas and Anthony Flew, *Did Jesus Rise From the Dead? The Resurrection Debate,* ed. Terry L. Miethe (New York: Harper and Row, 1987); Gary Habermas, "Resurrection of Christ," in *EDT,* pp. 938–41. An extensive

2. The Nature of Christ's Resurrection. Christ's resurrection was not simply a coming back from the dead, as had been experienced by others before, such as Lazarus (John 11:1–44), for then Jesus would have been subject to weakness and aging and eventually would have died again just as all other human beings die. Rather, when he rose from the dead Jesus was the "first fruits" (1 Cor. 15:20, 23) of a new kind of human life, a life in which his body was made perfect, no longer subject to weakness, aging, or death, but able to live eternally.

It is true that two of Jesus' disciples did not recognize him when they walked with him on the road to Emmaus (Luke 24:13–32), but Luke specifically tells us that this was because "their eyes were kept from recognizing him" (Luke 24:16), and later "their eyes were opened and they recognized him" (Luke 24:31). Mary Magdalene failed to recognize Jesus only for a moment (John 20:14–16), but it may have been still quite dark and she was not at first looking at him—she had come the first time "while it was still dark" (John 20:1), and she "turned" to speak to Jesus once she recognized him (John 20:16).

On other occasions the disciples seemed to have recognized Jesus fairly quickly (Matt. 28:9, 17; John 20:19–20, 26–28; 21:7, 12). When Jesus appeared to the eleven disciples in Jerusalem, they were initially startled and frightened (Luke 24:33, 37), yet when they saw Jesus' hands and his feet and watched him eat a piece of fish, they were convinced that he had risen from the dead. These examples indicate that there was a considerable degree of continuity between the physical appearance of Jesus before his death and after his resurrection. Yet Jesus did not look exactly as he had before he died, for in addition to the initial amazement of the disciples at what they apparently thought could not happen, there was probably sufficient difference in his physical appearance for Jesus not to be immediately recognized. Perhaps that difference in appearance was simply the difference between a man who had lived a life of suffering, hardship, and grief, and one whose body was restored to its full youthful appearance of perfect health: though Jesus' body was still a physical body, it was raised as a transformed body, never able again to suffer, be weak or ill, or die; it had "put on immortality" (1 Cor. 15:53). Paul says the resurrection body is raised "imperishable . . . in glory . . . in power . . . a spiritual body" (1 Cor. 15:42–44).[2]

The fact that Jesus had a physical body that could be touched and handled after the resurrection is seen in that the disciples "took hold of his feet" (Matt. 28:9), that he

---

compilation of arguments and quotations from recognized scholars affirming the overwhelming reliability of the evidence for Christ's resurrection is found in Josh McDowell, *Evidence that Demands a Verdict*, rev. ed., vol. 1 (San Bernardino, Calif.: Here's Life Publishers, 1979), pp. 179–263.

[2]By "spiritual body" Paul does not mean "immaterial," but rather "suited to and responsive to the guidance of the Spirit." In the Pauline epistles, the word "spiritual" (Gk. *pneumatikos*) seldom means "nonphysical" but rather "consistent with the character and activity of the Holy Spirit" (see, e.g., Rom. 1:11; 7:14; 1 Cor. 2:13, 15; 3:1; 14:37; Gal. 6:1 ["you who are spiritual"]; Eph. 5:19). The RSV translation, "It is sown a *physical* body, it is raised a *spiritual* body," is very misleading, because

Paul does not use the word that was available to him if he had meant to speak of a physical body (Gk. *sōmatikos*), but rather uses the word *psychikos*, which means, in this context, "natural" (so NIV, NASB), that is, a body that is living in its own life and strength and in the characteristics of this present age but is not fully subject to and conforming to the character and will of the Holy Spirit. Therefore, a clearer paraphrase would be, "It is sown a *natural* body subject to the characteristics and desires of this age, and governed by its own sinful will, but it is raised a *spiritual* body, completely subject to the will of the Holy Spirit and responsive to the Holy Spirit's guidance." Such a body is not at all "nonphysical," but it is a physical body raised to the degree of perfection for which God originally intended it.

appeared to the disciples on the road to Emmaus to be just another traveler on the road (Luke 24:15–18, 28–29), that he took bread and broke it (Luke 24:30), that he ate a piece of broiled fish to demonstrate clearly that he had a physical body and was not just a spirit, that Mary thought him to be a gardener (John 20:15), that "he showed them his hands and his side" (John 20:20), that he invited Thomas to touch his hands and his side (John 20:27), that he prepared breakfast for his disciples (John 21:12–13), and that he explicitly told them, "See my hands and my feet, that it is I myself; handle me, and see; for *a spirit has not flesh and bones as you see that I have*" (Luke 24:39). Peter said that the disciples "ate and drank with him after he rose from the dead" (Acts 10:41).

It is true that Jesus apparently was able to appear and disappear out of sight quite suddenly (Luke 24:31, 36; John 20:19, 26). Yet we should be careful not to draw too many conclusions from this fact, for not all the passages affirm that Jesus could suddenly appear or disappear; some just say that Jesus came and stood among the disciples. When Jesus suddenly vanished from the sight of the disciples in Emmaus, this may have been a special miraculous occurrence, such as happened when "the Spirit of the Lord caught up Philip; and the eunuch saw him no more" (Acts 8:39). Nor should we make too much of the fact that Jesus came and stood among the disciples on two occasions when the doors were "shut"[3] (John 20:19, 26), for no text says that Jesus "passed through walls" or anything like that. Indeed, on another occasion in the New Testament where someone needed to pass through a locked door, the door miraculously opened (see Acts 12:10).[4]

Murray Harris has recently proposed an alternative interpretation to the verses quoted above, especially the verses showing Jesus appearing and disappearing at different times: he says that these verses show that while Jesus could sometimes materialize into a physical body, his customary existence was in a nonphysical or nonfleshly form of his "spiritual body." Moreover, when he ascended into heaven after forty days, Jesus permanently gave up any more materializing into a physical body. Professor Harris says:

> The resurrection of Jesus was not his transformation into an immaterial body but his acquisition of a "spiritual body" which could materialize or dematerialize at will. When, on occasion, Jesus chose to appear to various persons in material form, this was just as really the "spiritual body" of Jesus as when he was not visible or tangible. . . . After the forty days, when his appearances on earth were ended, Jesus assumed the sole mode of being visible to the inhabitants of heaven but having a nonfleshly body. . . . In his risen state he transcended

---

[3]The Greek perfect participle *kekleismenon* may mean either that the doors were "shut" or that they were "locked."

[4]I do not wish to argue that it is impossible that Jesus' resurrection body somehow passed through the door or the wall to enter the room, only that no verse in the Bible says that. It is possible, but the possibility does not deserve the status of an assured conclusion that it has reached in much popular preaching and much evangelical scholarship—it is just one possible inference from these verses, among several. Leon Morris says, "Some suggest that Jesus came right through the closed door, or that the door opened of its own accord or the like. But Scripture says nothing of the mode of Jesus' entry into the room and we do well not to attempt too exact a definition" (*The Gospel According to John* [Grand Rapids: Eerdmans, 1971], p. 844). The problem with an affirmation that Jesus passed through walls is that it may cause people to think of Jesus' resurrection body as somehow nonmaterial, and this is contrary to the explicit affirmations of material characteristics that we have in several New Testament texts.

the normal laws of physical existence. He was no longer bound by material or spatial limitations.[5]

It is important to realize that Harris definitely affirms the physical, bodily resurrection of Jesus from the dead.[6] He says that the same body that died was also raised, but then it was transformed into a "spiritual body" with new properties.[7]

In response, while I do not consider this a doctrinal question of major significance (since it is simply a question about the nature of the resurrection body, about which we now know very little),[8] I nevertheless think the New Testament provides some persuasive evidence that would lead us to differ with Harris's view. Harris agrees that at several times Jesus had a physical body that could eat food and be touched and that had flesh and bones. He even agrees that at Jesus' ascension into heaven, "It was a real Jesus of 'flesh and bones' (Luke 24:39) who was taken up before the eyes of his disciples."[9] The only question is whether this body of Jesus at other times existed in nonphysical, nonfleshly form, as Harris claims. To answer that, we have to ask whether the New Testament texts about Jesus appearing and disappearing require this conclusion. It does not seem that they do.

Luke 24:31, which says that after Jesus broke bread and gave it to the two disciples, "he *disappeared* from their sight" (NIV), does not require this. The Greek expression used here for "disappeared" (*aphantos egeneto*) does not occur elsewhere in the New Testament, but when found in Diodorus Siculus (a historian who wrote from 60–30 B.C.), it is used once of a man named Amphiaraus who, with his chariot, fell into a chasm and "disappeared from sight," and the same expression is used in another place to talk about Atlas who was blown off a mountaintop by high winds and "disappeared."[10] In neither case does the expression mean that the person became immaterial or even invisible, but only that he was moved to a place hidden from people's sight.[11] So in Luke 24:31, all we can conclude is that the disciples no longer saw Jesus—perhaps the Spirit of the Lord took him away (as with Philip in Acts 8:39), or perhaps he was just hidden again from their sight (as with Moses and Elijah on the Mount of Transfiguration, Matt. 17:8, or as with the heavenly army around Elisha, 2 Kings 6:17, or [apparently] as with the disciples walking past the prison guards in Acts 5:19–23; 12:6, 10). In neither case do we need to conclude that Jesus' physical body became nonphysical, any more than we need to conclude that the disciples' bod-

---

[5]Murray Harris, *From Grave to Glory: Resurrection in the New Testament* (Grand Rapids: Zondervan, 1990), pp. 142–43.

[6]See Harris, ibid., pp. 351 and 353 (where he "unequivocally" affirms "the literal, physical resurrection of Jesus from the dead") and p. 365 ("I am happy to affirm that our Lord rose from the dead in the actual physical body he possessed before his death").

[7]He understands "spiritual" not to mean "nonphysical" but rather "animated and guided by the spirit" (or possibly "Spirit"), p. 195.

[8]See the lengthy report about Harris's view and those who have criticized it (and sometimes misrepresented it) in *CT*, April 5, 1993, pp. 62–66. Norman Geisler and some others have accused Harris of teaching serious heresy, but in this arti-

cle, J. I. Packer says that "both Harris and Geisler appear to be orthodox, and both of them equally so" (pp. 64–65). A report from three other evangelical theologians, Millard Erickson, Bruce Demarest, and Roger Nicole, says that Harris's views are "somewhat novel" but "are compatible with the doctrinal position [of Trinity Evangelical Divinity School, where Harris teaches, and] . . . of the wider evangelical movement" (p. 63).

[9]Harris, *From Grave to Glory*, p. 422.

[10]Diod. Sic. 4.65.9 (of Amphiaraus) and 3.60.3 (of Atlas).

[11]Another occurrence of the word *aphantos* has a similar sense: Plutarch (ca. A.D. 50–ca. 120) reports someone who said that if there is a "mid-center" of the earth or ocean, "it is known to the gods, but is hidden (*aphantos*) from mortals" (*Moralia* 409F). The sense is not "immaterial" but "hidden from sight, not visible."

ies became nonphysical when they walked past the guards (Acts 5:23; 12:10) and escaped from prison. So Luke 24:31 does not say that any transformation happened to Jesus' body; it merely says that the disciples could no longer see him.[12]

As for the claim that Jesus passed through material substances, this is not substantiated in the New Testament. As explained above, the fact that Jesus appeared in a room when the doors had been shut or locked (John 20:19, 26) may or may not mean that he passed through a door or wall. Especially relevant here is the first deliverance of the apostles from prison: they did not walk through the doors, but "an angel of the Lord opened the prison doors and brought them out" (Acts 5:19); yet the next morning the prison officers reported, "We found the prison securely locked and the sentries standing at the doors, but when we opened it we found no one inside" (Acts 5:23). The angel had opened the doors, the apostles had passed through, and the angel had closed and locked the doors again. Similarly, when Peter was rescued from prison, he did not dematerialize in order to pass through the locked chains around him, but "the chains fell off his hands" (Acts 12:7).[13] In the same way, it is certainly possible that the door miraculously opened for Jesus or even that he had entered the room with the disciples but was temporarily hidden from their eyes.

With regard to the nature of Jesus' resurrection body, much more decisive than the texts about Jesus' appearing and disappearing are the texts that show that Jesus clearly had a physical body with "flesh and bones" (Luke 24:39), which could eat and drink, break bread, prepare breakfast, and be touched. Unlike the texts on Jesus' appearing and disappearing, these texts are not capable of an alternative explanation that denies Jesus' physical body—Harris himself agrees that in these texts Jesus had a body of flesh and bones. But what were these physical appearances intended to teach the disciples if not that Jesus' resurrection body was definitely a physical body? If Jesus rose from the dead in the same physical body that had died, and if he repeatedly appeared to the disciples in that physical body, eating and drinking with them (Acts 10:41) over forty days, and if he ascended into heaven in that same physical body (Acts 1:9), and if the angel immediately told the disciples that "this Jesus, who was taken up from you into heaven, will come in the same way as you saw him go into heaven" (Acts 1:11), then Jesus was clearly teaching them that his resurrection body was *a physical body.* If the "customary form" of his resurrection body was nonphysical, then in these repeated physical appearances Jesus would be guilty of misleading

---

[12]Compare Luke 24:16, where it says that Jesus drew near to the disciples on the Emmaus Road, but "their eyes were kept from recognizing him." If God could cause the disciples' eyes to be partially blinded so that they could see Jesus but not recognize him, then certainly a few minutes later he could cause their eyes to be more fully blinded so they could not see him at all. The possibilities are too complex and our knowledge is too limited for us to insist that these texts require that Jesus became nonphysical.

[13]Harris says that Jesus passed through a sealed tomb, according to Matt. 28:2, 6, but the verses can just as easily mean that the stone was first rolled away, and then Jesus came out (cf. Luke 24:2). Similarly, John 20:4–7 only says that the grave cloths were lying where Jesus' body had been but does

not require that Jesus' body passed through the linen cloths: it could as readily mean that Jesus (or an angel) removed the cloths and placed them neatly in the tomb. Acts 10:40 says that Jesus was made "manifest" or visible to chosen witnesses (that is, they saw him), but again it says nothing about him materializing or being immaterial. In all of these verses, Harris seems to me to be concluding too much from too little data.

Finally, even if Jesus did pass through the door or the wall (as many Christians have concluded), this does not require us to say that his body was customarily nonmaterial, but could well be explained as a special miracle or as a property of resurrection bodies that we do not now understand, but that does not require that they be nonphysical or nonmaterial.

the disciples (and all subsequent readers of the New Testament) into thinking that his resurrection body remained physical when it did not. If he was customarily nonphysical and was going to become nonphysical forever at the ascension, then it would be very misleading for Jesus to say, "See my hands and my feet, that it is I myself; handle me, and see; for a spirit has not flesh and bones as you see that I have" (Luke 24:39). He did not say, ". . . flesh and bones, as you see that I temporarily have"! It would have been wrong to teach the disciples that he had a physical body when in his customary mode of existence he really did not.

If Jesus had wanted to teach them that he could materialize and dematerialize at will (as Harris argues), then he could easily have dematerialized before their eyes, so that they could clearly record this event. Or he could easily have passed through a wall while they watched, rather than just suddenly standing among them. In short, if Jesus and the New Testament authors had wanted to teach us that the resurrection body was customarily and essentially nonmaterial, they could have done so, but instead they gave many clear indications that it was customarily physical and material, even though it was a body that was perfected, made forever free from weakness, sickness, and death.

Finally, there is a larger doctrinal consideration. The physical resurrection of Jesus, and his eternal possession of a physical resurrection body, give clear affirmation of the goodness of the material creation that God originally made: "And God saw everything that he had made, and behold, *it was very good*" (Gen. 1:31). We as resurrected men and women will live forever in "new heavens and a new earth in which righteousness dwells" (2 Peter 3:13). We will live in a renewed earth that "will be set free from its bondage to decay" (Rom. 8:21) and become like a new Garden of Eden. There will be a new Jerusalem, and people "shall bring into it the glory and the honor of the nations" (Rev. 21:26), and there will be "the river of the water of life, bright as crystal, flowing from the throne of God and of the Lamb through the middle of the street of the city; also, on either side of the river, the tree of life with its twelve kinds of fruit, yielding its fruit each month" (Rev. 22:1–2). In this very material, physical, renewed universe, it seems that we will need to live as human beings with physical bodies, suitable for life in God's renewed physical creation. Specifically, Jesus' physical resurrection body affirms the goodness of God's original creation of man not as a mere spirit like the angels, but as a creature with a physical body that was "very good." We must not fall into the error of thinking that nonmaterial existence is somehow a better form of existence for creatures:[14] when God made us as the pinnacle of his creation, he gave us physical bodies. In a perfected physical body Jesus rose from the dead, now reigns in heaven, and will return to take us to be with himself forever.

3. Both the Father and the Son Participated in the Resurrection. Some texts affirm that God the Father specifically raised Christ from the dead (Acts 2:24; Rom. 6:4; 1 Cor. 6:14; Gal. 1:1; Eph. 1:20), but other texts speak of Jesus as participating in his own resurrection. Jesus says: "The reason my Father loves me is that I lay down my life — only to take it

[14]Professor Harris also wants to avoid this error, for he says, "There can be no dualism between spirit and matter. No New Testament writer envisages the salvation of the soul or spirit with the visible material world abandoned to oblivion" (p. 251). Yet I am concerned that his position may lead others to a depreciation of the value of the material creation and of the goodness of our physical bodies as created by God.

up again. No one takes it from me, but I lay it down of my own accord. I have authority to lay it down and authority to take it up again. This command I received from my Father" (John 10:17–18 NIV; cf. 2:19–21). It is best to conclude that both the Father and the Son were involved in the resurrection.[15] Indeed, Jesus says, "I am the resurrection and the life" (John 11:25; cf. Heb. 7:16).[16]

4. Doctrinal Significance of the Resurrection.

a. Christ's Resurrection Ensures Our Regeneration: Peter says that "we have been born anew to a living hope through the resurrection of Jesus Christ from the dead" (1 Peter 1:3). Here he explicitly connects Jesus' resurrection with our regeneration or new birth. When Jesus rose from the dead he had a new quality of life, a "resurrection life" in a human body and human spirit that were perfectly suited for fellowship and obedience to God forever. In his resurrection, Jesus earned for us a new life just like his. We do not receive all of that new "resurrection life" when we become Christians, for our bodies remain as they were, still subject to weakness, aging, and death. But in our spirits we are made alive with new resurrection power. Thus it is through his resurrection that Christ earned for us the new kind of life we receive when we are "born again." This is why Paul can say that God "made us alive together with Christ (by grace you have been saved), and *raised us up with him*" (Eph. 2:5–6; cf. Col. 3:1). When God raised Christ from the dead he thought of us as somehow being raised "with Christ" and therefore deserving of the merits of Christ's resurrection. Paul says his goal in life is "that I may know him and the power of his resurrection . . ." (Phil. 3:10). Paul knew that even in this life the resurrection of Christ gave new power for Christian ministry and obedience to God.

Paul connects the resurrection of Christ with the spiritual power at work within us when he tells the Ephesians that he is praying that they would know "what is the immeasurable greatness of his power in us who believe, according to the working of his great might which he accomplished in Christ when he raised him from the dead and made him sit at his right hand in the heavenly places" (Eph. 1:19–20). Here Paul says that the power by which God raised Christ from the dead is the same power at work within us. Paul further sees us as raised in Christ when he says, "We were buried therefore with him by baptism into death, so that as Christ was raised from the dead by the glory of the Father, we too might walk in newness of life. . . . So you also must consider yourselves dead to sin and alive to God in Christ Jesus" (Rom. 6:4, 11). This new resurrection power in us includes *power to gain more and more victory over remaining sin* in our lives—"sin will have no dominion over you" (Rom. 6:14; cf. 1 Cor. 15:17)—even though we will never be perfect in this life. This resurrection power also includes *power for ministry in the work of the kingdom.* It was after Jesus' resurrection that he promised his disciples, "You shall receive power when the Holy Spirit has come upon you; and you

---

[15]See the discussion of the participation of the Father and the Son in the resurrection in chapter 2, pp. 53–54.

[16]Because the works of God are usually works of the entire Trinity, it is probably true to say that the Holy Spirit also was involved in raising Jesus from the dead, but no text of Scripture affirms that explicitly (but see Rom. 8:11).

shall be my witnesses in Jerusalem and in all Judea and Samaria and to the end of the earth" (Acts 1:8). This new, intensified power for proclaiming the gospel and working miracles and triumphing over the opposition of the enemy was given to the disciples after Christ's resurrection from the dead and was part of the new resurrection power that characterized their Christian lives.

b. Christ's Resurrection Ensures Our Justification: In only one passage does Paul explicitly connect Christ's resurrection with our justification (or our receiving a declaration that we are not guilty but righteous before God). Paul says that Jesus "was put to death for our trespasses and *raised for our justification*" (Rom. 4:25). When Christ was raised from the dead, it was God's declaration of approval of Christ's work of redemption. Because Christ "humbled himself and became obedient unto death, even death on a cross" (Phil. 2:8), "God has highly exalted him . . ." (Phil. 2:9). By raising Christ from the dead, God the Father was in effect saying that he approved of Christ's work of suffering and dying for our sins, that his work was completed, and that Christ no longer had any need to remain dead. There was no penalty left to pay for sin, no more wrath of God to bear, no more guilt or liability to punishment—all had been completely paid for, and no guilt remained. In the resurrection, God was saying to Christ, "I approve of what you have done, and you find favor in my sight."

This explains how Paul can say that Christ was "raised for our justification" (Rom. 4:25). If God "raised us up with him" (Eph. 2:6), then, by virtue of our union with Christ, God's declaration of approval of Christ is also his declaration of approval of us. When the Father in essence said to Christ, "All the penalty for sins has been paid and I find you not guilty but righteous in my sight," he was thereby making the declaration that would also apply to us once we trusted in Christ for salvation. In this way Christ's resurrection also gave final proof that he had earned our justification.

c. Christ's Resurrection Ensures That We Will Receive Perfect Resurrection Bodies As Well: The New Testament several times connects Jesus' resurrection with our final bodily resurrection. "And God raised the Lord and will also raise us up by his power" (1 Cor. 6:14). Similarly, "he who raised the Lord Jesus will raise us also with Jesus and bring us with you into his presence" (2 Cor. 4:14). But the most extensive discussion of the connection between Christ's resurrection and our own is found in 1 Corinthians 15:12–58. There Paul says that Christ is the "first fruits of those who have fallen asleep" (1 Cor. 15:20). In calling Christ the "first fruits" (Gk. *aparchē*), Paul uses a metaphor from agriculture to indicate that we will be like Christ. Just as the "first fruits" or the first taste of the ripening crop show what the rest of the harvest will be like for that crop, so Christ as the "first fruits" shows what our resurrection bodies will be like when, in God's final "harvest," he raises us from the dead and brings us into his presence.

After Jesus' resurrection, he still had the nail prints in his hands and feet and the mark from the spear in his side (John 20:27). People sometimes wonder if that indicates that the scars of serious injuries that we have received in this life will also remain on our resurrection bodies. The answer is that we probably will not have any scars from injuries or wounds received in this life, but our bodies will be made perfect, "incorruptible" and raised "in glory." The scars from Jesus' crucifixion are unique because they are an eternal reminder of his sufferings and death for us.[17] The fact that he retains those scars does not necessarily mean that we shall retain ours. Rather, all will be healed, and all will be made perfect and whole.

5. Ethical Significance of the Resurrection. Paul also sees that the resurrection has application to our obedience to God in this life. After a long discussion of the resurrection, Paul concludes by encouraging his readers, "*Therefore,* my beloved brethren, be steadfast, immovable, always abounding in the work of the Lord, knowing that in the Lord your labor is not in vain" (1 Cor. 15:58). It is because Christ was raised from the dead, and we too shall be raised from the dead, that we should continue steadfastly in the Lord's work. This is because everything that we do to bring people into the kingdom and build them up will indeed have eternal significance, because we shall all be raised on the day when Christ returns, and we shall live with him forever.

Second, Paul encourages us, when we think about the resurrection, to focus on our future heavenly reward as our goal. He sees the resurrection as a time when all the struggles of this life will be repaid. But if Christ has not been raised and if there is no resurrection, then "your faith is futile and you are still in your sins. Then those also who have fallen asleep in Christ have perished. If for this life only we have hoped in Christ, we are of all men most to be pitied" (1 Cor. 15:17–19; cf. v. 32). But because Christ has been raised, and because we have been raised with him, we are to seek for a heavenly reward and set our mind on things of heaven:

> If then you have been raised with Christ, *seek the things that are above,* where Christ is, seated at the right hand of God. Set your minds on things that are above, not on things that are on earth. For you have died, and your life is hid with Christ in God. When Christ who is our life appears, then you also will appear with him in glory. (Col. 3:1–4)

A third ethical application of the resurrection is the obligation to stop yielding to sin in our lives. When Paul says we are to consider ourselves "dead to sin and alive to God in Christ Jesus" by virtue of the resurrection of Christ and his resurrection power within us (Rom. 6:11), he then goes on immediately to say, "*Let not sin therefore reign* in your mortal bodies. . . . Do not yield your members to sin" (Rom. 6:12–13). The fact that we have this new resurrection power over the domination of sin in our lives is used by Paul as a reason to exhort us not to sin any more.

B. Ascension into Heaven

1. Christ Ascended to a Place. After Jesus' resurrection, he was on earth for forty days (Acts 1:3), then he led them out to Bethany, just outside Jerusalem, and "lifting up his

---

[17]In fact, the evidences of the severe beating and disfigurement that Jesus suffered before his crucifixion were probably all healed, and only the scars in his hands, feet, and side remained as testimony to his death for us: Jesus was raised "in glory" (cf. 1 Cor. 15:43), not in horrible disfigurement just barely brought back to life.

hands, he blessed them. While he blessed them, he parted from them, and was carried up into heaven" (Luke 24:50–51).

A similar account is given by Luke in the opening section of Acts:

> And when he had said this, as they were looking on, he was lifted up, and a cloud took him out of their sight. And while they were gazing into heaven as he went, behold, two men stood by them in white robes, and said, "Men of Galilee, why do you stand looking into heaven? This Jesus, who was taken up from you into heaven, will come in the same way as you saw him go into heaven." (Acts 1:9–11)

These narratives describe an event that is clearly designed to show the disciples that Jesus went to a place. He did not suddenly disappear from them, never to be seen by them again, but gradually ascended as they were watching, and then a cloud (apparently the cloud of God's glory) took him from their sight. But the angels immediately said that he would come back *in the same way* in which he had gone into heaven. The fact that Jesus had a resurrection body that was subject to spatial limitations (it could be at only one place at one time) means that Jesus went *somewhere* when he ascended into heaven.

It is surprising that even some evangelical theologians hesitate to affirm that heaven is a place or that Jesus ascended to a definite location somewhere in the space-time universe. Admittedly we cannot now see where Jesus is, but that is not because he passed into some ethereal "state of being" that has no location at all in the space-time universe, but rather because our eyes are unable to see the unseen spiritual world that exists all around us. There are angels around us, but we simply cannot see them because our eyes do not have that capacity: Elisha was surrounded by an army of angels and chariots of fire protecting him from the Syrians at Dothan, but Elisha's servant was not able to see those angels until God opened his eyes so that he could see things that existed in that spiritual dimension (2 Kings 6:17). Similarly, when Stephen was dying, God gave him a special ability to see the world that is now hidden from our eyes, for he "gazed into heaven and saw the glory of God, and Jesus standing at the right hand of God; and he said, 'Behold, I see the heavens opened, and the Son of man standing at the right hand of God'" (Acts 7:55–56). And Jesus himself said, "In my Father's house are many rooms; if it were not so, would I have told you that I go to prepare *a place* for you? And when I go and prepare a place for you, I will come again and will take you to myself, that where I am you may be also" (John 14:2–3).

Of course we cannot now say exactly where heaven is. Scripture often pictures people as ascending up into heaven (as Jesus did, and Elijah) or coming down from heaven (as the angels in Jacob's dream, Gen. 28:12), so we are justified in thinking of heaven as somewhere "above" the earth. Admittedly the earth is round and it rotates, so where heaven is we are simply unable to say more precisely—Scripture does not tell us. But the repeated emphasis on the fact that Jesus went somewhere (as did Elijah, 2 Kings 2:11), and the fact that the New Jerusalem will come down out of heaven from God (Rev. 21:2), all indicate that there is clearly a localization of heaven in the space-time universe. Those who do not believe in Scripture may scoff at such an idea and wonder how it can be so, just as the first Russian cosmonaut who came back from space and declared that he did not see God or heaven anywhere, but that simply points to the blindness of their eyes toward the unseen spiritual world; it does not indicate that heaven does not exist in a certain place. In fact, the ascension of Jesus into heaven is designed to teach us that heaven does exist as a place in the space-time universe.

2. Christ Received Glory and Honor That Had Not Been His Before As the God-Man. When Jesus ascended into heaven he received glory, honor, and authority that had never been his before as one who was both God and man. Before Jesus died, he prayed, "Father, glorify me in your own presence with the glory which I had with you before the world was made" (John 17:5).[18] In his sermon at Pentecost Peter said that Jesus was "exalted at the right hand of God" (Acts 2:33), and Paul declared that "God has highly exalted him" (Phil. 2:9), and that he was "taken up in glory" (1 Tim. 3:16; cf. Heb. 1:4). Christ is now in heaven with the angelic choirs singing praise to him with the words, "Worthy is the Lamb who was slain, to receive power and wealth and wisdom and might and honor and glory and blessing!" (Rev. 5:12).[19]

3. Christ Was Seated at God's Right Hand (Christ's Session). One specific aspect of Christ's ascension into heaven and receiving of honor was the fact that he *sat down* at the right hand of God. This is sometimes called his *session* at God's right hand.[20]

The Old Testament predicted that the Messiah would sit at the right hand of God: "The LORD says to my lord: 'Sit at my right hand, till I make your enemies your footstool'" (Ps. 110:1). When Christ ascended back into heaven he received the fulfillment of that promise: "When he had made purification for sins, he *sat down* at the right hand of the Majesty on high" (Heb. 1:3). This welcoming into the presence of God and sitting at God's right hand is a dramatic indication of the completion of Christ's work of redemption. Just as a human being will sit down at the completion of a large task to enjoy the satisfaction of having accomplished it, so Jesus sat at the right hand of God, visibly demonstrating that his work of redemption was completed.

In addition to showing the completion of Christ's work of redemption, the act of sitting at God's right hand is an indication that he received authority over the universe. Paul says that God "raised him from the dead and made him sit at his right hand in the heavenly places, far above all rule and authority and power and dominion, and above every name that is named" (Eph. 1:20–21). Similarly, Peter says that Jesus "has gone into heaven and is at the right hand of God, with angels, authorities, and powers subject to him" (1 Peter 3:22). Paul also alludes to Psalm 110:1 when he says that Christ "must reign until he has put all his enemies under his feet" (1 Cor. 15:25).

One additional aspect of the authority that Christ received from the Father when he sat at his right hand was the authority to pour out the Holy Spirit on the church. Peter says on the Day of Pentecost, "Being therefore exalted at the right hand of God, and

---

[18]This verse shows that the glory Jesus received had been his before as eternal Son of God, but it had not been his before in his incarnate form as God-man.

[19]Some Lutheran theologians have also said that when Jesus ascended into heaven his human nature became ubiquitous (everywhere present): see the discussion in chapter 2, n. 36.

[20]The word *session* formerly meant "the act of sitting down," but it no longer has that meaning in ordinary English usage today.

having *received from the Father the promise of the Holy Spirit,* he has poured out this which you see and hear" (Acts 2:33).

The fact that Jesus now sits at the right hand of God in heaven does not mean that he is perpetually "fixed" there or that he is inactive. He is also seen as standing at God's right hand (Acts 7:56) and as walking among the seven golden lampstands in heaven (Rev. 2:1). Just as a human king sits on his royal throne at his accession to the kingship, but then engages in many other activities throughout each day, so Christ sat at the right hand of God as a dramatic evidence of the completion of his redemptive work and his reception of authority over the universe, but he is certainly engaged in other activities in heaven as well.

4. Christ's Ascension Has Doctrinal Significance for Our Lives. Just as the resurrection has profound implications for our lives, so Christ's ascension has significant implications for us. First, since we are united with Christ in every aspect of his work of redemption, Christ's going up into heaven foreshadows our future ascension into heaven with him. "We who are alive, who are left, shall be caught up together with them in the clouds to meet the Lord in the air; and so we shall always be with the Lord" (1 Thess. 4:17). The author of Hebrews wants us to run the race of life with the knowledge that we are following in Jesus' steps and will eventually arrive at the blessings of life in heaven that he is now enjoying: "Let us run with perseverance the race that is set before us, looking to Jesus the pioneer and perfecter of our faith, who for the joy that was set before him endured the cross, despising the shame, and is seated at the right hand of the throne of God" (Heb. 12:1–2). And Jesus himself says that he will one day take us to be with himself (John 14:3).

Second, Jesus' ascension gives us assurance that our final home will be in heaven with him. "In my Father's house are many rooms; if it were not so, would I have told you that I go to prepare a place for you? And when I go and prepare a place for you, I will come again and will take you to myself, that where I am you may be also" (John 14:2–3). Jesus was a man like us in every way yet without sin, and he has gone before us so that eventually we might follow him there and live with him forever. The fact that Jesus has already ascended into heaven and achieved the goal set before him gives great assurance to us that we will eventually go there also.

Third, because of our union with Christ in his ascension, we are able to share now (in part) in Christ's authority over the universe, and we will later share in it more fully. This is what Paul points to when he says that God "raised us up with him, and made us *sit with him in the heavenly places* in Christ Jesus" (Eph. 2:6). We are not physically present in heaven, of course, for we remain here on earth at the present time. But if Christ's session at God's right hand refers to his reception of authority, then the fact that God has made us sit with Christ means that we share in some measure in the authority that Christ has, authority to contend against "the spiritual hosts of wickedness in the heavenly places" (Eph. 6:12; cf. vv. 10–18) and to do battle with weapons that "have divine power to destroy strongholds" (2 Cor. 10:4). This sharing in Christ's authority over the universe will be made more fully our possession in the age to come: "Do you not know that we are to judge angels?" (1 Cor. 6:3). Moreover, we will share with Christ in his authority over the creation that God has made (Heb. 2:5–8).[21] Jesus promises, "He who conquers and who keeps my works until the end, I will give him power over the nations, and he shall rule them with a rod of iron, as when earthen pots are broken in pieces, even as I myself have received power from my Father" (Rev. 2:26–27). He also promises, "He who conquers, I will grant him to sit with me on my throne, as I myself conquered and sat down with my Father on his throne" (Rev. 3:21). These are amazing promises of our future sharing in Christ's sitting at the right hand of God, promises that we will not fully understand until the age to come.

C. States of Jesus Christ

In talking about the life, death, and resurrection of Christ, theologians have sometimes talked about the "states of Jesus Christ." By this they mean the different relationships Jesus had to God's law for mankind, to the possession of authority, and to receiving honor for himself. Generally two states (humiliation and exaltation) are distinguished. Thus, the doctrine of "the twofold state of Christ" is the teaching that Christ experienced first the state of humiliation, then the state of exaltation.

Within the humiliation of Christ are included his incarnation, suffering, death, and burial. Sometimes a fifth aspect (descent into hell) is included, but as explained above, the position taken in this book is that that concept is not supported in Scripture.

In the exaltation of Christ, there are also four aspects: his resurrection, ascension into heaven, session at the right hand of God, and return in glory and power. Many systematic theologies use the state of humiliation and the state of exaltation as broad categories to organize their discussion of Jesus' work.[22]

QUESTIONS FOR PERSONAL APPLICATION

1. As you read this chapter, what aspects of the Bible's teaching about a resurrection body were new to your understanding? Can you think of some characteristics of the resurrection body that you especially look forward to? How does the thought of having such a body make you feel?

2. What things would you like to do now but find yourself unable to do because of the weakness or limitations of your own physical body? Do you think these activities would be appropriate to your life in heaven? Will you be able to do them then?

3. When you were born again, you received new spiritual life within. If you think of this new spiritual life as part of the resurrection power of Christ working within you, how does that give you encouragement in living the Christian life and in ministering to people's needs?

---

[21]See discussion of Heb. 2:5–8 in chapter 2, p. 46.

[22]Although this is a useful method of organization, I have not used it in this book. For a detailed discussion, see W. Grudem, "States of Jesus Christ," *EDT*, pp. 1052–54.

4. The Bible says that you are now seated with Christ in the heavenly places (Eph. 2:6). As you meditate on this fact, how will it affect your prayer life and your engaging in spiritual warfare against demonic forces?

5. When you think of Christ now in heaven, does it cause you to focus more attention on things that will have eternal significance? Does it increase your assurance that you will someday be with him in heaven? How do you feel about the prospect of reigning with Christ over the nations and over angels as well?

SPECIAL TERMS

ascension	raised in power
exaltation of Christ	resurrection
humiliation of Christ	session
incorruptible	spiritual body
raised in glory	states of Jesus Christ

BIBLIOGRAPHY

Bray, G. L. "Ascension and Heavenly Session of Christ." In *NDT*, pp. 46–47.

Craig, William Lane. *The Son Rises: The Historical Evidence for the Resurrection of Jesus.* Chicago: Moody, 1981.

Fuller, Daniel P. *Easter Faith and History.* Grand Rapids: Eerdmans, 1965.

Gaffin, Richard B., Jr. *Resurrection and Redemption: A Study in Paul's Soteriology.* Formerly, *The Centrality of the Resurrection: A Study in Paul's Soteriology.* Phillipsburg, N.J.: Presbyterian and Reformed, 1978.

Habermas, G. R. "Resurrection of Christ." In *EDT*, pp. 938–41.

_____, and Anthony Flew. *Did Jesus Rise From the Dead? The Resurrection Debate.* Edited by Terry L. Miethe. New York: Harper and Row, 1987.

Harris, Murray J. *From Grave to Glory: Resurrection in the New Testament, Including a Response to Norman L. Geisler.* Grand Rapids: Zondervan, 1990.

_____. "Resurrection, General." In *NDT*, pp. 581–82.

Ladd, George E. *I Believe in the Resurrection of Jesus.* Grand Rapids: Eerdmans, 1975.

Macleod, D. "Resurrection of Christ." In *NDT*, pp. 582–85.

Morison, Frank. *Who Moved the Stone?* London: Faber and Faber, 1930; reprint, Grand Rapids: Zondervan, 1958.

O'Donovan, Oliver. *Resurrection and Moral Order.* Leicester: Inter-Varsity Press, 1986.

Ross, A. "Ascension of Christ." In *EDT*, pp. 86–87.

Swete, Henry Barclay. *The Ascended Christ: A Study in the Earliest Christian Teaching.* London: Macmillan, 1910.

Tenney, Merrill C. *The Reality of the Resurrection.* New York: Harper and Row, 1963.

Toon, Peter. *The Ascension of Our Lord.* Nashville: Thomas Nelson, 1984.

Wenham, John. *The Easter Enigma.* London: Paternoster, 1984.

SCRIPTURE MEMORY PASSAGE

1 Corinthians 15:20–23: *But in fact Christ has been raised from the dead, the first fruits of those who have fallen asleep. For as by a man came death, by a man has come also the resurrection of the dead. For as in Adam all die, so also in Christ shall all be made alive. But each in his own order: Christ the first fruits, then at his coming those who belong to Christ.*

HYMN

"Christ the Lord Is Risen Today"

"Christ the Lord is risen today," al-le-lu-ia!
Sons of men and angels say; al-le-lu-ia!
Raise your joys and triumphs high; al-le-lu-ia!
Sing, ye heav'ns, and earth reply; al-le-lu-ia!

Vain the stone, the watch, the seal; al-le-lu-ia!
Christ has burst the gates of hell: al-le-lu-ia!
Death in vain forbids him rise; al-le-lu-ia!
Christ hath opened paradise. Al-le-lu-ia!

Lives again our glorious King; al-le-lu-ia!
Where, O death, is now thy sting? Al-le-lu-ia!
Once he died, our souls to save; al-le-lu-ia!
Where thy victory, O grave? Al-le-lu-ia!

Soar we now where Christ has led, al-le-lu-ia!
Following our exalted Head; al-le-lu-ia!
Made like him, like him we rise; al-le-lu-ia!
Ours the cross, the grave, the skies. Al-le-lu-ia!

Hail, the Lord of earth and heav'n! Al-le-lu-ia!
Praise to thee by both be giv'n; al-le-lu-ia!
Thee we greet triumphant now; al-le-lu-ia!
Hail, the resurrection thou! Al-le-lu-ia!

AUTHOR: CHARLES WESLEY, 1739

Chapter 5

THE OFFICES OF CHRIST

How is Christ prophet, priest, and king?

EXPLANATION AND SCRIPTURAL BASIS

There were three major offices among the people of Israel in the Old Testament: the *prophet* (such as Nathan, 2 Sam. 7:2), the *priest* (such as Abiathar, 1 Sam. 30:7), and the *king* (such as King David, 2 Sam. 5:3). These three offices were distinct. The prophet spoke God's words to the people; the priest offered sacrifices, prayers, and praises to God on behalf of the people; and the king ruled over the people as God's representative. These three offices foreshadowed Christ's own work in different ways. Therefore we can look again at Christ's work, now thinking about the perspective of these three offices or categories.[1] Christ fulfills these three offices in the following ways: as *prophet* he reveals God to us and speaks God's words to us; as *priest* he both offers a sacrifice to God on our behalf and is himself the sacrifice that is offered; and as *king* he rules over the church and over the universe as well. We now turn to discuss each of these offices in more detail.

A. Christ As Prophet

The Old Testament prophets spoke God's words to the people. Moses was the first major prophet, and he wrote the first five books of the Bible, the Pentateuch. After Moses there was a succession of other prophets who spoke and wrote God's words. But Moses predicted that sometime another prophet like himself would come.

The LORD your God will raise up for you a *prophet like me* from among you, from your brethren—him you shall heed—just as you desired of the LORD

---

[1]John Calvin (1509–64) was the first major theologian to apply these three categories to the work of Christ (see his *Institutes of the Christian Religion*, Book 2, Chapter 15). The categories have been adapted by many subsequent theologians as a helpful way of understanding various aspects of Christ's work.

your God. . . . And the LORD said to me . . . "I will raise up for them a prophet like you from among their brethren; and I will put my words in his mouth, and he shall speak to them all that I command him." (Deut. 18:15–18)

However, when we look at the gospels we see that Jesus is not *primarily* viewed as a prophet or as *the* prophet like Moses, though there are occasional references to this effect. Often those who call Jesus a "prophet" know very little about him. For instance, various opinions of Jesus were circulating: "Some say John the Baptist, others say Elijah, and others Jeremiah *or one of the prophets*" (Matt. 16:14; cf. Luke 9:8). When Jesus raised the son of the widow of Nain from the dead, the people were afraid and said, "A great *prophet* has arisen among us!" (Luke 7:16). When Jesus told the Samaritan woman at the well something of her past life, she immediately responded, "Sir, I perceive that you are *a prophet*" (John 4:19). But she did not then know very much at all about him. The reaction of the man born blind who was healed in the temple was similar: "He is a prophet" (John 9:17; note that his belief in Jesus' messiahship and deity did not come until v. 37, after a subsequent conversation with Jesus).[2] Therefore, "prophet" is not a primary designation of Jesus or one used frequently by him or about him.

Nevertheless, there was still an expectation that *the* prophet like Moses would come (Deut. 18:15, 18). For instance, after Jesus had multiplied the loaves and fish, some people exclaimed, "This is indeed *the prophet* who is to come into the world!" (John 6:14; cf. 7:40). Peter also identified Christ as the prophet predicted by Moses (see Acts 3:22–24, quoting Deut. 18:15). So Jesus is indeed the prophet predicted by Moses.

Nevertheless, it is significant that in the Epistles Jesus is never called a prophet or *the* prophet. This is especially significant in the opening chapters of Hebrews, because there was a clear opportunity to identify Jesus as a prophet if the author had wished to do so. He begins by saying, "In many and various ways God spoke of old to our fathers *by the prophets;* but in these last days he has spoken to us *by a Son*" (Heb. 1:1–2). Then after discussing the greatness of the Son, in chapters 1–2, the author concludes this section not by saying, "Therefore, consider Jesus, the greatest prophet of all," or something like that, but rather by saying, "Therefore, holy brethren, who share in a heavenly call, consider Jesus, *the apostle* and high priest of our confession" (Heb. 3:1).

Why did the New Testament epistles avoid calling Jesus a prophet? Apparently because, although Jesus is the prophet whom Moses predicted, yet he is also far greater than any of the Old Testament prophets, in two ways:

1. He is the one *about whom* the prophecies in the Old Testament were made. When Jesus spoke with the two disciples on the road to Emmaus, he took them through the entire Old Testament, showing how the prophecies pointed to him: "And beginning with Moses *and all the prophets*, he interpreted to them in all the scriptures the things concerning himself" (Luke 24:27). He told these disciples that they were "slow of heart to believe *all that the prophets had spoken*," showing that it was "necessary that the Christ should suffer these things and enter into his glory" (Luke 24:25–26; cf. 1 Peter 1:11, which says that the

---

[2]In Luke 24:19 the two travelers on the road to Emmaus also refer to Jesus as a "prophet," thus putting him in a general category of religious leaders sent from God, perhaps for the benefit of the stranger whom they presumed to have little knowledge of the events surrounding Jesus' life.

Old Testament prophets were "predicting the sufferings of Christ and the subsequent glory"). Thus, the Old Testament prophets looked *forward* to Christ in what they wrote, and the New Testament apostles looked *back* to Christ and interpreted his life for the benefit of the church.

2. Jesus was not merely a messenger of revelation from God (like all the other prophets), but was himself the *source* of revelation from God. Rather than saying, as all the Old Testament prophets did, "Thus says the LORD," Jesus could begin divinely authoritative teaching with the amazing statement, "But I *say* unto you" (Matt. 5:22, et al.). The word of the Lord *came to* the Old Testament prophets, but Jesus spoke on his own authority as the eternal Word of God (John 1:1) who perfectly revealed the Father to us (John 14:9; Heb. 1:1 – 2).

In the broader sense of *prophet,* simply meaning one who reveals God to us and speaks to us the words of God, Christ is of course truly and fully a prophet. In fact, he is the one whom all the Old Testament prophets prefigured in their speech and in their actions.

B. Christ As Priest

In the Old Testament, the priests were appointed by God to offer sacrifices. They also offered prayers and praise to God on behalf of the people. In so doing they "sanctified" the people or made them acceptable to come into God's presence, albeit in a limited way during the Old Testament period. In the New Testament Jesus becomes our great high priest. This theme is developed extensively in the letter to the Hebrews, where we find that Jesus functions as priest in two ways.

1. Jesus Offered a Perfect Sacrifice for Sin. The sacrifice which Jesus offered for sins was not the blood of animals such as bulls or goats: "For it is impossible that the blood of bulls and goats should take away sins" (Heb. 10:4). Instead, Jesus offered himself as a perfect sacrifice: "But as it is, he has appeared once for all at the end of the age to put away sin *by the sacrifice of himself*" (Heb. 9:26). This was a completed and final sacrifice, never to be repeated, a theme frequently emphasized in the book of Hebrews (see 7:27; 9:12, 24 – 28; 10:1 – 2, 10, 12, 14; 13:12). Therefore Jesus fulfilled all the expectations that were prefigured, not only in the Old Testament sacrifices, but also in the lives and actions of the priests who offered them: he was both the sacrifice and the priest who offered the sacrifice. Jesus is now the "great high priest who has passed through the heavens" (Heb. 4:14) and who has appeared "in the presence of God on our behalf" (Heb. 9:24), since he has offered a sacrifice that ended for all time the need for any further sacrifices.

2. Jesus Continually Brings Us Near to God. The Old Testament priests not only offered sacrifices, but also in a representative way they came into the presence of God from time to time on behalf of the people. But Jesus does much more than that. As our perfect high priest, he continually *leads us* into God's presence so that we no longer have need of a Jerusalem temple, or of a special priesthood to stand between us and God. And Jesus does not come into the inner part (the holy of holies) of the earthly temple in Jerusalem, but he has gone into the heavenly equivalent to the holy of holies, the very presence of God himself in heaven (Heb. 9:24). Therefore we have a hope that follows him there: "We have this as a sure and steadfast anchor of the soul, a hope that *enters into the inner shrine behind the curtain,* where Jesus has gone as a forerunner on our behalf, having become a high priest for ever" (Heb. 6:19–20). This means that we have a far greater privilege than those people who lived at the time of the Old Testament temple. They could not even enter into the first room of the temple, the holy place, for only the priests could go there. Then into the inner room of the temple, the holy of holies, only the high priest could go, and he could only enter there once a year (Heb 9:1–7). But when Jesus offered a perfect sacrifice for sins, the curtain or veil of the temple that closed off the holy of holies was torn in two from top to bottom (Luke 23:45), thus indicating in a symbolic way on earth that the way of access to God in heaven was opened by Jesus' death. Therefore the author of Hebrews can make this amazing exhortation to all believers:

> Therefore, brethren, since we have confidence to *enter the sanctuary* [lit. 'the holy places,' meaning both the 'holy place' and the 'holy of holies' itself] by the blood of Jesus . . . and since we have a great priest over the house of God, *let us draw near with a true heart in full assurance of faith.* (Heb. 10:19–22)

Jesus has opened for us the way of access to God so that we can continually "draw near" into God's very presence without fear but with "confidence" and in "full assurance of faith."

3. Jesus As Priest Continually Prays for Us. One other priestly function in the Old Testament was to pray on behalf of the people. The author of Hebrews tells us that Jesus also fulfills this function: "He is able for all time to save those who draw near to God through him, since he always lives *to make intercession for them*" (Heb. 7:25). Paul affirms the same point when he says Christ Jesus is the one "who indeed *intercedes for us*" (Rom. 8:34).

Some have argued that this work of high priestly intercession is only the act of remaining in the Father's presence as a continual reminder that he himself has paid the penalty for all our sins. According to this view, Jesus does not actually make specific prayers to God the Father about individual needs in our lives, but "intercedes" only in the sense of remaining in God's presence as our high priestly representative.

However, this view does not seem to fit the actual language used in Romans 8:34 and Hebrews 7:25. In both cases, the word *intercede* translates the Greek term *entygchanō*. This word does not mean merely "to stand as someone's representative before another person," but clearly has the sense of making specific requests or petitions before someone. For example, Festus uses this word to say to King Agrippa, "You see this man about whom the whole Jewish people *petitioned* me" (Acts 25:24). Paul also uses it of Elijah when he "*pleads* with God against Israel" (Rom. 11:2). In both cases the requests are very specific, not just general representations.[3]

---

[3]Literature outside the New Testament provides further examples of *entygchanō* used to mean "to bring requests or petitions." See, e.g., Wisd. 8:21 ("I *asked* the Lord, and made petition to him"); 1 Macc. 8:32; 3 Macc. 6:37 ("They *requested* the King, that he send them back to their home"); 1 Clem. 56:1; Epistle of Polycarp to the Philippians 4:3; Josephus, *Antiquities* 12:18; 16:170 (the Jews in Cyrene *petition* Marcus Agrippa concerning people in their land who are falsely collecting taxes). More examples could be found as well (cf. also Rom. 8:27, and, using a cognate word, v. 26).

We may conclude, then, that both Paul and the author of Hebrews are saying that Jesus continually lives in the presence of God to make specific requests and to bring specific petitions before God on our behalf. This is a role that Jesus, as God-man, is uniquely qualified to fulfill. Although God could care for all our needs in response to direct observation (Matt. 6:8), yet it has pleased God, in his relationship to the human race, to decide to act instead in response to prayer, apparently so that the faith shown through prayer might glorify him. It is especially the prayers of men and women created in his image that are pleasing in God's sight. In Christ, we have a true man, a perfect man, praying and thereby continually glorifying God through prayer. Thus, human manhood is raised to a highly exalted position: "There is one God, and there is one mediator between God and men, *the man* Christ Jesus" (1 Tim. 2:5).

Yet in his human nature alone Jesus could not of course be such a great high priest for all his people all over the world. He could not hear the prayers of persons far away, nor could he hear prayers that were only spoken in a person's mind. He could not hear all requests simultaneously (for in the world at any one moment there are millions of people praying to him). Therefore, in order to be the perfect high priest who intercedes for us, he must be God as well as man. He must be one who in his divine nature can both know all things and bring them into the presence of the Father. Yet because he became and continues to be man he has the right to represent us before God and he can express his petitions from the viewpoint of a sympathetic high priest, one who understands by experience what we go through.

Therefore, Jesus is the only person in the whole universe for all eternity who can be such a heavenly high priest, one who is truly God and truly man, exalted forever above the heavens.

The thought that Jesus is continually praying for us should give us great encouragement. He always prays for us according to the Father's will, so we can know that his requests will be granted. Berkhof says:

> It is a consoling thought that Christ is praying for us, even when we are negligent in our prayer life; that He is presenting to the Father those spiritual needs which were not present to our minds and which we often neglect to include in our prayers; and that He prays for our protection against the dangers of which we are not even conscious, and against the enemies which threaten us, though we do not notice it. He is praying that our faith may not cease, and that we may come out victoriously in the end.[4]

C. Christ As King

In the Old Testament the king has authority to rule over the nation of Israel. In the New Testament, Jesus was born to be King of the Jews (Matt. 2:2), but he refused any attempt by people to try to make him an earthly king with earthly military and political power (John 6:15). He told Pilate, "My kingship is not of this world; if my

---

[4]Louis Berkhof, *Systematic Theology* (Grand Rapids: Eerdmans, 1939, 1941), p. 403.

kingship were of this world, my servants would fight, that I might not be handed over to the Jews; but my kingship is not from the world" (John 18:36). Nonetheless, Jesus did have a kingdom whose arrival he announced in his preaching (Matt. 4:17, 23; 12:28, et al.). He is in fact the true king of the new people of God. Thus, Jesus refused to rebuke his disciples who cried out at his triumphal entry into Jerusalem, "Blessed is *the King* who comes in the name of the Lord!" (Luke 19:38; cf. vv. 39–40; also Matt. 21:5; John 1:49; Acts 17:7).

After his resurrection, Jesus was given by God the Father far greater authority over the church and over the universe. God raised him up and "made him sit at his right hand in the heavenly places, *far above all rule and authority and power and dominion,* and above every name that is named, not only in this age but also in that which is to come; and he has put all things under his feet and has made him the head over all things for the church" (Eph. 1:20–22; Matt. 28:18; 1 Cor. 15:25). That authority over the church and over the universe will be more fully recognized by people when Jesus returns to earth in power and great glory to reign (Matt. 26:64; 2 Thes. 1:7–10; Rev. 19:11–16). On that day he will be acknowledged as "*King of kings* and Lord of lords" (Rev. 19:16) and every knee shall bow to him (Phil. 2:10).

D. Our Roles As Prophets, Priests, and Kings

If we look back at the situation of Adam before the fall and forward to our future status with Christ in heaven for eternity, we can see that these roles of prophet, priest, and king had parallels in the experience that God originally intended for man, and will be fulfilled in our lives in heaven.

In the Garden of Eden, Adam was a "prophet" in that he had true knowledge of God and always spoke truthfully about God and about his creation. He was a "priest" in that he was able freely and openly to offer prayer and praise to God. There was no need of a sacrifice to pay for sins, but in another sense of sacrifice Adam and Eve's work would have been offered to God in gratitude and thanksgiving, and so would have been a "sacrifice" of another sort (cf. Heb. 13:15). Adam and Eve were also "kings" (or king and queen) in the sense of having been given dominion and rule over the creation (Gen. 1:26–28).

After sin entered into the world, fallen human beings no longer functioned as prophets, for they believed false information about God and spoke falsely about him to others. They no longer had priestly access to God because sin cut them off from his presence. Instead of ruling over the creation as kings, they were subject to the harshness of the creation and tyrannized by flood, drought, and unproductive land, as well as by tyrannical human rulers. The nobility of man as God had created him — to be a true prophet, priest, and king — was lost through sin.

There was a partial recovery of the purity of these three roles in the establishment of the three offices of prophet, priest, and king in the kingdom of Israel. From time to time godly men occupied these offices. But there were also false prophets, dishonest priests, and ungodly kings, and the original purity and holiness with which God intended man to fulfill these offices were never fully realized.

When Christ came, we saw for the first time the fulfillment of these three roles, since he was the perfect prophet, who most fully declared God's words to us, the perfect high priest, who offered the supreme sacrifice for sins and who brought his people near to God, and the true and rightful king of the universe, who will reign forever with a scepter of righteousness over the new heavens and new earth.

But amazingly we as Christians even now begin to imitate Christ in each of these roles, though in a subordinate way. We have a "prophetic" role as we proclaim the gospel to the world and thereby bring God's saving Word to people. In fact, whenever we speak truthfully about God to believers or to unbelievers we are fulfilling a "prophetic" function (using the word *prophetic* in a very broad sense).

We are also priests, because Peter calls us "a royal priesthood" (1 Peter 2:9). He invites us to be built into a spiritual temple and "to be a holy priesthood" as well as "to offer spiritual sacrifices acceptable to God through Jesus Christ" (1 Peter 2:5). The author of Hebrews also views us as priests who are able to enter into the holy of holies (Heb. 10:19, 22) and able to "continually offer up a sacrifice of praise to God, that is, the fruit of lips that acknowledge his name" (Heb. 13:15). He also tells us that our good works are sacrifices pleasing to God: "Do not neglect to do good and to share what you have, for such *sacrifices* are pleasing to God" (Heb. 13:16). Paul also has a priestly role in mind for us when he writes, "I appeal to you therefore, brethren, by the mercies of God, to present your bodies *as a living sacrifice,* holy and acceptable to God, which is your spiritual worship" (Rom. 12:1).

We also share in part now in the kingly reign of Christ, since we have been raised to sit with him in the heavenly places (Eph. 2:6), thus sharing to some degree in his authority over evil spiritual forces that may be arrayed against us (Eph. 6:10–18; James 4:7; 1 Peter 5:9; 1 John 4:4). God has even now committed to us authority over various areas in this world or in the church, giving to some authority over much and to some authority over little. But when the Lord returns those who have been faithful over little will be given authority over much (Matt. 25:14–30).

When Christ returns and rules over the new heavens and new earth, we will once again be true "prophets" because our knowledge will then be perfect and we shall know as we are known (1 Cor. 13:12). Then we will speak only truth about God and about his world, and in us the original prophetic purpose which God had for Adam will be fulfilled. We will be priests forever, for we will eternally worship and offer prayer to God as we behold his face and dwell in his presence (Rev. 22:3–4). We will continually offer ourselves and all that we do or have as sacrifices to our most worthy king.

Yet we shall also, in subjection to God, share in ruling over the universe, for with him we shall "reign forever and ever" (Rev. 22:5). Jesus says, "He who conquers, I will grant him *to sit with me on my throne,* as I myself conquered and sat down with my Father on his throne" (Rev. 3:21). In fact, Paul tells the Corinthians, "Do you not know that *the saints will judge the world?* . . . Do you not know that *we are to judge angels?*" (1 Cor. 6:2–3). Therefore for all eternity, we shall forever function as subordinate prophets, priests, and kings, yet always subject to the Lord Jesus, the supreme prophet, priest, and king.

QUESTIONS FOR PERSONAL APPLICATION

1. Can you see some ways in which an understanding of Christ's role as prophet, priest, and king will help you understand more fully the functions of prophets, priests, and kings in the Old Testament? Read the description of Solomon's kingdom in 1 Kings 4:20–34 and 1 Kings 10:14–29. Do you see in Solomon's kingdom any foreshadowing of the three offices of Christ? Any foreshadowing of Christ's eternal kingdom? Do you think that you have greater or lesser privileges living now as a member of the church in the new covenant age?

2. Can you see any fulfillment of the role of prophet in your life now? Of the role of priest? Of the role of king? How could each of these functions be developed in your life?

SPECIAL TERMS

intercession   priest
king   prophet

BIBLIOGRAPHY

Baker, J. P. "Offices of Christ." In *NDT,* pp. 476–77.
Clowney, Edmund P. *The Unfolding Mystery: Discovering Christ in the Old Testament.* Phillipsburg, N.J.: Presbyterian and Reformed, 1988.
Letham, Robert. *The Work of Christ.* Downers Grove, Ill.: InterVarsity Press, 1993.
Reymond, R. L. "Offices of Christ." In *EDT,* p. 793.

SCRIPTURE MEMORY PASSAGE

1 Peter 2:9–10: *But you are a chosen race, a royal priesthood, a holy nation, God's own people, that you may declare the wonderful deeds of him who called you out of darkness into his marvelous light. Once you were no people but now you are God's people; once you had not received mercy but now you have received mercy.*

HYMN

"Rejoice the Lord Is King"

This powerful hymn encourages us to rejoice at Christ's present and future kingship. (An excellent hymn about Christ's role as priest is "Arise, My Soul, Arise," also by Charles Wesley, and this may be used as an alternative hymn. Another alternative is "How Sweet the Name of Jesus Sounds," by John Newton, esp. v. 4.)

Rejoice, the Lord is King: your Lord and King adore;
   Rejoice, give thanks and sing, and triumph evermore:
Lift up your heart, lift up your voice;
   Rejoice, again I say, rejoice.

Jesus, the Savior, reigns, the God of truth and love;
   When he had purged our stains, he took his seat above:
Lift up your heart, lift up your voice;
   Rejoice, again I say, rejoice.

His kingdom cannot fail, he rules o'er earth and heav'n;
   The keys of death and hell are to our Jesus giv'n:
Lift up your heart, lift up your voice;
   Rejoice, again I say, rejoice.

He sits at God's right hand till all his foes submit,
   And bow to his command, and fall beneath his feet:
Lift up your heart, lift up your voice;
   Rejoice, again I say, rejoice.

AUTHOR: CHARLES WESLEY, 1746

Chapter 6

THE WORK OF THE HOLY SPIRIT

What are the distinctive activities of the Holy Spirit throughout the history of the Bible?

EXPLANATION AND SCRIPTURAL BASIS

In the previous chapters we have discussed at some length the person and work of God the Son, Jesus Christ. We have also examined the biblical evidence for the deity and distinct personality of the Holy Spirit (in connection with the doctrine of the Trinity). It is appropriate now in this chapter that we focus on the distinctive work of the Holy Spirit. Among the different activities of the members of the Trinity, what activities are said to be especially the work of God the Holy Spirit?

In this chapter we shall attempt to gain an overview of the teaching of all of Scripture on the work of the Holy Spirit in order to understand more fully what kinds of activities have been especially delegated to the Holy Spirit by God the Father and God the Son.

We may define the work of the Holy Spirit as follows: *The work of the Holy Spirit is to manifest the active presence of God in the world, and especially in the church.* This definition indicates that the Holy Spirit is the member of the Trinity whom the Scripture most often represents as being *present* to do God's work in the world. Although this is true to some extent throughout the Bible, it is particularly true in the new covenant age. In the Old Testament, the presence of God was many times manifested in the glory of God and in theophanies, and in the gospels Jesus himself manifested the presence of God among men. But after Jesus ascended into heaven, and continuing through the entire church age, the Holy Spirit is now the *primary* manifestation of the presence of the Trinity among us. He is the one who is most prominently *present* with us now.[1]

---

[1] In this discussion, when I use the word "present" I mean "present to 'bless.'" Of course, since he is fully God, the *being* of the Holy Spirit is always present everywhere (he is omnipres- ent), but he does not always show his presence in activities that bring blessing.

From the very beginning of creation we have an indication that the Holy Spirit's work is to complete and sustain what God the Father has planned and what God the Son has begun, for in Genesis 1:2, "the *Spirit of God* was moving over the face of the waters." And at Pentecost, with the beginning of the new creation in Christ, it is the Holy Spirit who comes to grant power to the church (Acts 10:38; 2:4, 17–18). Because the Holy Spirit is the person of the Trinity through whom God particularly manifests his presence in the new covenant age, it is appropriate that Paul should call the Holy Spirit the "first fruits" (Rom. 8:23) and the "guarantee" (or "down payment," 2 Cor. 1:22; 5:5) of the full manifestation of God's presence that we will know in the new heavens and new earth (cf. Rev. 21:3–4).

Even in the Old Testament, it was predicted that the presence of the Holy Spirit would bring abundant blessings from God: Isaiah predicted a time when the Spirit would bring great renewal.

> For the palace will be forsaken, the populous city deserted . . . *until the Spirit is poured upon us from on high,* and the wilderness becomes a fruitful field, and the fruitful field is deemed a forest. Then justice will dwell in the wilderness, and righteousness abide in the fruitful field. And the effect of righteousness will be peace, and the result of righteousness, quietness and trust for ever. My people will abide in a peaceful habitation, in secure dwellings, and in quiet resting places. (Isa. 32:14–18)

Similarly, God prophesied through Isaiah to Jacob, "For I will pour water on the thirsty land, and streams on the dry ground; *I will pour my Spirit upon your descendants,* and my blessing on your offspring" (Isa. 44:3).

By contrast, the departure of the Holy Spirit removed the blessing of God from a people: "But they rebelled and *grieved his holy Spirit;* therefore he turned to be their enemy, and himself fought against them" (Isa. 63:10). Nonetheless, several prophecies in the Old Testament predicted a time when the Holy Spirit would come in greater fullness, a time when God would make a new covenant with his people (Ezek. 36:26–27; 37:14; 39:29; Joel 2:28–29).

In what specific ways does the Holy Spirit bring God's blessing? We may distinguish four aspects of the work of the Holy Spirit to bring evidence of God's presence and to bless: (1) the Holy Spirit *empowers;* (2) the Holy Spirit *purifies;* (3) the Holy Spirit *reveals;* (4) the Holy Spirit *unifies.* We will examine each of these four activities below. Finally, we must recognize that these activities of the Holy Spirit are not to be taken for granted, and they do not just happen automatically among God's people. Rather, the Holy Spirit reflects the pleasure or displeasure of God with the faith and obedience—or unbelief and disobedience—of God's people. Because of this, we need to look at a fifth aspect of the Holy Spirit's activity: (5) the Holy Spirit *gives stronger or weaker evidence* of the presence and blessing of God, according to our response to him.

A. The Holy Spirit Empowers

1. He Gives Life. In the realm of nature it is the role of the Holy Spirit to give life to all animate creatures, whether on the ground or in the sky and sea, for "When you send forth your Spirit, they are created" (Ps. 104:30). Conversely, if God "should take back his spirit to himself, and gather to himself his breath, all flesh would perish together, and man would return to dust" (Job 34:14–15). Here we see the role of the Spirit in the giving and sustaining of human and animal life.

Parallel with this is the role of the Holy Spirit to give us new life in regeneration.[2] Jesus told Nicodemus, "That which is born of the flesh is flesh, and that which is *born of the Spirit* is spirit. Do not marvel that I said to you, 'You must be born anew'" (John 3:6–7; cf. vv. 5, 8; 6:63; 2 Cor. 3:6). He also said, "It is *the Spirit who gives life; the flesh profits nothing*" (John 6:63 NASB; cf. 2 Cor. 3:6; Acts 10:44–47; Titus 3:5).[3] Consistent with this life-giving function of the Holy Spirit is the fact that it was the Holy Spirit who conceived Jesus in the womb of Mary his mother (Matt. 1:18, 20; Luke 1:35). And on the day when Christ returns, it is the same Holy Spirit who will complete this life-giving work by giving new resurrection life to our mortal bodies: "If the Spirit of him who raised Jesus from the dead dwells in you, he who raised Christ Jesus from the dead will give life to your mortal bodies also *through his Spirit* which dwells in you" (Rom. 8:11).

2. He Gives Power for Service.

a. Old Testament: In the Old Testament, the Holy Spirit frequently empowered people for special service. He empowered Joshua with leadership skills and wisdom (Num. 27:18; Deut. 34:9), and empowered the judges to deliver Israel from their oppressors (note how "the Spirit of the LORD came upon" Othniel in Judg. 3:10, Gideon in 6:34, Jephthah in 11:29, and Samson in 13:25; 14:6, 19; 15:14). The Holy Spirit came mightily upon Saul to arouse him to battle against the enemies of Israel (1 Sam. 11:6), and when David was anointed as king, "the Spirit of the LORD came mightily upon David from that day forward" (1 Sam. 16:13), equipping David to fulfill the task of kingship to which God had called him.[4] In a slightly different kind of empowering, the Holy Spirit endowed Bezalel with artistic skills for the construction of the tabernacle and its equipment (Ex. 31:3; 35:31), and with the ability to teach these skills to others (Ex. 35:34).[5]

The Holy Spirit also protected God's people and enabled them to overcome their enemies. For example, God put his Spirit in the midst of them at the time of the exodus (Isa. 63:11–12) and later, after their return from exile, put his Spirit in the midst of

---

[2]The phrase "baptism in the Holy Spirit" is used by the New Testament (for example, in 1 Cor. 12:13) to speak of the Holy Spirit's work at the time we become Christians (though many evangelicals today, especially in charismatic and Pentecostal groups, would understand "baptism in the Holy Spirit" to refer to something the Holy Spirit does after conversion).

[3]Related to the life-giving work of the Holy Spirit is the fact that he also seals his work to us so that he keeps true believers from falling away from God and losing their salvation (Eph. 1:13).

[4]It is apparently in the sense of equipping for kingship that David asks that the Holy Spirit not be withdrawn from him when he prays, "Cast me not away from your presence, and *take not your holy Spirit from me*" (Ps. 51:11). Just as the Holy Spirit in his role of anointing Saul for kingship had departed from Saul at the same time as he came upon David (cf. 1 Sam. 16:13 with v. 14), so David, after his sin with Bathsheba (see Ps. 51, title), prayed that the Holy Spirit would not similarly be taken from him.

[5]The Holy Spirit also empowered the Old Testament prophets by giving them revelations to speak, but I have included that function under Section C below ("The Holy Spirit Reveals").

them to protect them and keep them from fear (Hag. 2:5). When Saul was attempting to capture David by force, the Holy Spirit came upon Saul's messengers (1 Sam. 19:20) and eventually upon Saul himself (v. 23), causing them involuntarily to fall to the ground and to prophesy for hours, thus defeating Saul's purpose and humiliating him in response to his malicious show of force against David and Samuel. In a similar way, while Ezekiel was prophesying judgment by the power of the Holy Spirit against some of the leaders of Israel (Ezek. 11:5), one of the leaders named Pelatiah actually died (Ezek. 11:13). In this way the Holy Spirit brought immediate judgment on him.

Finally, the Old Testament predicted a time when the Holy Spirit would anoint a Servant-Messiah in great fullness and power:

> And the *Spirit of the* LORD *shall rest upon him,* the spirit of wisdom and understanding, the spirit of counsel and might, the spirit of knowledge and the fear of the LORD. And his delight shall be in the fear of the LORD. (Isa. 11:2–3)

Isaiah prophesied that God would say of this coming Servant, "I have put my Spirit upon him" (Isa. 42:1), and he himself would say, "The Spirit of the Lord GOD is upon me, because the LORD has anointed me" (Isa. 61:1; cf. Luke 4:18).

Before leaving this discussion of the empowering of the Holy Spirit in the Old Testament, we should note that it sometimes is said that there was no work of the Holy Spirit *within* people in the Old Testament. This idea has mainly been inferred from Jesus' words to the disciples in John 14:17, "He dwells with you, and will be *in* you." But we should not conclude from this verse that there was no work of the Holy Spirit within people before Pentecost. Although the Old Testament does not frequently speak of people who had the Holy Spirit in them or who were filled with the Holy Spirit, there are a few examples: Joshua is said to have the Holy Spirit within him (Num. 27:18; Deut. 34:9), as are Ezekiel (Ezek. 2:2; 3:24), Daniel (Dan. 4:8–9, 18; 5:11), and Micah (Mic. 3:8).[6] This means that when Jesus says to his disciples that the Holy Spirit "dwells with you and will be in you" (John 14:17), he cannot mean that there was an absolute "within/without" difference between the old and new covenant work of the Holy Spirit. Nor can John 7:39 ("as yet the Spirit had not been given, because Jesus was not yet glorified") mean that there was *no* activity of the Holy Spirit in people's lives before Pentecost. Both of these passages must be different ways of saying that the more powerful, fuller work of the Holy Spirit that is characteristic of life after Pentecost had not yet begun in the lives of the disciples. The Holy Spirit had not come within them in the way in which God had promised to put the Holy Spirit within his people when the new covenant would come (see Ezek. 36:26, 27; 37:14), nor had the Holy Spirit been poured out in the great abundance and fullness that would characterize the new covenant age (Joel 2:28–29). In this powerful new covenant sense, the Holy Spirit was not yet at work within the disciples.

b. New Testament: The empowering work of the Holy Spirit in the New Testament is seen first and most fully in his anointing and empowering of Jesus as the Messiah. The

---

[6]Before Pentecost in the New Testament we also find that John the Baptist (Luke 1:15), Elizabeth (Luke 1:41), and Zechariah (Luke 1:67) were all said to be filled with the Holy Spirit.

Holy Spirit descended upon Jesus at his baptism (Matt. 3:16; Mark 1:11; Luke 3:22). John the Baptist said, "I saw the Spirit descend as a dove from heaven, and it remained on him" (John 1:32). Therefore Jesus entered into the temptation in the wilderness "full of the Holy Spirit" (Luke 4:1), and after his temptation, at the beginning of his ministry, "Jesus returned *in the power of the Spirit* into Galilee" (Luke 4:14). When Jesus came to preach in the synagogue at Nazareth, he declared that Isaiah's prophecy was fulfilled in himself: "The Spirit of the Lord is upon me, because he has anointed me to preach good news to the poor. He has sent me to proclaim release to the captives and recovering of sight to the blind, to set at liberty those who are oppressed, to proclaim the acceptable year of the Lord" (Luke 4:18–19). The power of the Holy Spirit in Jesus' life was then seen in his subsequent miracles, as he cast out demons with a word and healed all who came to him (Luke 4:36, 40–41). The Holy Spirit was pleased to dwell in Jesus and empower him, for he fully delighted in the absolute moral purity of Jesus' life. In the context of talking about his own ministry, and the Father's blessing on that ministry, Jesus says, "It is not by measure that he gives the Spirit; the Father loves the Son, and has given all things into his hand" (John 3:34–35). Jesus had an anointing of the Holy Spirit without measure, and this anointing "remained on him" (John 1:32; cf. Acts 10:38).

The Holy Spirit also empowered Jesus' disciples for various kinds of ministry. Jesus had promised them, "You shall *receive power when the Holy Spirit has come upon you;* and you shall be my witnesses in Jerusalem and in all Judea and Samaria and to the end of the earth" (Acts 1:8).[7] There are several specific examples of the Holy Spirit's empowering the early Christians to work miracles as they proclaimed the gospel (note Stephen in Acts 6:5, 8; and Paul in Rom. 15:19; 1 Cor. 2:4). But the Holy Spirit also gave great power to the preaching of the early church so that when the disciples were filled with the Holy Spirit they proclaimed the Word boldly and with great power (Acts 4:8, 31; 6:10; 1 Thess. 1:5; 1 Peter 1:12). In general, we can say that the Holy Spirit speaks through the gospel message as it is effectively proclaimed to people's hearts. The New Testament ends with an invitation from both the Holy Spirit and the church, who together call people to salvation: "The Spirit and the Bride say, 'Come.' And let him who hears say, 'Come'" (Rev. 22:17). In fact, not only in the preaching of the gospel message, but also in the reading and teaching of Scripture, the Holy Spirit continues to speak to people's hearts each day (see Heb. 3:7 and 10:15, where the author quotes an Old Testament passage and says that the Holy Spirit is now speaking that passage to his readers).

---

[7]The word here translated "power" (*dynamis*) occurs nine other times in Acts. In one case (4:33), it is unclear whether this "power" refers to powerful preaching that convicted the hearers or to miraculous signs that accompanied the preaching. But in the other eight examples (2:22; 3:12; 4:7; 6:8; 8:10 [in this verse referring to pagan miracle-working power], 13; 10:38; 19:11) it refers to *power to work miracles.* This meaning of the term *dynamis* is further confirmed by its frequent use in Luke's gospel to refer to miracle-working power. Therefore when Jesus promised the disciples in Acts 1:8 that they would receive "power" when the Holy Spirit came upon them, it seems likely that they would have understood him to mean at least the power of the Holy Spirit to work miracles that would attest to the truthfulness of the gospel. Because the immediate context of the sentence talks about being witnesses for Jesus, they may also have understood him to mean that they would receive the power of the Holy Spirit to work through their preaching and bring conviction of sins and awaken faith in people's hearts. This power in their preaching was evident in subsequent events, as when Peter's hearers "were cut to the heart" (Acts 2:37), or when "many of those who heard the word believed; and the number of the men came to about five thousand"(Acts 4:4).

Another aspect of empowering Christians for service is the Holy Spirit's activity of giving spiritual gifts to equip Christians for ministry. After listing a variety of spiritual gifts, Paul says, "But *one and the same Spirit works all these things,* distributing to each one individually just as He wills" (1 Cor. 12:11 NASB). Since the Holy Spirit is the one who shows or manifests God's presence in the world, it is not surprising that Paul can call spiritual gifts "manifestations" of the Holy Spirit (1 Cor. 12:7).[8] When spiritual gifts are active, it is another indication of the presence of God the Holy Spirit in the church.[9]

In the prayer lives of individual believers, we find that the Holy Spirit empowers prayer and makes it effective. "We do not know how to pray as we ought, but the Spirit himself intercedes for us with sighs too deep for words" (Rom. 8:26). And Paul says that we "have access in one Spirit to the Father" (Eph. 2:18). One specific kind of prayer that the New Testament says is empowered by the Holy Spirit is the gift of prayer in tongues (1 Cor. 12:10–11; 14:2, 14–17).

Yet another aspect of the Holy Spirit's work in empowering Christians for service is empowering people to overcome spiritual opposition to the preaching of the gospel and to God's work in people's lives. This power in spiritual warfare was first seen in the life of Jesus, who said, "If it is *by the Spirit of God* that I cast out demons, then the kingdom of God has come upon you" (Matt. 12:28). When Paul came to Cyprus he encountered opposition from Elymas the magician, but he, "*filled with the Holy Spirit,* looked intently at him and said, 'You son of the devil, you enemy of all righteousness, full of all deceit and villainy, will you not stop making crooked the straight paths of the Lord? And now, behold, the hand of the Lord is upon you, and you shall be blind and unable to see the sun for a time.' Immediately mist and darkness fell upon him and he went about seeking people to lead him by the hand" (Acts 13:9–11). The gift of "distinguishing between spirits" (1 Cor. 12:10), given by the Holy Spirit, is also to be a tool in this warfare against the forces of darkness, as is the Word of God, which functions as the "sword of the Spirit" (Eph. 6:17) in spiritual conflict.

B. The Holy Spirit Purifies

Since this member of the Trinity is called the *Holy* Spirit, it is not surprising to find that one of his primary activities is to cleanse us from sin and to "sanctify us" or make us more holy in actual conduct of life. Even in the lives of unbelievers there is some restraining influence of the Holy Spirit as he convicts the world of sin (John 16:8–11; Acts 7:51). But when people become Christians the Holy Spirit does an initial cleansing work in them, making a decisive break with the patterns of sin that were in their lives before.[10] Paul says of the Corinthians, "You were washed, *you were sanctified,* you were justified in the name of the Lord Jesus Christ and *in the Spirit of our God*" (1 Cor. 6:11; see

---

[8]The Greek word translated "manifestation" is *phanerōsis,* which means something that discloses, something that makes publicly evident or clear. The related adjective *phaneros* means "visible, clear, plainly to be seen, open, plain, evident, known" (BAGD, p. 852).

[9]The Holy Spirit also empowers obedience to God during

the Christian life (see discussion below on the Holy Spirit's work of purification).

[10]See discussion of this in John Murray, "Definitive Sanctification," in *Collected Writings of John Murray* (Edinburgh and Carlisle, Pa.: Banner of Truth, 1977), pp. 277–84.

also Titus 3:5). This cleansing and purifying work of the Holy Spirit is apparently what is symbolized by the metaphor of fire when John the Baptist says that Jesus will baptize people "with the Holy Spirit and with fire" (Matt. 3:11; Luke 3:16).

After the initial break with sin that the Holy Spirit brings about in our lives at conversion, he also produces in us growth in holiness of life. He brings forth the *"fruit of the Spirit"* within us ("love, joy, peace, patience, kindness, goodness, faithfulness, gentleness, self-control," Gal. 5:22–23), those qualities that reflect the character of God. As we continually "are being changed into his likeness from one degree of glory to another," we should be reminded that "this comes from the Lord who is the Spirit" (2 Cor. 3:18). Sanctification comes by the power of the Holy Spirit (2 Thess. 2:13; 1 Peter 1:2; cf. Rom. 8:4, 15–16), so that it is *"by the Spirit"* that we are able to "put to death the deeds of the body" and grow in personal holiness (Rom. 8:13; see 7:6; Phil. 1:19).

Some people today say a purifying (or healing) work of the Holy Spirit occurs when they are "slain in the Spirit," an experience in which they suddenly fall to the ground in a semi-conscious state and remain there for minutes or hours. Although the phrase "slaying in the Spirit" is nowhere in Scripture, there are instances when people fell to the ground, or fell into a trance, in the presence of God.[11] Contemporary experiences should be evaluated according to what lasting results ("fruit") they bear in people's lives (see Matt. 7:15–20; 1 Cor. 14:12, 26c).

C. The Holy Spirit Reveals

1. Revelation to Prophets and Apostles. Let us now examine the work of the Holy Spirit in revealing God's words to the Old Testament prophets and New Testament apostles, in many cases so that these words could be put into Scripture (see, for example, Num. 24:2; Ezek. 11:5; Zech. 7:12, et al.). The whole of the Old Testament Scriptures came about because "men spoke from God as they were carried along by the Holy Spirit" (2 Peter 1:21 NIV). Several other passages mention this work of the Holy Spirit in Old Testament prophets (see Matt. 22:43; Acts 1:16; 4:25; 28:25; 1 Peter 1:11). The New Testament apostles and others who wrote words of New Testament Scripture were also guided "into all the truth" by the Holy Spirit (John 16:13), who also spoke to the apostles what he heard from the Father and the Son, and declared to them "the things that are to come" (John 16:3; cf. Eph. 3:5). Others who were filled with the Holy Spirit also spoke or sang words that became part of Scripture, such as Elizabeth (Luke 1:41), Zechariah (Luke 1:67), and Simeon (Luke 2:25).

2. He Gives Evidence of God's Presence. Sometimes it has been said that the work of the Holy Spirit is not to call attention to himself but rather to give glory to Jesus and to God the Father. But this seems to be a false dichotomy, not supported by Scripture. Of course the Holy Spirit does glorify Jesus (John 16:14) and bear witness to him (John 15:26; Acts 5:32; 1 Corinthians 12:3; 1 John 4:2). But this does not mean that he does not make his

[11]See Gen. 15:12; Exod. 40:35; 1 Sam. 19:24; 1 Kings 8:11; Ezek. 1:28; 3:23; Dan. 8:27; John 18:6; Acts 9:4; 10:10; Rev. 1:17; 4:10 (compare angelic encounters in Dan. 8:17–18; 10:7–17).

own actions and words known! The Bible has hundreds of verses *talking about the work of the Holy Spirit,* making his work known, and the Bible is itself spoken or inspired by the Holy Spirit!

Moreover, *the Holy Spirit frequently made himself known by phenomena that indicated his activity,* both in the Old Testament and in the New Testament periods. This was true when the Holy Spirit came upon the seventy elders with Moses and they prophesied (Num. 11:25–26), and when the Holy Spirit came upon the judges to enable them to do great works of power (Judg. 14:6, 19; 15:14, et al.). In these instances people could see the effect of the Holy Spirit coming on the Lord's servants. This was also true when the Holy Spirit came mightily upon Saul and he prophesied with a band of prophets (1 Sam. 10:6, 10), and it was frequently true when he empowered the Old Testament prophets to give public prophecies.

The Holy Spirit also made his presence evident in a visible way when he descended as a dove on Jesus (John 1:32), or came as a sound of a rushing wind and with visible tongues of fire on the disciples at Pentecost (Acts 2:2–3). In addition, when people had the Holy Spirit poured out on them and began to speak in tongues or praise God in a remarkable and spontaneous way (see Acts 2:4; 10:44–46; 19:6), the Holy Spirit certainly made his presence known as well. And Jesus promised that the Holy Spirit within us would be so powerful he would be like a river of living water flowing out from our inmost beings (see John 7:39)—a simile that suggests that people would be aware of a presence that would somehow be perceptible.

In the lives of individual believers, the Holy Spirit does not entirely conceal his work, but makes himself known in various ways. He bears witness with our spirit that we are children of God (Rom. 8:16), and cries, "Abba! Father!" (Gal. 4:6). He provides a guarantee or a down payment of our future fellowship with him in heaven (2 Cor. 1:22; 5:5), and reveals his desires to us so that we can be led by those desires and follow them (Rom. 8:4–16; Gal. 5:16–25). He gives gifts that manifest his presence (1 Cor. 12:7–11). And from time to time he works miraculous signs and wonders that strongly attest to the presence of God in the preaching of the gospel (Heb. 2:4; cf. 1 Cor. 2:4; Rom. 15:19).

It seems more accurate, therefore, to say that although the Holy Spirit does glorify Jesus, he also frequently calls attention to his work and *gives recognizable evidences that make his presence known.* Indeed, it seems that one of his primary purposes in the new covenant age is *to manifest the presence of God,* to give indications that make the presence of God known. And when the Holy Spirit works in various ways that can be perceived by believers and unbelievers, this encourages people's faith that God is near and that he is working to fulfill his purposes in the church and to bring blessing to his people.

3. He Guides and Directs God's People. Scripture gives many examples of direct guidance from the Holy Spirit to various people. In fact, in the Old Testament, God said that it was sin for the people to enter into agreements with others when those agreements were "not of my Spirit" (Isa. 30:1). Apparently the people had been deciding on the basis of their own wisdom and common sense rather than seeking the guidance of God's Holy Spirit before they entered into such agreements. In the New Testament, the Holy Spirit led Jesus into the wilderness for his period of temptation (Matt. 4:1; Luke 4:1); in fact, so strong was this leading of the Holy Spirit that Mark can say that "The Spirit immediately drove him out into the wilderness" (Mark 1:12).[12]

In other contexts the Holy Spirit gave direct words of guidance to people, saying to Philip, for example, "Go up and join this chariot" (Acts 8:29), or telling Peter to go with three men who came to him from Cornelius' household (Acts 10:19–20; 11:12), or directing the Christians at Antioch, "Set apart for me Barnabas and Saul for the work to which I have called them" (Acts 13:2).

Also in the category of "giving guidance," but of a much more direct and compelling kind, are several examples where the Holy Spirit actually transported a person from one place to another. This was so when "the Spirit of the Lord caught up Philip; and the eunuch saw him no more. . . . But Philip was found at Azotus" (Acts 8:39–40)—the guidance in this case could hardly have been more clear! But similar things happened to some Old Testament prophets, for those who knew Elijah seemed to expect that the Spirit of God would snatch him up and transport him somewhere (1 Kings 18:12; 2 Kings 2:16: "It may be that the Spirit of the LORD has caught him up and cast him upon some mountain or into some valley"). The Spirit of the Lord several times, Ezekiel says, "lifted me up" and brought him to one place or another (Ezek. 11:1; 37:1; 43:5), an experience that was also part of John's later visions in Revelation (Rev. 17:3; 21:10).[13]

But in the vast majority of cases the leading and guiding by the Holy Spirit is not nearly as dramatic as this. Scripture talks rather about a day-to-day guidance by the Holy Spirit—being "led" by the Holy Spirit (Rom. 8:14; Gal. 5:18), and walking according to the Spirit (Rom. 8:4; Gal. 5:16). Now it is possible to understand Paul here to be referring only to obedience to the moral commands of Scripture, but this interpretation seems quite unlikely, especially since the entire context is dealing with emotions and desires which we perceive in a more subjective way, and because Paul here contrasts being led by the Spirit with following the desires of the flesh or the sinful nature:

> But I say, *walk by the Spirit,* and do not gratify the desires of the flesh. For the desires of the flesh are against the Spirit, and the *desires of the Spirit* are against the flesh. . . . Now the works of the flesh are plain: fornication, impurity, licentiousness, idolatry, sorcery, enmity, strife, jealousy, anger. . . . But the fruit of the Spirit is love, joy, peace, patience, kindness, goodness, faithfulness, gentleness, self-control. . . . If we live by the Spirit, let us also walk by the Spirit. Let us have no self-conceit, no provoking of one another, no envy of one another. (Gal. 5:16–26)

The contrast between "desires of the flesh" and "desires of the Spirit" implies that our lives should be responding moment by moment to the desires of the Holy Spirit, not to the desires of the flesh. Now it may be that a large part of responding to those desires is the intellectual process of understanding what love, joy, peace (and so forth) are, and

---

[12]The verb here translated "drove out" is a strong term, *ekballō,* which means "drive out, expel," and more literally can mean "throw out."

[13]It is possible that Ezekiel and John are speaking of trans-

portation in a vision (as in Ezek. 8:3 and 11:24) rather than literal physical travel. Paul allows for both possibilities in 2 Cor. 12:2–3.

then acting in a loving or a joyful or peaceful way. But this can hardly constitute the whole of such guidance by the Spirit because these emotions are not simply things we think about; they are things we also feel and sense at a deeper level. In fact, the word translated "desires" (Gk. *epithymia*) is a word that refers to strong human desires, not simply to intellectual decisions. Paul implies that we are to follow these desires as they are produced by the Holy Spirit in us. Moreover, the idea of being "led" by the Holy Spirit (Gal. 5:18) implies an active *personal* participation by the Holy Spirit in guiding us. This is something more than our reflecting on biblical moral standards, and includes an involvement by the Holy Spirit in relating to us as persons and leading and directing us.

There are specific examples of the Holy Spirit guiding people directly in the book of Acts. After the decision of the Jerusalem council, the leaders wrote in their letter to the churches, "It has *seemed good to the Holy Spirit* and to us to lay upon you no greater burden than these necessary things" (Acts 15:28). This verse suggests that the council must have had a sense of the good pleasure of the Holy Spirit in these areas: they knew what "seemed good to the Holy Spirit." On Paul's second missionary journey, Luke writes that they were "forbidden by the Holy Spirit to speak the word in Asia" and then that "they attempted to go into Bithynia, but the Spirit of Jesus did not allow them" (Acts 16:6–7). Of course, no written principle from the Old Testament Scriptures would have led them to conclude that they could not preach in Asia or Bithynia. The Holy Spirit must rather have communicated his direct guidance to them in some specific way, whether through words heard audibly or in the mind, or through strong subjective impressions of a lack of the Holy Spirit's presence and blessing as they attempted to travel to these different areas. Later, when Paul is on his way to Jerusalem, he says, "I am going to Jerusalem, *bound in the Spirit,* not knowing what shall befall me there; except that the Holy Spirit testifies to me in every city that imprisonment and afflictions await me" (Acts 20:22–23). Paul did not think he had another choice—so clearly did the Holy Spirit manifest his presence and desires to him, that Paul could speak of having been "bound" in the Spirit.[14]

In other cases the Holy Spirit gave guidance to establish people in various ministries or church offices. So the Holy Spirit said to some in the church at Antioch, "Set apart for me Barnabas and Saul for the work to which I have called them" (Acts 13:2). And Paul could say that the Holy Spirit had established the elders of the Ephesian church in their office because he said, "Take heed to yourselves and to all the flock, in which the Holy Spirit has made you overseers" (Acts 20:28). Finally, the Holy Spirit did provide some guidance through the means of spiritual gifts such as prophecy (1 Cor. 14:29–33).[15]

---

[14]The word translated "bound" is a perfect passive participle of *deō,* and signifies an earlier completed event (perhaps a strong conviction from the Holy Spirit that settled Paul's mind on the trip to Jerusalem once for all), but an event that also has continuing results in the present, so that Paul remained "bound" when he spoke (the event still influenced Paul so strongly that he had no other choice but to continue forward toward Jerusalem).

[15]However, it is always dangerous to follow spontaneous prophecies alone for guidance in this church age, since we are never to think of any prophecies as inerrant or 100 percent accurate today. Mistakes can especially come in the area of personal guidance. But all that does not allow us to say that there can be no guidance that comes through prophecy.

4. He Provides a Godlike Atmosphere When He Manifests His Presence. Because the Holy Spirit is fully God, and shares all the attributes of God, his influence will be to bring a Godlike character or atmosphere to the situations in which he is active. Because he is the *Holy* Spirit he will at times bring about a conviction of sin, righteousness, and judgment (John 16:8–11). Because God is love, the Holy Spirit pours God's love into our hearts (Rom. 5:5; 15:30; Col. 1:8) and often the strongly manifested presence of the Holy Spirit will create an atmosphere of love. Because God is "not a God of confusion but of peace" (1 Cor. 14:33), the Holy Spirit brings an atmosphere of peace into situations: "The kingdom of God is not food and drink, but righteousness and peace and joy in the Holy Spirit" (Rom. 14:17; cf. Gal. 5:22). This last verse also teaches that the Holy Spirit imparts an atmosphere of joy (see also Acts 13:52; 1 Thess. 1:6). Although the list is not exhaustive, Paul summarized many of these Godlike qualities that the Holy Spirit produces when he listed the various elements of the fruit of the Spirit in Galatians 5:22–23.

Other elements of the atmosphere that the Holy Spirit can impart are truth (John 14:17; 15:26; 16:13; 1 John 5:7), wisdom (Deut. 34:9; Isa. 11:2), comfort (Acts 9:31), freedom (2 Cor. 3:17), righteousness (Rom. 14:17), hope (Rom. 15:13; cf. Gal. 5:5), an awareness of sonship or adoption (Rom. 8:15–16; Gal. 4:5–6), and even glory (2 Cor. 3:8). The Holy Spirit also brings unity (Eph. 4:3), and power (Acts 10:38; 1 Cor. 2:4; 2 Tim. 1:7; cf. Acts 1:8). All of these elements of the Holy Spirit's activity indicate the various aspects of an atmosphere in which he makes his own presence—and thereby his own character—known to the people.

5. He Gives Us Assurance. The Holy Spirit bears witness "with our spirits that we are children of God" (Rom. 8:16), and gives evidence of the work of God within us: "And by this we know that he abides in us, by the Spirit which he has given us" (1 John 3:24). "By this we know that we abide in him and he in us, *because he has given us of his own Spirit*" (1 John 4:13). The Holy Spirit not only witnesses to us that we are God's children, but also witnesses that God abides in us and that we are abiding in him. Once again more than our intellect is involved: the Spirit works to give us assurance at the subjective level of spiritual and emotional perception as well.

6. He Teaches and Illumines. Another aspect of the Holy Spirit's revealing work is teaching certain things to God's people and illumining them so that they can understand things. Jesus promised this teaching function especially to his disciples when he said that the Holy Spirit "will *teach* you all things, and bring to your remembrance all that I have said to you" (John 14:26), and said, "he will guide you into all the truth" (John 16:13). Moreover, he promised that when his disciples were put on trial because of persecution, the Holy Spirit would teach them at that time what to say (Luke 12:12; cf. Matt. 10:20; Mark 13:11). At other times the Holy Spirit revealed specific information to people—showing Simeon that he would not die until he saw the Messiah, for example (Luke 2:26), or revealing to Agabus that a famine would occur (Acts 11:28) or that Paul would be taken captive in Jerusalem (Acts 21:11). In other cases the Holy Spirit revealed to Paul that he would suffer in Jerusalem (Acts 20:23; 21:4) and expressly said to Paul things that would happen in the latter days (1 Tim. 4:1), and revealed to him what God has prepared for those who love him (1 Cor. 2:10).

The illuminating work of the Holy Spirit is seen in the fact that he enables us to understand: "We have received not the spirit of the world, but the Spirit which is from God, *that we might understand* the gifts bestowed on us by God" (1 Cor. 2:12). Therefore, "The unspiritual man does not receive the gifts (literally, things) of the Spirit of God" but "The spiritual man judges all things" (1 Cor. 2:14–15). We should pray that the Holy Spirit would give us his illumination and thereby help us to understand rightly when we study Scripture or when we ponder situations in our lives. Although he did not mention the Holy Spirit specifically, the psalmist prayed for such illumination when he asked God, "Open my eyes, that I may behold wondrous things out of your law" (Ps. 119:18). Similarly, Paul prayed for the Christians in and around Ephesus,

> . . . that the God of our Lord Jesus Christ, the Father of glory, may give you a spirit [or: "the Spirit," NIV] of wisdom and of revelation in the knowledge of him, having the eyes of your hearts enlightened, that you may know what is the hope to which he has called you, what are the riches of his glorious inheritance in the saints, and what is the immeasurable greatness of his power in us who believe, according to the working of his great might. (Eph. 1:17–19)

D. The Holy Spirit Unifies

When the Holy Spirit was poured out on the church at Pentecost, Peter proclaimed that the prophecy of Joel 2:28–32 was fulfilled:

> But this is what was spoken by the prophet Joel:
>
> "And in the last days it shall be, God declares,
> that I will pour out my Spirit upon all flesh,
> and your sons and your daughters shall prophesy,
> and your young men shall see visions,
> and your old men shall dream dreams;
> yes, and on my menservants and my maidservants in those days
> I will pour out my Spirit; and they shall prophesy." (Acts 2:16–18)

There is an emphasis on the Holy Spirit coming on a community of believers—not just a leader like Moses or Joshua, but sons and daughters, old men and young men, menservants and maidservants—all will receive the outpouring of the Holy Spirit in this time.[16]

In the event of Pentecost, the Holy Spirit created a new community which was the church. The community was marked by unprecedented unity, as Luke reminds us:

[16]This was also a fulfillment of Moses' wish that the Lord would put his Spirit on all his people (Num. 11:29), and of the vision of the valley of dry bones revived by the Spirit in Ezek.

37. See also Donald Guthrie, *New Testament Theology* (Leicester: Inter-Varsity Press, 1981), pp. 512–13, 540, 562.

And all who believed were together and had all things in common; and they sold their possessions and goods and distributed them to all, as any had need. And day by day, attending the temple together and breaking bread in their homes, they partook of food with glad and generous hearts, praising God and having favor with all the people. (Acts 2:44–47)

Paul blesses the Corinthian church with a blessing that seeks the unifying fellowship of the Holy Spirit for all of them when he says, "The grace of the Lord Jesus Christ and the love of God and the *fellowship of the Holy Spirit*[17] be with you all" (2 Cor. 13:14). It is significant that in this trinitarian verse he especially attributes the deepening of fellowship among believers not to the Father or the Son but to the Holy Spirit, a statement consistent with the overall unifying work of the Spirit in the church.

This unifying function of the Holy Spirit is also evident when Paul tells the Philippians, "If therefore there is any encouragement in Christ, if there is any consolation of love, if there is any *fellowship of the Spirit* . . . make my joy complete by being of the same mind, maintaining the same love, united in spirit, intent on one purpose" (Phil. 2:1–2 NASB).[18] In a similar way, when he emphasizes the new unity between Jews and Gentiles in the church, he says that "through him we both have access in one Spirit to the Father" (Eph. 2:18), and says that in the Lord they are built into the one new house of God "in the Spirit" (Eph. 2:22). When he wants to remind them of the unity they should have as Christians he exhorts them to be "eager to maintain *the unity of the Spirit in the bond of peace*" (Eph. 4:3).

Paul's discussion of spiritual gifts also repeats this theme of the unifying work of the Holy Spirit. Whereas we might think that people who have differing gifts would not readily get along well with each other, Paul's conclusion is just the opposite: differing gifts draw us together, because we are forced to depend on each other. "The eye cannot say to the hand, 'I have no need of you,' nor again the head to the feet, 'I have no need of you'" (1 Cor. 12:21). These differing gifts, Paul tells us, are empowered by "one and the same Spirit, who apportions to each one individually as he wills" (1 Cor. 12:11), so that in the church, "To each is given the *manifestation of the Spirit* for the common good" (1 Cor. 12:7). In fact, "in one Spirit we were all baptized into one body—Jews or Greeks, slaves or free—and all were made to drink of one Spirit" (1 Cor. 12:13, author's translation).

The idea that the Holy Spirit unifies the church is also evident in the fact that "strife . . . disputes, dissensions, factions" (Gal. 5:20 NASB) are desires of the flesh that are opposed to being "led by the Spirit" (Gal. 5:18; cf. v. 25). The Holy Spirit is the one who produces love in our hearts (Rom. 5:5; Gal. 5:22; Col. 1:8), and this love "binds everything together in perfect harmony" (Col. 3:14). Therefore when the Holy Spirit is working strongly in a church to manifest God's presence, one evidence will be a beautiful harmony in the church community and overflowing love for one another.

---

[17]The word *koinōnia*, "fellowship," could also mean "participation in the Holy Spirit," but it would make little sense for Paul to wish for them something they already had as believers (participation in the Holy Spirit). It is better to translate the verse, "fellowship of the Holy Spirit," thus emphasizing a blessing from the Holy Spirit that Paul hoped would increase in the Corinthian church.

[18]The Greek word *koinōnia* is also best translated "fellowship" here because Paul's purpose in Phil. 2:1–11 is to encourage unity in the Philippian church. (See the preceding footnote also.)

E. The Holy Spirit Gives Stronger or Weaker Evidence of the Presence and Blessing of God According to Our Response to Him

Many examples in both the Old and New Testament indicate that the Holy Spirit will bestow or withdraw blessing according to whether or not he is pleased by the situation he sees. It is noteworthy that Jesus was completely without sin and the Holy Spirit "remained on him" (John 1:32) and was given to him without measure (John 3:34). In the Old Testament the Holy Spirit came mightily upon Samson several times (Judg. 13:25; 14:6, 19; 15:14), but ultimately left him when he persisted in sin (Judg. 16:20). Similarly, when Saul persisted in disobedience the Holy Spirit departed from him (1 Sam. 16:14). And when the people of Israel rebelled and grieved the Holy Spirit he turned against them (Isa. 63:10).

Also in the New Testament the Holy Spirit can be grieved and cease to bring blessing in a situation. Stephen rebuked the Jewish leaders, saying, "You always *resist the Holy Spirit*" (Acts 7:51). Paul warns the Ephesian Christians, "Do not *grieve the Holy Spirit of God,* in whom you were sealed for the day of redemption" (Eph. 4:30), and exhorts the Thessalonian church, "Do not *quench the Spirit*" (1 Thess. 5:19; cf. the metaphor of delaying to open the door and thereby disappointing one's lover in Song of Sol. 5:3, 6). In a similar vein, Paul gives a serious warning to Christians not to defile their bodies by joining them to a prostitute because the Holy Spirit lives within their bodies: "Do you not know that your body is a temple of the Holy Spirit within you, which you have from God? You are not your own; you were bought with a price. So glorify God in your body" (1 Cor. 6:19–20).

Even more serious than grieving or quenching the Holy Spirit is a deeper, more hardened disobedience to him that brings strong judgment. When Peter rebuked Ananias, "Why has Satan filled your heart to lie to the Holy Spirit and to keep back part of the proceeds of the land?" (Acts 5:3), he fell down dead. Similarly, when Peter said to Ananias's wife Sapphira, "How is it that you have agreed together to tempt the Spirit of the Lord?" (Acts 5:9), she immediately fell down dead as well. The book of Hebrews warns those who are in danger of falling away that severe punishment is deserved by the man "who has spurned the Son of God, and profaned the blood of the covenant by which he was sanctified, and *outraged the Spirit of grace*" (Heb. 10:29). For such a person there only remains "a fearful prospect of judgment" (Heb. 10:27).[19]

Finally, there remains one more level of offense against the Holy Spirit. This kind of offense is even more serious than grieving him or acting with the hardened disobedience to him that brings discipline or judgment. It is possible so to offend the Holy Spirit that his convicting work will not be brought to bear again in a person's life.

> Every sin and blasphemy will be forgiven men, but the *blasphemy against the Spirit* will not be forgiven. And whoever says a word against the Son of man will be forgiven; but whoever speaks against the Holy Spirit will not be forgiven, either in this age or in the age to come. (Matt. 12:31–32; cf. Mark 3:29; Luke 12:10)

---

[19]This passage could also be put in the next category, discussed in the following paragraph.

These statements are made in a context in which the Pharisees willfully and maliciously attribute to Satan the powerful work of the Holy Spirit that was evident in the ministry of Jesus. Since the Holy Spirit so clearly manifested the presence of God, those who willfully and maliciously spoke against him and attributed his activity instead to the power of Satan were guilty, Jesus said, "of an eternal sin" (Mark 3:29).

All of these passages indicate that we must be very careful not to grieve or offend the Holy Spirit. He will not force himself on us against our wills (see 1 Cor. 14:32), but if we resist and quench and oppose him, then his empowering will depart and he will remove much of the blessing of God from our lives.

On the other hand, in the life of Christians whose conduct is pleasing to God, the Holy Spirit will be present to bring great blessing. The Holy Spirit was "poured out" in fullness at Pentecost (see Acts 2:17–18) and he now dwells within all true believers, making them temples of the living God (1 Cor. 3:16; 6:19–20). We can know close fellowship and partnership with the Holy Spirit in our lives (2 Cor. 3:14; Phil. 2:1). He entrusts gifts (1 Cor. 12:11) and truth (2 Tim. 1:14) and ministries (Acts 20:28) to us. In fact, so full and abundant will be his presence that Jesus could promise that he will flow out of our inmost being like "rivers of living water" (John 7:38–39). Peter promises that his presence especially rests on those who suffer for the sake of Christ: "If you are reproached for the name of Christ, you are blessed, because the spirit of glory and of God rests upon you" (1 Peter 4:14).

Therefore it is important that all our ministry be done *in the Holy Spirit,* that is, that we consciously dwell in the Godlike atmosphere created by the Holy Spirit—the atmosphere of power, love, joy, truth, holiness, righteousness, and peace. But greater than these characteristics of the atmosphere created by the Holy Spirit is the sense of the presence of the Holy Spirit himself—*to be in the Holy Spirit is really to be in an atmosphere of God's manifested presence.* This is why people in the New Testament can walk in the comfort of the Holy Spirit (Acts 9:31), and why it is possible just to be "in the Spirit" as John was on the Lord's day (Rev. 1:10; cf. 4:2).

It is surprising how many particular activities are said in the New Testament to be done "in" the Holy Spirit: it is possible to *rejoice* in the Holy Spirit (Luke 10:21), to *resolve* or decide something in the Holy Spirit (Acts 19:21), to have one's *conscience bear witness* in the Holy Spirit (Rom. 9:1), to have *access to God* in the Holy Spirit (Eph. 2:18), to *pray* in the Holy Spirit (Eph. 6:18; Jude 20), and to *love* in the Holy Spirit (Col. 1:8). In the light of these texts, we might ask ourselves, for how many of these activities during each day are we consciously aware of the Holy Spirit's presence and blessing?

It is also possible to be filled with the Holy Spirit (Eph. 5:18; cf. Luke 1:15, 41, 67; 4:1; Acts 2:4; 4:8; 6:3, 5; 7:55; 9:17; 11:24; 13:9). To be filled with the Holy Spirit is to be filled with the immediate presence of God himself, and it therefore will result in feeling what God feels, desiring what God desires, doing what God wants, speaking by God's power, praying and ministering in God's strength, and knowing with the knowledge which God himself gives. In times when the church experiences revival the Holy Spirit produces these results in people's lives in especially powerful ways.

Therefore in our Christian lives it is important that we depend on the Holy Spirit's power, recognizing that any significant work is done "Not by might, nor by power, *but by my Spirit,* says the LORD of hosts" (Zech. 4:6). Paul is emphatic in telling the Galatians that the Holy Spirit was received by faith in the beginning of their Christian life (Gal. 3:2) and would continue to work according to their faith in their lives subsequent to conversion: "Having begun with the Spirit, are you now ending with the flesh? . . . Does he who supplies the Spirit to you and works miracles among you do so by works of the law, or by hearing with faith?" (Gal. 3:3, 5).

Therefore we are to walk according to the guidance of the Holy Spirit (Rom. 8:12–16; Gal. 5:16–26) and set our minds on the things of the Spirit (Rom. 8:4–6). All our ministry, whatever form it may take, is to be done in the power of the Holy Spirit.

QUESTIONS FOR PERSONAL APPLICATION

1. In the past, has it been hard for you to think of the Holy Spirit as a person rather than simply as a presence or force? What items (if any) in this chapter have helped you think more readily of the Holy Spirit as a person? Do you think that you have a consciousness of relating to the Holy Spirit as a person who is distinct from God the Father and God the Son? What might help you be more aware of this distinction among the members of the Trinity as they relate to you?

2. Do you perceive any difference in the way the Father, Son, and Holy Spirit relate to you in your Christian life? If so, can you explain what that difference is or how you are aware of it?

3. Have you ever been especially aware of the Holy Spirit's empowering in a specific situation of ministry? (This could have been while doing evangelism or counseling, Bible teaching or preaching, prayer or worship, or in some other ministry situation.) How did you perceive the presence of the Holy Spirit at that time, or what made you aware of his presence?

4. In your own experience, in what ways does the guidance of the Holy Spirit come to you? Is it primarily (or exclusively) through the words of Scripture? If so, are there times when certain Scripture passages seem to come alive or speak with great relevance and forcefulness to you at the moment? How do you know when this is happening? If the Holy Spirit's guidance has come to you in other ways in addition to speaking through the words of Scripture, what have those other ways been?

5. Do you have a sense from time to time of the pleasure or displeasure of the Holy Spirit at some course of action that you are taking? Is there anything in your life right now that is grieving the Holy Spirit? What do you plan to do about it?

6. Did the Holy Spirit immediately leave Samson when he began to sin (see Judg. 13:25; 14:6, 19; 15:14)? Why or why not? Is the presence of spiritual power in someone's ministry a guarantee that the Holy Spirit is pleased with all of that person's life?

SPECIAL TERMS

blasphemy against the Holy Spirit
filled with the Holy Spirit
Holy Spirit

in the Holy Spirit
manifestation of God's active
presence

BIBLIOGRAPHY

Bruner, Frederick Dale. *A Theology of the Holy Spirit.* Grand Rapids: Eerdmans, 1970.

Carson, D. A. *Showing the Spirit: A Theological Exposition of 1 Corinthians 12–14.* Grand Rapids: Baker, 1987.

Carter, Charles. *The Person and Ministry of the Holy Spirit.* Grand Rapids: Baker, 1974.

Caulley, T. S. "Holy Spirit." In *EDT,* pp. 521–27.

Gaffin, Richard B., Jr. "The Holy Spirit." *WTJ* 43:1 (Fall 1980), pp. 58–78.

Green, Michael. *I Believe in the Holy Spirit.* Grand Rapids: Eerdmans, 1975.

Hawthorne, Gerald. *The Presence and the Power: The Significance of the Holy Spirit in the Life and Ministry of Jesus.* Dallas: Word, 1991.

Hoekema, Anthony A. "The Role of the Holy Spirit." In *Saved By Grace.* Grand Rapids: Eerdmans, and Exeter: Paternoster, 1989, pp. 28–53.

Horton, S. M. *What the Bible Says About the Holy Spirit.* Springfield, Mo.: Gospel Publishing House, 1976.

Ladd, George E. *The Presence of the Future: The Eschatology of Biblical Realism.* Grand Rapids: Eerdmans, 1974.

Moule, C. F. D. *The Holy Spirit.* Grand Rapids: Eerdmans, 1978.

Pache, Rene. *The Person and Work of the Holy Spirit.* Chicago: Moody, 1954.

Packer, J. I. "Holy Spirit." In *NDT,* pp. 316–19.

_____. *Keep in Step with the Spirit.* Old Tappan, N.J.: Revell, 1984.

Palmer, Edwin H. *The Person and Ministry of the Holy Spirit.* Grand Rapids: Baker, 1958.

Ryrie, C. C. *The Holy Spirit.* Chicago: Moody, 1965.

Smeaton, G. *The Doctrine of the Holy Spirit.* 2d ed. Edinburgh: T. and T. Clark, 1889.

Sproul, R. C. *The Mystery of the Holy Spirit.* Wheaton, Ill.: Tyndale, 1990.

Stott, John R. W. *Baptism and Fullness: The Work of the Holy Spirit Today.* Downers Grove, Ill.: InterVarsity Press, 1964.

Swete, Henry B. *The Holy Spirit in the New Testament.* 2d ed. London: Macmillan, 1910.

White, John. *When the Spirit Comes with Power.* Downers Grove, Ill.: InterVarsity Press, 1988.

Wood, Leon J. *The Holy Spirit in the Old Testament.* Grand Rapids: Zondervan, 1976.

SCRIPTURE MEMORY PASSAGE

Romans 8:12–14: *So then, brethren, we are debtors, not to the flesh, to live according to the flesh—for if you live according to the flesh you will die, but if by the Spirit you put to death the deeds of the body you will live. For all who are led by the Spirit of God are sons of God.*

HYMN

"Come, O Creator Spirit"

This is one of the oldest hymns in any hymnal, written by an anonymous author in the tenth century or earlier. It directly addresses the Holy Spirit and asks him to come and bring blessing in our hearts, filling us with joy and love and praise, and giving us protection from the enemy and peace in our lives.

Come, O Creator Spirit blest,
And in our hearts take up thy rest;
Spirit of grace, with heav'nly aid
Come to the souls whom thou hast made.

Thou art the Comforter, we cry,
Sent to the earth from God Most High,
Fountain of life and fire of love,
And our anointing from above.

Bringing from heav'n our sev'n-fold dow'r,
Sign of our God's right hand of pow'r,
O blessed Spirit, promised long,
Thy coming wakes the heart to song.

Make our dull minds with rapture glow,
Let human hearts with love o'erflow;
And, when our feeble flesh would fail,
May thine immortal strength prevail.

Far from our souls the foe repel,
Grant us in peace henceforth to dwell;
Ill shall not come, nor harm betide,
If only thou wilt be our guide.

Show us the Father, Holy One,
Help us to know th' eternal Son;
Spirit divine, for evermore
Thee will we trust and thee adore.

ANON., TENTH CENTURY

Alternative Hymn:
"Spirit of God, Descend Upon My Heart"

Spirit of God, descend upon my heart;
Wean it from earth, through all its pulses move;
Stoop to my weakness, mighty as thou art,
And make me love thee as I ought to love.

Hast thou not bid us love thee, God and King?
 All, all thine own, soul, heart, and strength and mind.
I see thy cross - there teach my heart to cling:
 O let me seek thee, and O let me find.

Teach me to feel that thou art always nigh;
 Teach me the struggles of the soul to bear,
To check the rising doubt, the rebel sigh;
 Teach me the patience of unanswered prayer.

Teach me to love thee as thine angels love,
 One holy passion filling all my frame;
The baptism of the heav'n descended Dove,
 My heart an altar, and thy love the flame.

AUTHOR: GEORGE CROLY, 1854

We want to hear from you. Please send your comments about this book to us in care of zreview@zondervan.com. Thank you.

ZONDERVAN.com/
AUTHORTRACKER
follow your favorite authors